ADAPTIVE TECHNOLOGIES FOR LEARNING & WORK ENVIRONMENTS

JOSEPH J. LAZZARO

AMERICAN LIBRARY ASSOCIATION
CHICAGO AND LONDON 1993

Managing editor: Joan A. Grygel

Cover design by Richmond Jones
Text design by Mark Hoover

Composed by Digital Graphics, Inc., in Trump Mediæval and Syntax using
TEX. Reproduction copy set on a Varityper 5300P phototypesetter

Printed on 50-pound Glatfelter Natural, a pH-neutral stock, and bound in
10 point C1S cover stock by Braun-Brumfield, Inc.

The paper used in this publication meets the minimum requirements of
American National Standard for Information Sciences—Permanence of Paper
for Printed Library Materials, ANSI Z39.48–1984. ∞

Library of Congress Cataloging-in-Publication Data

Lazzaro, Joseph J.
    Adaptive technologies for learning and work environments / by
Joseph J. Lazzaro.
      p. cm.
    Includes bibliographical references and index.
    ISBN 0-8389-0615-X
    1. Computers and the handicapped—United States. 2. Computerized
self-help devices for the handicapped—United States. I. Title.
HV1569.5.L38   1993
362.4'048—dc20   92-46993

Printed in the United States of America.

97 96 95 94 93   5 4 3 2 1

Contents

Preface   *ix*

Introduction   *xiii*

1 Breaking Barriers with Adaptive Technology   *1*

Blindness and Visual Impairment   2
  Barriers for Persons Who Are Blind
  or Visually Impaired   2
  Overview of Adaptive Technologies for Persons Who
  Are Blind or Visually Impaired   3
Deafness and Hearing Impairment   3
  Barriers for Persons Who Are Deaf or Hearing Impaired   4
  Overview of Adaptive Technologies for Persons Who
  Are Deaf or Hearing Impaired   5
Motor and/or Speech Impairment   5
  Barriers for Persons with Motor and/or Speech
  Impairments   5
  Overview of Adaptive Technologies for Persons
  with Motor and/or Speech Impairments   6
The Americans with Disabilities Act   7
  On-the-Job Discrimination   9
  Public Accommodations and Transportation   10
  ADA Technical Assistance Centers   10
Conclusion   13

2 The Personal Computer   *14*

From Abacus to Apple   15
Computer Hardware   20
  The Central Processing Unit   20

Input Devices   21
Output Devices   23
Input/Output Ports   25
Modems   26
Computer Memory   27
Storage Devices   27
Expansion Slots and Circuit Cards   29
Software   32
The Disk Operating System   33
Applications Programs   34
Personal Computer Manufacturers   36
The Apple IIGS   37
The Apple Macintosh   38
IBM PC and Compatibles   38
Laptops and Notebooks   39
Selecting a Personal Computer   41

3 Technology for Persons with Vision Impairments   *45*
Speech Synthesis   46
Internal Speech Synthesis Hardware   46
External Speech Synthesis Hardware   49
Speech Synthesis Software   51
Screen Readers for Graphics   54
Other Adaptive Speech Applications   59
Magnification Systems   61
Optical Aids   61
Large Monitors   62
Closed Circuit Television Systems   62
Software-Based Magnification Programs   65
Hardware-Based Magnification Systems   69
Braille Systems   71
From Early Braille to Computer Technology   71
Braille Translation Software   72
Braille Printers   75
Refreshable Braille Displays   78
Pocket Braille Computers   80
Optical Character Recognition Systems   81
From the Kurzweil Reading Machine
to Today's OCR Devices   81
Scanning Text into a Word Processor   83
Products for Persons with Vision Impairments   84

Speech Synthesis Providers 84
Magnification System Providers 86
Braille Printer and Display Providers 87
Optical Character Recognition System Providers 88

4 Technology for Persons with Hearing Impairments 89

Text Telephones 90
Talking on a Text Telephone 91
Braille Text Telephones 93
Relay Services 96
Facsimile Communication 96
Computer-Assisted Access 97
Baudot/ASCII Modems 97
Text Telephone Software 100
Talking on a Baudot/ASCII Modem 102
Visual Beep Indicator Software 102
Computer-Aided Transcription 103
Computerized Sign Language Training 104
Signaling Systems 106
Captioning Systems 109
Making Captioned Videotapes 110
Electronic Amplification Systems 111
Hearing Aids 112
Assistive Listening Devices 113
Telephone Amplification Systems 114
Products for Persons Who Are Deaf or
  Hearing Impaired 115
Text Telephone Providers 115
Computer-Based Access Product Providers 116
Sign Language Training Software Providers 117
Signaling System Providers 117
Captioning System Providers 118
Electronic Amplification System Providers 118
Products for Persons Who Are Deaf-Blind 119

5 Technology for Persons with Motor and/or Speech Impairments 121

Adapted Keyboards 122
Keyboard Keyguards 124
Keyboard Modification Software 125
Macro Software 125
Sticky Keys and Key Modifier Software 127

Alternative Input Systems   130
  Adapted Switches and Scanning Keyboards   130
  Morse Code Systems   132
  Word-Prediction Software   134
Voice Recognition Systems   136
  Voice Recognition Hardware   136
  Installing and Training Voice Recognition Software   137
Alternative Communications Devices   141
Environmental Control Systems   143
Products for Persons with Motor and/or Speech
  Impairments   145
  Adapted Keyboard Providers   145
  Keyboard Modification Software Providers   147
  Alternative Input Hardware and Software Providers   149
  Voice Recognition System Providers   151
  Alternative Communication System Providers   153
  Environmental Control System Providers   154

6 **Applications for Adaptive Technology**   *157*
Local Area Networks   157
  Network Hardware   158
  Network Software   161
  Installing Adaptive Technologies on a Local Area
    Network   164
The Online World   165
  Online Services   165
  Bulletin Boards   165
  Electronic Mail   166
  Fax   167
  Live Chatting Online   167
  Calling an Online Service or Bulletin Board   167
  Electronic Conferencing   171
  The Internet   171
  Interfacing Adaptive Technology for Online Services   172
Compact Disks   173
  CD-ROM Hardware and Software   174
  Interfacing Adaptive Technology with a CD-ROM   175
Telecommunications Services and CD-ROM Products   176
  Online Service Providers   176
  Disability-Related Bulletin Board Providers   178
  Public Access Internet Sites   181
  CD-ROM Providers   182

7 Rehabilitation Engineering, Training, and Technical Support   184

Rehabilitation Engineering   *184*
  Job-Site Analysis   186
  Coordinating the Adaptation of the Workplace   190
Training   *190*
  Classroom Training   191
  On-the-Job Training   191
  Continuing Training   192
  Training Materials   192
Technical Support   *193*
  Vendor Technical Support   194
  Third-Party Technical Support   194
  Users' Groups and Special Interest Groups   194
  Help Screens   195

8 Funding Adaptive Technology   197

Cost-Saving Ideas   *198*
Personal Funding Sources   *199*
  Family and Friends   199
  Lending Institutions and Credit Unions   199
  Credit Cards   200
Government-Sponsored Funding Sources   *200*
Private-Sector Funding Sources   *204*
Financial Aid Resources   *206*
  Address of Funding Sources   206
  Books on Funding Sources   207

Appendixes

A Organizational Resources for Persons
   with Disabilities   *209*
B Assistive Technology Conferences   *218*
C Journals and Newsletters on Assistive Technology   *222*
D Technology Assistance States   *224*

Index   231

Preface

The human spirit is fluid and dynamic, capable of adapting to any situation. The dictionary defines the word *adapt* in terms of accommodation and adjustment, of growing comfortable under a new set of circumstances. After becoming legally blind more than twenty years ago, my personal adaptation was a long time in coming. But come it eventually did, thanks to the help of family and friends. Without their constant support, I would never have written this book. My thanks also to the pioneers who created the personal computer. A talking computer has permitted me to pursue a professional career.

Since early childhood, the hard sciences have been a great passion. As a young adult, I spent hours absorbing physics and science texts. After losing my vision, the hope of a career and productive life seemed to be slipping away, but technology was soon to come to the rescue. My life was changed forever when a friend brought me a newsletter article. The newsletter, devoted to adaptive technology for persons with disabilities, contained an advertisement discussing talking computers for persons with vision impairments. Encouraged, I sent away for a brochure. When the information finally arrived on audiotape, I wasted no time playing it back.

The tape began with a description of the Apple II computer, and how it could be converted to a talking computer system. It discussed how a talking computer could be used to write letters, file names and addresses, and even play games. I concluded that the Apple computer was a device I could operate independently because all keystrokes were spoken as typed and everything displayed on the screen also was verbalized. Finally, I was able to purchase an Apple computer equipped with an Echo speech synthesizer and a talking word-processing program.

The talking Apple allowed me to finish college. Within a matter of a few months, the computer totally changed my standard mode of operation at the university. For the first time I could write and edit papers without assistance, which meant that I created more professional, higher-quality work. I also took an interest in computer programming and found that I could create computer software. Several months after obtaining the talking Apple, an editor at *Byte* magazine invited me to write an article about speech synthesis, "The Search for Speech," published in December 1984. As a result of this article, I was invited to help the University of Massachusetts create an Adaptive Computing Center.

Because of the wonders of adaptive technology, my life has been changed forever. Thanks to the talking computer, I have been able to adapt to my new life and to find a place of worth in the community, which is more than anyone can ask. I hope this book will help others open new doors just as the talking computer opened vast horizons for me.

Acknowledgments

Many friends and colleagues assisted me during the writing of this manuscript. My greatest thanks goes to Cynthia Tumilty Lazzaro for providing inspiration throughout this and other writing projects; her technical skill is second to none. I also wish to thank Kim Charlson, assistant director of the Braille and Talking Book Library at Perkins School for the Blind, for advice and for proofreading the manuscript. A special acknowledgment goes to F. Alexander Brejcha for brainstorming sessions and constant support throughout the project.

Individuals who provided assistance on specific sections of the manuscript also deserve a very special thanks. These include John Robichaud, Donald Breda, and Brian Charlson for reading the portions of the manuscript dedicated to engineering and training; Steven Mendelsohn and Patricia Beattie for their advice on financing adaptive technology; Robert McGillivray for his assistance regarding magnification systems; and Judi Harkin and Wayne Howell for their help on technology for persons with hearing impairments.

My appreciation also extends to The Computer Museum, Boston, for providing photographs of early computers. The Trace Research and Development Center's DOS-ABLEDATA CD-ROM database was very beneficial for researching groups of assistive devices. Closing the Gap and the Rehabilitation Engineering Center for the National Rehabilitation Hospital in Washington, D.C., provided valuable assistance in compiling lists of resources. Special thanks to the following BIX staff for all their assistance: Kirk Odle, Henry Brugsch, Tony Lockwood, and Sandra Prow. Thanks also go to Allison Feldhusen for transcribing, reading, and giving moral support. A tip of the hat to William McGarry and Gordon Gillespy for assistance in compiling lists of disability-oriented bulletin boards. Grateful thanks to Daniel Searing of the U.S. Department of Justice and Scott Marshall of the American Foundation for the Blind for information about the Americans with Disabilities Act of 1990. Special thanks to Janina Sajka of the World Institute on Disability for proofreading and endless moral support. Professor Jack Looney of the University of Massachusetts at Boston provided endless amounts of his personal time, both in and out of the classroom. Finally, grateful thanks to my editors, Herbert Bloom and Joan Grygel, for long hours above and beyond the call of duty on this project.

Readers who wish to do so may contact me at my Internet electronic mail addresses:

LAZZARO@WORLD.STD.COM or
LAZZARO@BIX.COM

Introduction

Adaptive Technologies for Learning and Work Environments focuses on personal computers and the adaptive technology designed to assist persons with disabilities at home, work, and school. The technologies discussed in this book focus on information access, which is critical to top performance in the office or classroom. The book is intended for individuals with visual, hearing, motor, and speech disabilities as well as their friends, family, coworkers, and anyone who relates to persons with disabilities. Managers and supervisors who may need to provide adaptive technology to comply with the Americans with Disabilities Act (ADA) will also find much useful information within the following chapters.

For individuals with disabilities, adaptive technology can grant independence and self-sufficiency, even when faced with a seemingly insurmountable barrier. The term *disability*, as used in this book, means any physical condition that seriously limits an individual from performing life-support tasks such as seeing, hearing, walking, or speaking. (Other disabilities can impair a person's ability to process information, but they are beyond the scope of this book.) For our purposes, *adaptive technology* is any device that allows an individual to work or gain access to information independently. The adaptive technologies focused upon in this book consist of those that are compatible with personal computers and those that are used for information access. If you're concerned about complying with the Americans with Disabilities Act, *Adaptive Technologies for Learning and Work Environments* will instruct you about the various forms of assistive technology being employed on the job, at home, in public facilities, and in the classroom.

The list of adaptive technologies includes devices to verbalize and magnify the computer screen, print hard-copy braille, read printed books aloud, talk on the telephone, access video programming, command computers through spoken commands or through a few keystrokes, and speak to or hear family and friends without human assistance. The text also discusses useful applications for personal computers already equipped with adaptive technology, such as linking computers into networks, accessing online databanks, or using compact disk reference systems. The book also describes how to analyze the environment for the appropriate adaptive technology as well as how to provide training and ongoing technical support. Sources of financial aid for adaptive technologies are also presented.

Throughout the book, more than 120 specific adaptive products are highlighted as examples of the myriad adaptive technologies available. Practical, how-to-do-it sections explain installation procedures and provide examples of how to use different technologies. Extensive end-of-chapter lists of adaptive technology providers together with the four appendixes provide names and addresses of useful resources. (If this book is read onto audiotape, readers may wish to record the end-of-chapter lists with the appendix material. This will increase listening comprehension of the basic text.)

Chapter 1 introduces the concept of barriers faced by persons with disabilities, including vision impairments, hearing impairments, and speech and motor impairments, and provides an overview of adaptive technologies that can assist in overcoming such barriers. The chapter concludes with an overview of the Americans with Disabilities Act, focusing chiefly on the employment aspects of this ground-breaking legislation.

Chapter 2 focuses on the history of computing machines from the abacus to the Apple. It introduces the reader to personal computer terminology and provides a look inside a typical desktop computer system. The chapter lays a foundation for the discussion of adaptive technologies in the following chapters. A checklist of computer considerations serves as a guide for purchasing the right mainstream and adaptive systems.

Chapters 3 through 5 discuss technologies for persons with vision, hearing, and motor and/or speech impairments, respectively. Each technology is discussed in detail, and various representative products are highlighted to demonstrate the wealth of options available.

Chapter 6 outlines powerful applications for adapted computer systems, including networks, the online world, and CD-ROM access. These applications grant the user access to vast storehouses of information.

Chapter 7 discusses engineering and training. These important considerations focus on how job sites are adapted and consumers are trained on mainstream and assistive systems.

Chapter 8 details financial aid for purchasing adaptive technology. Various sources are cited, including those from the government and private sector. A number of model grants and programs are examples of the variety of funding sources available.

The text concludes with appendixes that list organizations, conferences, journals and newsletters, and state-run programs that can further assist the reader in finding out more about adaptive technology and its applications. A subject and product index provides quick access to the topics herein.

Aimed at information access, the text demonstrates how to adapt personal computers for different disabilities and how to gain equal access to information in our knowledge-intensive society.

Barriers can also be quite different for individuals with differing degrees of a disability. The barriers faced by totally blind persons versus those with limited vision, by persons who are totally deaf versus individuals who have limited hearing, or by persons using a wheelchair versus those employing a walker or crutches all differ. The next sections explore specific disabilities to increase an understanding of the kinds of barriers each individual may experience. Once we have a good understanding of the barriers, we can employ adaptive technology to overcome those obstacles.

Blindness and Visual Impairment

The term *legally blind* refers to individuals who have a serious restriction in their field of vision or in the distance they can see effectively. When many people hear the word *blind*, they almost immediately think of total darkness. This often is not the case—many persons who are classified legally blind may have useful vision. Although the term *visually impaired* often is used to describe persons who are legally blind, it more accurately describes persons with low vision. No matter how much vision an individual happens to possess, he or she can often function independently when equipped with the appropriate adaptive equipment and training.

Barriers for Persons Who Are Blind or Visually Impaired

Numerous barriers face persons who are blind or visually impaired; inaccessible printed text is one of the most formidable. Although the printed word is the chief mode of communication for most people, little printed matter is available in accessible form for persons who are visually impaired. If they wish to read magazines or books, persons who are visually impaired must have the material transcribed into braille—a task that can take days or weeks—or have someone read it aloud. This communications barrier prevents persons with vision impairments from obtaining timely information, an especially objectionable barrier for students and workers.

Another barrier faced by persons who are visually impaired involves personal and business correspondence. Many persons who are blind rely on friends and family to read their mail and other printed material. This dependency compels persons who are blind not only to arrange their lives around the schedules of their readers but also to sacrifice their privacy. Writing letters and other documents can cause difficulty, as standard typewriters do not offer feedback of keystrokes or of errors. Among the other barriers faced by persons with vision impairments include the identification of money and the management of finances. Television programming can create a barrier, especially during periods of silence in a broadcast. Getting from place to place can often raise difficulty, but mobility aids are beyond the scope of information access.

Overview of Adaptive Technologies for Persons Who Are Blind or Visually Impaired

Many of the barriers faced by persons who are blind or visually impaired can be reduced through the application of adaptive technology. Numerous technologies are available, and many assistive systems attach to personal computers. Talking computer systems can be programmed to verbalize keystrokes and the information displayed on the video screen. With the assistance of a talking computer, individuals can read and write correspondence, manage business and personal matters, access databanks of information, manage financial resources, etc. Magnification systems can enlarge text and graphics displayed on the computer video screen and enlarge books and other printed material for comfortable reading. Braille printers can generate hard-copy braille documents and work hand-in-hand with most computer systems. Refreshable braille displays attached to personal computers allow information access via the braille alphabet. Optical scanning systems can read printed documents aloud and scan the information directly into a personal computer. For a complete description of these and other adaptive technologies and vendors to assist persons with vision impairments, consult Chapter 3.

Deafness and Hearing Impairment

The terms *deaf* or *hearing impaired* indicate individuals who have serious restrictions in their abilities to perceive sounds. The amount of hearing impairment an individual has can be quantified by measuring the amount of boosting a signal requires to be audible. The measurement of hearing loss can sometimes be deceptive, as it is possible for an individual to have keen hearing in one frequency while having a hearing impairment in another. Throughout this book, the term *deaf* denotes those with no hearing and *hearing impaired* describes individuals with some remaining hearing. As with blindness and visual impairment, the nondisabled person often incorrectly defines the condition of deafness, tending to classify all persons with hearing losses as totally deaf.

In the past, deafness or hearing impairment meant living a life of isolation, cut off from most human interaction. This has changed a great deal in recent times due to increased public awareness and the benefits of adaptive technologies.

Barriers for Persons Who Are Deaf or Hearing Impaired

The telephone presents a communications barrier to persons who are deaf or hard of hearing. Persons who are totally deaf cannot use an unmodified telephone. Those who are hearing impaired may not be able to use the telephone either because the sound level may be too low for accurate perception or it may emphasize frequencies the individual cannot hear easily.

Public gatherings and meetings can often present barriers to persons who are deaf or hearing impaired. As with the telephone, public gatherings present different barriers depending on the amount of hearing an individual possesses. Since most public gatherings involve speech as a method for conveying thoughts, persons who are deaf cannot readily access the verbal portion of the information being presented. These limits can be quite formidable unless the individual takes full advantage of assistive technology, sign language, or lip reading. Those with hearing impairments may not be able to hear the words of the speaker clearly without amplification. The background noise and chatter of the attending audience and room and equipment noises may also mask the words of the speaker or distort sound energy.

Television programming presents a barrier to persons who are deaf and those with hearing impairments. While the visual portion of the program presents no barriers, the audio soundtrack can be a barrier.

The inability to detect various sounds in the environment may present a barrier for persons who are either deaf or hearing impaired, especially if these sounds signal danger or some other important message. Common sounds such as a ringing telephone, buzzing doorbell, crying baby, or screeching smoke alarm must be monitored and dealt with. However, they might go unanswered if the proper adaptive equipment is not present.

Overview of Adaptive Technologies for Persons Who Are Deaf or Hearing Impaired

A myriad of devices can assist persons who are deaf or who have hearing impairments. Text telephones allow persons to talk on the telephone, using keyboards and printers to send messages back and forth. Computers provide equal access, and mainstream technologies such as fax and online databanks level the playing field. Hearing aids and other amplification devices bring the world of sound a little closer, permitting equal access to verbal, face-to-face, and telephone communications. Signaling systems monitor the environment and flash room lamps when important sound sources are present. Captioning systems allow equal access to video programming, providing text messages for the audio portion of programming. For a complete description of assistive technology and vendors of the adaptive devices for persons who are deaf or hearing impaired, consult Chapter 4.

Motor and/or Speech Impairment

The term *motor impairment* describes physical conditions that limit movement of the hands, arms, legs, or any other voluntary muscles. Persons can be affected below the waist or both above and below the waist. Motor impairment also can impede fine-motor coordination.

Speech impairment can be the result of many different causes, for example, physical or neurological conditions. Some individuals who are deaf may also have speech impairments. However, for purposes of our discussion, speech impairment will be grouped with motor disabilities because many motor disabilities often result in speech impairments. In the past, persons with speech impairments were forced to communicate with eye movements or even cruder gestures. For individuals with motor or speech impairments, adaptive technology to communicate with others is widely available.

Barriers for Persons with Motor and/or Speech Impairments

As with vision- and hearing-related disabilities, motor and speech impairments range from simple to severe. Less-severe conditions may require individuals to use canes for mobility. A slightly more severe condition would require individuals to employ a wheelchair for mobility even though they maintain upper body movement. More severe conditions may compel individuals to use a wheelchair and leave them unable to use the upper body for tasks. Depending on the nature of an individual's mobility restrictions, the exact barriers that are faced can vary.

For those with speech impairments, there is also a range of involvement, from slurred speech to total inability to speak. The following are some general examples of barriers, but they vary from individual to individual.

For wheelchair users, self-care may not be a major problem because these individuals often can use their hands for activities of daily living. The most significant problems facing this population are the architectural barriers that can prevent individuals from attending work, school, church, or other social functions. Architectural barriers, however, are beyond the scope of this book, as we are chiefly concerned with technology for information access.

For the person who has little or no reliable hand and arm control and reduced upper-body strength, activities of daily life may require more effort and planning. In many cases these individuals must use personal-care attendants to assist with housekeeping, operating kitchen appliances, and other functions around the home and workplace. Telephones also present barriers to persons with little or no reliable hand and arm movement. Computers may not be accessed easily due to lack of adaptive equipment; similarly, a host of office equipment, such as photocopiers, fax machines, word processors, and typewriters, may be difficult to access.

Overview of Adaptive Technologies for Persons with Motor and/or Speech Impairments

The list of adaptive technologies designed to assist persons with motor or speech impairments is extensive. Computers can be adapted to respond to spoken commands, permitting equal access to jobs and information. Adapted keyboards can be customized for persons with minimal typing ability, and special switches can respond to the wink of an eye or even breath control; in fact, any reliable body movement can be used to control a personal computer. Morse code also can operate a personal computer, and an adapted switch of almost any configuration can produce the dots and dashes. Portable communications devices at home, school, office, or in public situations can speak for those who have no voice. Environmental control systems can turn electronic equipment on and off and control heating and lighting around the home or office. For a complete description of these technologies and their vendors, consult Chapter 5.

Stimulated by the personal computer, it almost goes without saying that we can look forward to more powerful and less expensive adaptive technology to assist persons with disabilities. Clearly, adaptive technology can do much to create greater independence and opportunity, especially when coupled with legislation to mandate equal opportunity for persons with disabilities.

The Americans with Disabilities Act

The Americans with Disabilities Act (ADA), signed into law on July 26, 1990, is the most comprehensive civil rights legislation to protect persons with disabilities against discrimination. The bulk of the ADA is based on Section 504 of the Rehabilitation Act of 1973 and the Civil Rights Act of 1964. Broken down into five basic sections, the ADA outlaws discrimination against individuals with disabilities in private employment, state and local government employment and services, public accommodations, transportation, and telephone communications. For our purposes, we have greatly simplified the ADA. This information is not intended to circumvent the advice of an attorney or published government regulations. We have attempted to provide an overview as it relates to employment. The following discussion, based on booklets provided by the U.S. Equal Employment Opportunity Commission (EEOC) and the Department of Justice in Washington, D.C., deals mainly with Title I, job discrimination aspects of the ADA.

The ADA makes it illegal to discriminate against qualified disabled persons in both the private and public sector. This means that private companies are now covered by civil rights legislation. In the past mainly federally funded institutions were mandated to comply. Job discrimination against people with disabilities is illegal if practiced by private employers, state and local governments, employment agencies, labor organizations, and labor-management committees. The ADA is enforced by the EEOC and by state and local civil-rights enforcement agencies that work with the EEOC.

The ADA currently outlaws job discrimination by private employers with 25 or more employees. After July 26, 1994, companies with 15 or more employees will fall under ADA jurisdiction. Another part of the ADA in effect as of January 26, 1992, prohibits discrimination in state and local government programs and services, including job discrimination by all state and local governments, regardless of the number of employees.

According to the ADA, it is illegal not to hire a disabled person solely on the basis of a disability. Under the ADA, persons are considered disabled if they have a physical or mental impairment that substantially limits a major life activity. To be protected under the ADA, persons must have a record of impairment or be regarded as having a substantial, as opposed to a minor, impairment. A *substantial impairment* is one that significantly limits or restricts a major life activity such as hearing, seeing, speaking, walking, breathing, performing manual tasks, caring for oneself, learning, or working. Only long-term disabling conditions are covered under the ADA. Individuals who break a leg, for example, are not covered under the ADA because this is a temporary condition.

Under the ADA, businesses are not required to hire unqualified individuals just because they are disabled. Therefore, the person in question must satisfy the employer's requirements for the job, such as education, employment experience, skills, or licenses.

The candidate also must be qualified to perform the essential functions or duties of a job. *Essential functions* are the fundamental job duties that the person must be able to perform independently or with the help of a reasonable accommodation. An employer cannot refuse to hire persons who are disabled because their disabilities prevent them from performing duties that are not essential to the job.

The term *reasonable accommodation* is one that has become a buzzword of late, but it is a concept that is helpful in the world of disabilities. Reasonable accommodation is any change or adjustment to a job or work environment that permits a qualified applicant or employee with a disability to participate in the job-application process, to perform the essential functions of a job, or to enjoy benefits and privileges of employment equal to those enjoyed by employees without disabilities. Some relatively simple and common examples of reasonable accommodation include providing or modifying equipment or devices; restructuring a job; allowing part-time or modified work schedules; reassigning the individual to a vacant position; adjusting or modifying examinations, training materials, or policies; providing readers and interpreters; and making the workplace readily accessible to and usable by people with disabilities. Many forms of adaptive technology are considered reasonable accommodation. This book describes many such adaptive devices to guide the employer and employee toward the appropriate reasonable accommodation.

The employer is required to provide a reasonable accommodation to a qualified applicant or employee with a disability unless the employer can prove that the accommodation would be an undue hardship. Thus, the employer would have to prove that providing the reasonable accommodation would cause significant difficulty or expense.

On-the-Job Discrimination

The ADA also protects employees against on-the-job discrimination in all its other forms; for example, it is illegal to fail to promote persons solely on the basis of a disability, and so forth. It also is illegal to discriminate in recruitment, firing, hiring, training, job assignments, pay benefits, layoff leave, and all other employment-related activities. The Act also protects a person if he or she is a victim of discrimination because of family, business, social, or other relationships or associations with an individual with a disability. Furthermore, it is unlawful for an employer to retaliate against people for asserting their rights under the ADA.

Job-Application Questions and Practices

An employer cannot ask job applicants if they are disabled or ask about the nature or severity of a disability. However, an employer can ask if applicants can perform the duties of the job with or without reasonable accommodation and ask applicants to describe or to demonstrate how, with or without reasonable accommodation, they would perform the duties of the job.

Prior to offering a job, an employer cannot require applicants to take a medical examination. Following a job offer, an employer can condition the offer on the applicant's passing a required medical examination, but this is permissible only if *all* entering employees for that job category have to take the examination. However, an employer cannot reject persons because of information about a disability revealed by the medical examination unless the reasons for rejection are job-related and necessary for the conduct of the employer's business.

Employee Medical Examination Issues

Once a person has been hired and has started on the job, the employer cannot require that the employee take a medical examination or ask questions about the employee's disability unless the questions or examinations are related to the job and are necessary for the conduct of the employer's business. The employer may conduct voluntary medical examinations as part of an employee health program and may provide medical information required by state workers' compensation laws to the agencies that administer such laws. The key point here is that the employer may not examine an individual based only on the fact that the employee has a disability.

Filing Charges of Discrimination

People who suspect that they have been discriminated against in employment on the basis of disability should contact the EEOC promptly. Those who have been discriminated against are entitled to a remedy that will place them in the position they would have been in if the discrimination had never occurred. They may be entitled to hiring, promotion, reinstatement, back pay, or reasonable accommodation, including reassignment. A person may also be entitled to attorney's fees and to monetary damages in certain circumstances.

Public Accommodations and Transportation

In addition to protecting persons from job discrimination, the ADA requires that public facilities and transportation be accessible to individuals with disabilities. The Act requires that places of public accommodation must offer accessible facilities to persons with disabilities. This includes hotels, restaurants, theaters, auditoriums, banks, shopping malls, hospitals, train and bus stations, libraries, museums, amusement parks, recreation facilities, and other public facilities. Newly constructed facilities must be fully accessible to persons with disabilities. If an existing facility is scheduled for significant alteration, the renovated facility must be accessible to persons with disabilities. In addition to public facilities, the ADA requires that transportation be accessible. Because this book focuses on adaptive technology for employment and education, a full description of this portion of the ADA is beyond its scope.

ADA Technical Assistance Centers

Congress mandated the National Institute on Disability and Rehabilitation Research (NIDRR) to establish ten regional centers to provide information, training, and technical assistance to employers, people with disabilities, and other organizations. The centers act as a central source of information on ADA issues in employment, public accommodations, public services, and communications. The toll-free number to contact the nearest center is 800-949-4232. The individual centers also can be contacted directly by phone or by mail.

The regional technical assistance centers can provide further information on how to comply with the ADA. The Department of Justice in Washington, D.C., is also another source of information on the ADA. The Department of Justice maintains a computer bulletin board that contains the full text of the ADA and its applicable regulations. The board also contains the "Title II Technical Assistance Manual" that gives details concerning the state and local government provisions of the ADA for free downloading. The number of the bulletin board is 202-514-6193. The voice number of the Department of Justice is 202-514-0301, and the TDD number is 202-514-0381.

Region I
Connecticut, Maine, Massachusetts, New Hampshire, Rhode Island, Vermont

New England Disability and Business Technical Assistance Center
145 Newbury St., Portland, ME 04101
207-874-6535 Voice or TDD

Region II
New Jersey, New York, Puerto Rico, Virgin Islands

Northeast Disability and Business Technical Assistance Center
354 South Broad St., Trenton, NJ 08608
609-392-4004 Voice; 609-392-7044 TDD

Region III
Delaware, D.C., Maryland, Pennsylvania, Virginia, West Virginia

Mid-Atlantic Disability and Business Technical Assistance Center
2111 Wilson Blvd., Ste. 400, Arlington, VA 22201
703-525-3268; Voice or TDD

Region IV
Alabama, Florida, Georgia, Kentucky, Mississippi, North Carolina, South Carolina, Tennessee

Southeast Disability and Business Technical Assistance Center
1776 Peachtree St., Ste. 310 N., Atlanta, GA 30309
404-888-0022 Voice; 404-888-9007 TDD

Region V

Illinois, Indiana, Michigan, Minnesota, Ohio, Wisconsin

Great Lakes Disability and Business Technical Assistance Center
1640 West Roosevelt Rd. (M/C 627), Chicago, IL 60608
312-413-1407 Voice; 312-413-0453 TDD

Region VI

Arkansas, Louisiana, New Mexico, Oklahoma, Texas

Southwest Disability and Business Technical Assistance Center
2323 South Shepherd Blvd., Ste. 1000, Houston, TX 77019
713-520-0232 Voice; 713-520-5136 TDD

Region VII

Iowa, Kansas, Nebraska, Missouri

Great Plains Disability and Business Technical Assistance Center
4816 Santana Dr., Columbia, MO 65203
314-882-3600 Voice or TDD

Region VIII

Colorado, Montana, North Dakota, South Dakota, Utah, Wyoming

Rocky Mountain Disability and Business Technical Assistance Center
3630 Sinton Rd., Ste. 103, Colorado Springs, CO 80907-5072
719-444-0252 Voice; 719-444-0268 TDD

Region IX

Arizona, California, Hawaii, Nevada

Pacific Coast Disability and Business Technical Assistance Center
440 Grand Ave., Ste. 500, Oakland, CA 94610
510-465-7884 Voice; 510-465-3172 TDD

Region X

Alaska, Idaho, Oregon, Washington

Northwest Disability and Business Technical Assistance Center
605 Woodview Dr., Lacey, WA 98503
206-438-3168 Voice; 206-438-3167 TDD

Additional information on employment issues is available in *A Technical Assistance Manual on the Employment Provisions (Title I) of the Americans with Disabilities Act* issued by the Equal Employment Opportunity Commission. A copy of this document can be obtained from the EEOC by calling 800-669-EEOC for voice, or 800-800-3302 for TDD.

Conclusion

One of the most fearsome barriers that must be dealt with—and the most difficult to circumvent—is not physical: it is the barrier of negative attitude created unwittingly by a lack of information or old-fashioned narrow-mindedness. A negative attitude on the part of the mainstream community can range from misplaced pity and a desire to "protect" to a simple false belief that the disabled are unable to achieve. Such mental barriers also can reside in the minds of persons with disabilities, robbing them of the ability to achieve their fullest potential. Prompted by fear or insecurity, a negative attitude can keep individuals who have disabilities from allowing themselves the chance to grow and adjust to a new way of living. Regardless of who holds this attitude, it can prevent persons with disabilities from having a chance to sink or swim on their own merits.

With the application of adaptive technology, users can move boldly and powerfully—assistive technology can empower persons with disabilities to become more productive and prosperous. Because of the flood of computer-based adaptive technology, persons with a wide range of disabilities can become more independent and employable. The opportunity to achieve meaningful employment is closer than ever, now that the Americans with Disabilities Act is on the books and enforced. With the proper adaptive equipment and a personal computer, persons with disabilities can work alongside their nondisabled counterparts, experiencing the satisfaction and rewards offered through the pursuit of career and educational goals.

2

The Personal Computer

The personal computer has virtually transformed the way work is performed in the classroom and in the office. Nowhere is this more obvious than in the lives of persons with disabilities who rely on sophisticated computer-based technologies on a daily basis. Many adaptive technologies consist of advanced hardware and software for personal computers, and they draw on the power of the computer for their assistive tasks.

Computers were originally intended to perform rapid mathematical calculations, but today's personal computers execute more than computational tasks. People use modern personal computers to write documents, manage budgets, draw diagrams and other graphics, create animated presentations, compile mailing lists, search remote computerized databases, send and receive mail electronically, and even play games. Students use computers to tackle homework and classroom assignments, and employees perform work at the business site and at home on computers. In fact, computers are an integral part of the workplace—most businesses have computerized their operations to increase productivity and profits.

More than ten years ago computers such as the Apple II, IBM PC, and Macintosh represented the beginning of the personal computer revolution. Today, the cost of personal computer systems is decreasing steadily while their power and capability is increasing sharply. It is now possible to purchase complete personal computer systems for about one or two thousand dollars, and some machines are even less expensive. For persons with disabilities, these developments mean increased access to information and the work environment.

From Abacus to Apple

Since the dawn of recorded civilization, humans have long sought devices to quickly and accurately perform mathematical calculations. The first generation of computing machines were mechanical. The abacus, a 2,000-year-old apparatus, is one of the earliest attempts to build a device specifically for performing numerical operations. This ancestor of the modern computer consisted of movable beads strung on parallel wires held in place on a wooden rack.

In 1822 Charles Babbage, a mathematics professor from Cambridge, England, constructed a working model of a mechanical calculator that he called the Difference Engine. Babbage conceived his Difference Engine to be steam powered and capable of performing rapid numerical calculations, but it was never commercially manufactured.

Just before the turn of the twentieth century, still pursuing the dream of the computer, the United States government used a mechanical card-sorting machine to process data collected from the census of 1890. The computer-like device used punched cards to organize and sort information, greatly reducing the time to complete the census count. Although the card-sorting machine proved somewhat workable, true programmable computers did not exist until the next century.

In 1946 the first successful electronic digital computer was realized. Known as ENIAC (*E*lectronic *N*umerical *I*ntegrator *A*nd *C*alculator), it employed almost 20,000 vacuum tubes in its construction. The early computer systems were unlike the user-friendly machines we now possess. The relatively primitive data-storage methods—punched cards—required huge mechanical feeders and sorters capable of processing several hundred punched cards per minute (an extremely slow process compared to the standards of today). Early computers were operated by complex switches, and the operator had to be familiar with binary notation. (Modern computers are programmed through English-like syntax.) Reprogramming these early computers sometimes required that they be rewired. These early computers were also massive, chiefly because they relied on vacuum-tube technology for their operation. The computers of the day were the size of auditoriums, and only programmers, engineers, and scientists had access. But these embryonic systems led to computers that changed the face of the business world.

The Babbage Difference Engine was a primitive mechanical computer that was never commercially manufactured. True computers had to wait for the dawn of the electronics industry in the twentieth century before they were fully practical. *Courtesy of The Computer Museum, Boston.*

In the early 1960s the mainframe computer entered the marketplace, allowing more institutions to enjoy the benefits of computing machines. (A mainframe computer is a large centralized computer connected to a network of video terminals, each taking its turn at the main computer in a process known as time sharing.) Mainframe computers stored their information on vast reels of magnetic tape. Although an improvement over punched cards, magnetic tape had to be searched in a linear fashion to locate

The huge Univac computer of 1951 had a magnetic-tape storage system and keyboard console. *Courtesy of The Computer Museum, Boston.*

a specific item of information, a process that could take many minutes. IBM, then the leader in mainframe sales, sold complete mainframe systems for as much as twenty million dollars each. Although mainframes were out of the financial reach of private individuals, many colleges, businesses, and medium-sized institutions were able to computerize their operations with mainframe computers.

The development of the transistor and the integrated circuit resulted in smaller electronic devices and greatly contributed to the success of the computer and electronics industry. The transistor was much smaller than the older vacuum tube technology, and integrated circuits could include thousands of transistors on a wafer-thin chip about the size of a postage stamp. Armed with transistor and integrated circuit based components, engineers constructed smaller circuit cards and, thus, were able to build more miniature and reliable radios, televisions, and, finally, computers.

In the late 1960s the minicomputer, a smaller and less-expensive version of the mainframe, evolved. Because it was within the budget of smaller organizations, the minicomputer

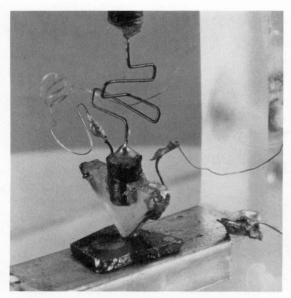

In 1947 the transistor was first assembled at Bell Labs. This "point-contact" transistor amplified electrical signals by passing them through a solid semiconductor material. This process revolutionized the electronics industry and was a giant leap toward smaller and more reliable electronic devices. *Courtesy of The Computer Museum, Boston.*

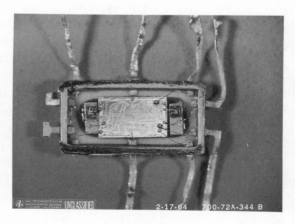

In the late 1950s the integrated circuit was developed, leading to even greater miniaturization and reliability of electronic devices. The first customers for these wafer-thin chips were numerous commercial firms, NASA, and the U.S. Air Force for integration into defense-related systems. *Courtesy of The Computer Museum, Boston.*

The Altair, a low-cost computer, was first assembled from a kit. The photo shows its internal system cooling fan, power supply, circuit boards, and front panel control switches, all of which had to be wired, soldered, assembled, and/or mounted. *Courtesy of The Computer Museum, Boston.*

enabled smaller businesses and other institutions to computerize their operations. Like the mainframe, the minicomputer could drive networks of terminals, bringing time sharing to a larger population.

In the mid-1970s the first personal computers, smaller and less expensive than minicomputers or mainframes, were sold in kit form to be assembled by hobbyists who were interested in electronics and engineering. These kit computers led to commercially manufactured computer systems from a variety of vendors. Apple, Radio Shack, and IBM rolled out personal computers that more of the general public could afford. In the late 1970s and early 1980s, the Apple II, IBM PC, and Macintosh created a market for computers and computer programs that forever altered business and education. The new generation of commercially successful personal computers has brought a new independence to persons with disabilities, perhaps the greatest positive change in the history of rehabilitation.

Computer Hardware

Personal computers have much in common with their older mainframe and minicomputer counterparts. Today's personal computers have capabilities, power, and speed similar to those of mainframe computers. Many of the same components found on mainframes are also on personal computers—but on a smaller scale.

Hardware consists of all the physical components of a computer. The following sections define and describe basic hardware components of a typical personal computer: central processing unit, input devices, output devices, memory, storage systems, and expansion slots and circuit cards.

The Central Processing Unit

The central processing unit (CPU), also called a microprocessor, is the engine that drives the computer. It is the heart of any computer system. The CPU interprets and carries out instructions according to specific software programs. It resides on the mother board—the main circuit board for a computer system. In the past, the CPU of a mainframe computer filled a room, but the CPUs that drive current personal computers are wafer-thin chips about an inch square.

The type of CPU is of immense significance because the speed of the chip will determine the amount of work the computer can perform and how long it will take to accomplish a given task. The speed of the CPU is measured in millions of cycles per second, or megahertz (MHz). This measurement is the clock speed of the computer. The faster the clock speed, the more calculations per unit of time the machine can perform. Modern personal computers have clock speeds of up to 50 MHz, and even faster clock speeds are contemplated for future models. The average clock speed for a typical personal computer system is around 15 to 20 MHz. The user can tell how fast a computer is by the number assigned to the CPU. For example, IBM-compatible computers use 286, 386, and 486 processors, with the higher number indicating the faster CPU.

Persons with disabilities should purchase computers with fast CPUs because computers fitted with adaptive equipment will need additional power to deal with both mainstream and adaptive hardware and software. If the CPU is using a significant portion of its power running the mainstream application, it will have little power left over to deal with the adaptive equipment. The reverse

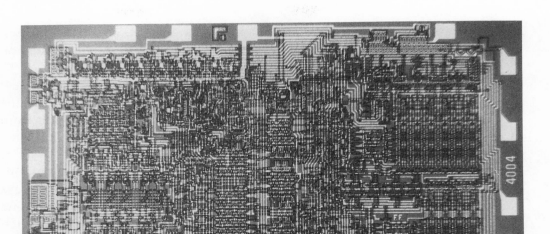

In 1971 the first microprocessor, the 4004 manufactured by Intel Corporation (shown), contained 2,300 miniature circuits. By 1981 more than 100,000 transistors could be placed on chips the same size. *Courtesy of The Computer Museum, Boston.*

is also true. Thus, a fast CPU will prevent the adapted system from being slowed down.

Input Devices

Computers process information—but only the information selected by the user. Before information can be processed, it has to be entered, or input, into the computer's memory. Modern personal computers use a typewriter-style keyboard as an input device. The user types on the keyboard, and the information thus is entered into the computer one character at a time. The mouse is another type of input device that is used to point to objects on the screen. The next sections discuss these input devices in detail and point out their possible barriers that can be overridden by adaptive technologies.

Keyboards

Keyboards are input devices that allow users to enter data to be processed by the CPU. Based on the time-honored design of the typewriter, each computer keyboard contains roughly 100 individual alpha-numeric keys similar to the print symbols present on a standard typewriter.

Although somewhat similar to typewriters, computer keyboards contain some keys not found on typewriters. These unique keys allow the user to enter information in a way different from that of typewriters, to move the lighted pointer—the cursor—through documents, and to issue specific commands to the system. For example, a numeric keypad contains numbers and calculator-style arithmetic operators for performing calculations. Arrow keys move the cursor up and down one line at a time or left and right one character at a time. Other keys rapidly move the cursor through documents in larger increments if desired: The Pageup and Pagedown keys move the cursor up or down one page at a time. The Home key moves the cursor to the top of the current document, and the End key moves it to the end of a document. When the Insert key is struck, the user can inject characters, words, sentences, or blocks of text into the space occupied by the cursor.

Included on a computer keyboard are unique keys for command and control functions. The Control and Alt keys provide users with an alternative Shift key, allowing commands to be sent directly to the CPU. For example, to print a document, the user depresses the Control key while holding down the P key. Ten to twelve function keys, labeled F1 through F10 or F12, are arranged either across the top or along the left edge of the keyboard. These function keys can be programmed to execute multiple keystrokes and complex command sequences. Pressing a single function key can issue strings of complex commands in rapid succession.

A keyboard either can be attached directly to the main housing of the computer or connected by cables. Detachable keyboards are often easier to use as they can be positioned close to the user or at a more desirable work angle.

The keyboard may present a great barrier or no barrier at all. For persons with vision impairments, the keyboard itself presents few barriers, and speech, magnification, and braille adaptive technologies provide verbal, visual, or tactile feedback of individual keystrokes. For persons who are hearing impaired, the keyboard offers few barriers. For persons with motor disabilities, the keyboard can present a significant barrier, but adapted keyboards and other assistive systems can help an individual hurdle many of these barriers. Because of its major role in using a personal computer, the keyboard is the focus of many adaptive technologies in removing potential barriers.

Mice

Mice are palm-sized instruments with a roller ball on their underside and with two or three control buttons to click on top. Users maneuver mice around on desktops in conjunction with their keyboards to move the cursor around the screen similar to the actions produced by the arrow keys. When a mouse is moved, the cursor follows its speed and direction on the screen, and the cursor quickly points to the place desired.

Mice can present barriers for persons who are visually or motor impaired. However, technologies that circumvent or emulate a mouse can overcome these barriers.

Output Devices

All computers require a way to present information to the user either during processing or after processing is completed. Modern personal computers use a video monitor screen as an output device, allowing the computer to display both text and graphics. Other output devices are printers that provide hard-copy paper documents to the user. The next sections describe these and other output devices in detail, along with the barriers they may present and the role of adaptive technologies in overcoming the barriers for persons with certain disabilities.

Monitors

Data to be processed is typed into a system through a keyboard and displayed on a video monitor, a device based on the cathode ray tube. The monitor contains a gun that fires a beam of electrons at a light-emitting layer on the interior face of the tube. When an electron strikes this layer, a dot of light appears on the screen. Monitors can be purchased in monochrome or color formats. By using different chemicals in the photosensitive layer, all the colors of the spectrum can be produced. Monitors have separate controls for brightness and contrast similar to the controls on a standard television set. Typical monitors are external units that connect to computers via cables.

Depending on the individual disability, a monitor can introduce an immense barrier or no barrier whatsoever. For a person with vision impairments, the monitor presents a great barrier in its unmodified form. The technologies of speech synthesis, magnification systems, and braille can translate the output from a monitor into a verbal, enlarged, or tactile format, allowing persons with vision impairments greater access. For persons who are hearing

Pictured is the typical configuration of IBM-PC compatible computers. The monitor is separate from but shown on top of the CPU cabinet. Floppy disk bays are on the right of the cabinet, and the keyboard is shown in front. *Courtesy of Paul Avis.*

impaired or those who have motor and/or speech disabilities, the monitor offers few barriers.

Printers

The printer is a common output device that produces hard-copy paper documents. Most printers can print on single sheets of paper. Tractor-feed printers print on fanfold paper stock with perforated strips that guide the paper along. Printers are external devices that connect to the computer with a cable. There are a number of basic types of printers on the market.

Dot matrix printers are among the least expensive models. These printers use individual inked dots to print text and graphics. The dots are printed close together, giving the appearance of a solid line. Dot matrix printers are appropriate for printing letters and other long or short documents. Because they use individual dots to produce characters, dot matrix printers also can print graphics (pictures). To produce "letter quality" text, dot matrix printers use more dots per square inch for an image with finer detail.

Letter quality printers, sometimes referred to as daisy wheel printers, use rotating print wheels to print text. These printers can only reproduce the characters present on their print wheels; therefore, they cannot construct graphics or other special symbols. Thus, their output is more like that from electric typewriters than is output from other computer printers. The print wheel turns under software control. When a certain text character is desired, the wheel rotates to strike that particular character against a ribbon that transfers the character to the paper. As with a typewriter, the letter quality printer uses an ink cartridge or ribbon.

Laser printers use a photoreaction process similar to that of photocopiers. First, the laser printer creates a graphic image in its memory of the page to be printed, then it reproduces that image using a laser beam to write the image line-by-line onto a rotating cylinder. After passing under the laser beam, the cylinder is covered with a chemical known as toner. Toner adheres to the cylinder wherever the laser beam was present. The cylinder is then covered with ink and pressed to the paper to produce the image. Ink will only transfer to the paper where the toner was present. The laser printer can print text and graphics in any number of type sizes and character sets.

As its name implies, an ink-jet printer uses controlled streams of ink to spray shapes of letters and other symbols directly on the paper. Ink-jet printers can be used to print both text and graphics and are a less-expensive alternative to laser printers.

Input/Output Ports

A computer port is a place to plug in standard cables that connect the computer to a printer, other computers, or adaptive devices. A computer's ports send and receive information to communicate with the external device. Input/output ports are configured as serial, parallel, or SCSI.

Serial and Parallel Ports

With serial ports, data travels in a fashion similar to that of a train: each data bit follows the one in front. With parallel ports, data travels in parallel wires, side-by-side as on a multiple-lane superhighway. It is important to know which kind of port is required to interface external devices and adaptive hardware. For example, mice connect via serial ports. Printers can connect to either serial or parallel ports, but most printers today use parallel ports. Many adaptive devices attach to these ports as well.

Computers can have more than one serial and more than one parallel port. Computers that will be adapted should have at least one serial port if not two. If more than one printer is to be connected, then the computer may need more than one parallel port.

SCSI Ports

Another type of input/output port, the small computer systems interface (SCSI) port can be used to communicate with other internal or external devices. For example, adaptive devices such as voice recognition systems attach to some brands of computers through the SCSI port. A single SCSI port can be used to control multiple devices. A SCSI port can be added to an IBM-compatible, whereas the Macintosh comes from the factory with its own SCSI port.

Modems

The modem, a popular addition to most computer systems, is used to send and receive information at high speeds over the telephone system. The term *modem* stands for *MOdulator/DEModulator*. The pulsed signals produced by a modem are transmitted over the telephone lines and are decoded at the other end by a receiving modem. Computer-to-computer interchanges via telephone lines use the American Standard Code for Information Interchange language, or ASCII for short. A computer connected to the phone via modem can call other computers to send and receive data. This information might be the latest stock prices, the morning newspaper, an encyclopedia, a graphic image, a text document, or electronic mail from the office. A modem is a powerful option to attach to any personal computer because it can broaden greatly the user's information horizons.

Numerous types and brands of modems are on the market. They can be purchased as either external or internal devices for computers. Some modems also may double as facsimile (fax) machines, allowing users to send and receive faxes from their keyboards.

Modems that transmit data at faster rates of speed are more expensive than their slower counterparts. The speed of a modem is measured by its baud rate—the speed at which data flows through a cable or connector. (The term *baud rate* also is used with other computer devices.) Current high-end modems can transmit at speeds as high as 14,400 baud. Higher speeds are also possible. The average speed for a modem is currently 2400 baud.

Computer Memory

Memory is the physical work space of a computer system and the place where documents are held while work is performed on them. The limitation of memory defines the amount of work that can be performed by a particular system; memory is one of the yardsticks against which performance is measured.

There are two different types of memory: alterable and unalterable. Memory that is alterable by the user is called random-access memory (RAM), and memory that is unalterable is called read-only memory (ROM). RAM and ROM are measured in units called bytes. The terms *bytes* and *bits* are used a great deal in the world of computers. A byte is one character of information, such as a letter, number, or punctuation mark. Bytes are composed of even smaller units known as bits. It takes eight bits to make one byte. Metric prefixes denote quantities of storage for memory and other units. Thus, a kilobyte (K) is 1,000 bytes of information, and a megabyte (MB) is 1,000,000 bytes. (It's a bit more complicated than that, but this serves as an approximation.)

Memory is of prime concern to the person using adaptive hardware and software. For persons who are visually impaired and who use speech, magnification, or braille adaptations, the demands on a computer's memory are fairly high—consuming about 64K of memory. For a typical personal computer, this might be one-tenth of the total system memory. For the user who is deaf or hard of hearing, memory consumption is also of great concern, as communications software will consume valuable RAM space. For the user who is motor or speech impaired, memory usage is also of prime importance because many assistive programs, such as software to lock down individual keyboard keys, applications to predict the word a user wants to type, software designed to either use or bypass the mouse, and applications designed to generate hundreds of keystrokes with the strike of a single key, can use a great deal of memory. These software utilities can be stacked in memory, one on top of another, making it vital to run them on a system with as much memory as possible.

Storage Devices

All computers need a place to permanently store information. The disk drive is one of the most important subsystems of the personal computer, as it is here that documents and files will be stored while the system is not in use. The disk drive is a high-speed data recorder capable of storing and retrieving large quantities of information. Tape drives also store data, but are now mainly used to make duplicate copies of a disk drive for safekeeping. However, disk drives have much in common with their tape-based cousins—both types of devices rely on magnetic oxide media and recording heads to store information. A typical disk drive records data on an oxide-coated spinning platter similar to a phonograph record.

The amount of disk storage, measured in kilobytes or megabytes, is of prime importance. The larger the amount of storage, the more information can be accessed by the user. Since there are strong trends for providing text and other information in disk-based formats, and since information stored on disk is more accessible than printed material, disk storage is especially important to persons with disabilities. Therefore, persons with disabilities should gravitate toward purchasing personal computers with as much disk storage space as possible, keeping both present and future disk storage needs in mind.

Floppy Disks and Hard Disks

The two basic types of disk storage devices for personal computers are floppy disks and hard disks. A floppy disk drive uses removable disks for storage; thus, the user can record information on blank disks, similar to recording information on blank tape cassettes. The most common floppy disk sizes are 3.5-inch and 5.25-inch formats. A 5.25-inch disk can hold as little as 360K or as much as 1.2MB of storage. A 3.5-inch disk can hold as little as 720K or as much as 1.4MB of information. To visualize these amounts, consider that an average paperback book will fit almost perfectly in 720K.

Floppy disks allow users to transport information from one computer system to another. Hard disks, on the other hand, are not movable across computers because they are internal devices. The primary advantage of hard disks is that they have a much greater capacity to store information than floppy disks. The typical hard disk drive is a sealed unit that can hold hundreds of megabytes of data.

Computers can have varying combinations of hard and floppy disk drives. That is, a computer may have one floppy drive, two of the same size, a combination of the two sizes, or any of the preceding combined with a hard disk drive.

For people with disabilities, especially persons with vision impairments, information stored on disk is a very accessible format; thus, they may store large quantities of information on disk as a standard practice. Therefore, a large hard drive is recommended.

For some individuals, such as persons with motor impairments, inserting and removing disks may be a barrier, so a computer is more accessible if everything is stored on one hard disk drive.

Compact Disks

Compact disks also can be used to store information on personal computers. These are known as CD-ROM for compact disk read-only memory. As their name implies, information on a CD-ROM disk can be read but not added to or deleted. A CD-ROM disk can hold hundreds of megabytes of information because it is cut with a laser beam rather than with a magnetic pulse. With its data bits much closer together, more information per unit of space resides on the CD-ROM disk than is possible on other storage media. For example, a single CD-ROM disk may store an entire dictionary, encyclopedia, or a virtual library of information. Chapter 6 describes CD-ROM systems and their implications for persons with disabilities.

Tape Drives

Tape drives were once the chief storage system for mainframe and minicomputers, and even personal computers used tape drives in the 1970s. Today, however, they are used chiefly for backup purposes—to make extra copies of data for safekeeping. A typical tape drive is similar in concept to a standard cassette recorder, allowing the contents of a hard disk to be quickly and easily copied. Current tape drives can compress information as it is stored, allowing larger amounts of information to fit on the backup tape. Access to an individual bit of data is not fast on a tape drive because the user must wind through segments of tape to find a specific item. Tape drives can be purchased either as internal units or as external mechanisms with separate enclosures.

Expansion Slots and Circuit Cards

Expansion slots and circuit cards are important computer hardware considerations. Inside nearly every personal computer are expansion slots that allow users to add new equipment to the system by plugging in new circuit cards (also called circuit boards or, simply, boards). An expansion slot provides both data and electrical connections for a given circuit card.

Circuit cards perform a wide range of functions that can increase the overall power and capability of an existing computer system. For example, circuit cards can be inserted into the com-

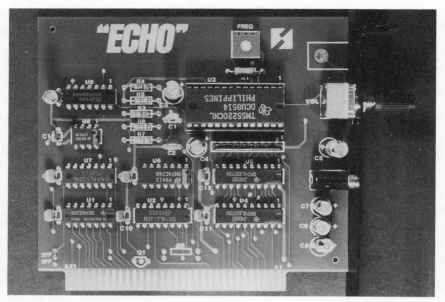

The Echo speech synthesizer card (see speech synthesis in Chapter 3) contains microprocessor chips and an edge connector that plugs into an expansion slot on the mother board of IBM PC-compatible computers. *Courtesy of Phillip Rounseville.*

puter to add speech synthesizers, magnification systems, voice recognition systems, input and output devices, modems, etc.

Although they are not found on every brand of computer system, expansion slots are standard equipment on most computers. For example, the family of IBM PC-compatible personal computers have between three and eight expansion slots each, the Apple IIGS has seven, and the Macintosh computer has between one and six expansion slots, depending on the particular model.

Installing a Circuit Card

When a circuit card is plugged into the system, it is as if it had been installed at the factory. To install a circuit card into an expansion slot, first turn off the power to avoid shock or damaging the circuit card itself. Next, open the computer case with a screwdriver to expose the expansion slots. The slots generally can be found along the rear of the case, and the circuit cards are plugged into the slots in a vertical position. Some computer systems have slots arranged in a horizontal configuration, and the circuit cards are inserted on their sides rather than upright. The rear of the circuit card often has a metal plate that contains an interface jack or other type of connector. These connectors are used to attach cables to the circuit card. For example, a voice recognition circuit card plugged

This interior view of the ALR personal computer shows the power supply (upper right corner) with its warning labels. The mother board has one circuit card plugged into an expansion slot (upper left corner). The 3.5-inch disk drive appears in the right-central position at the bottom of the photo. *Courtesy of Paul Avis.*

into a computer would then connect to a microphone through its interface jacks on the rear of the circuit card.

When installing a circuit card, some technical considerations are in order. Each circuit card must be assigned a unique number known as an interrupt. An interrupt may be thought of as a phone number. Each card must have its own unique number, and no two cards can share the same interrupt, otherwise the system will fail to operate. A circuit card interrupt can be set by flipping tiny switches on the card. These switches are called dip switches.

As with interrupts, cards can be set to occupy unique memory addresses. No two cards can share the same memory address, otherwise the system will fail. Some computers automatically adjust the address locations of the installed circuit cards to prevent conflicts with other cards, while others must be manually configured. Although a full discussion of interrupts and memory addresses is beyond the scope of this book, it should be generally known that these kinds of conflicts are a major source of potential problems when adapting personal computers with circuit-card–based adaptive technology.

Expansion slots and circuit cards are the foundation for adaptive technology, allowing off-the-shelf personal computers to be adapted for persons with disabilities. Since many adaptive devices are circuit cards, personal computers can readily be adapted with many different types of assistive technology.

Software

Whereas hardware may be considered the physical body of the computer, software may be thought of as the brains behind the hardware. Without software, the hardware would merely be idle with no tasks to perform and no instructions to follow. Computer software consists of a list of instructions that the computer executes in a deliberate order. The instructions can be carried out in sequential order, or they can be initiated out of sequence according to the rules of a particular programming language. When the user turns on his or her computer, the software controls how the video display will look and governs the interaction with the personal computer.

The bulk of personal computer software available on the open market is being sold commercially for a profit. Commercial software can be purchased in computer stores and through mail order outlets. The user is not allowed to copy commercial software, as this violates the standard user agreement against piracy and copyright law. Users who willingly copy commercial software and give it to others may be subject to a fine or other penalty under the law.

Another class of software is known as shareware. As its name implies, shareware can be copied freely and shared. This type of software usually can be purchased by mail through the vendor. Shareware most often is distributed by small software houses that use online databanks and word-of-mouth to spread the word about their programs. Contrary to popular belief, shareware software is not free but is offered on a try-before-you-buy basis. Users who find the software to be of value are encouraged to send the vendor a nominal registration fee that entitles users to technical support and possibly to the latest version of the program. This is done on the honor system.

Freeware, frequently called public domain software, is software that can be copied freely by the user. There is never any charge for this software. Freeware is often distributed on bulletin boards, online services, and at computer clubs and groups.

A fourth classification of software might be called vaporware. This term applies to any product that has been announced publicly by a vendor but that does not have a specific release or shipping date.

The following sections describe some of the various forms of software found on most personal computers. These are classified by their basic functions: disk operating systems and applications packages including word processors, databases, spreadsheets, utilities, telecommunications packages, and programming languages.

The Disk Operating System

The disk operating system is a software program that allows the computer to manage information stored on the disk drives. Once the disk operating system is running, other software can be accessed to perform a specific task.

The operating system performs many important functions and handles all files created on the computer system. (A file on a computer is like a labeled manila folder; it contains electronic data such as a letter or group of letters, a balance sheet, a mailing list, or other data.) The disk operating system keeps track of all files created on the system, displays lists of select files, and copies, deletes, renames, moves, and sorts files. The operating system also loads, saves, and executes software programs.

Although there are many operating systems on the market designed for specific personal computers, the two basic types are text-based and graphics-based systems. Text-based operating systems rely on a command line in which the user enters commands at a system prompt and presses the return, or Enter, key to execute the command.

The graphical user interface relies on graphics and icons, or pictures of objects, to send commands to the computer. Graphics-based operating systems also rely on a mouse as a pointing device to highlight objects to be selected. Task switching, in which more than one program can be run at a time, is another aspect of a graphical user interface. Each program has its own separate window, or small region, on screen.

The disk operating system for IBM PC and compatible computers is known as MS-DOS, from Microsoft, or PC-DOS, from IBM. MS-DOS can be controlled through a command-line interface or through a graphical user interface. The graphical user interface for MS-DOS is known as Microsoft Windows. OS/2, another product of IBM, is a graphics-based operating system that runs on IBM PC and compatible computers. For the Apple Macintosh, the operating system is System 7, which is a graphics-oriented operating system that uses both the mouse and the keyboard to control the system. For the Apple IIGS, GS/OS is a graphics-based operating system, also employing a mouse for many functions. UNIX is an operating system that can support multiple users, and can use both a text interface and a graphics interface.

Applications Programs

Most software packages are application programs. For example, applications programs allow the user to write letters, perform budget calculations, manage mailing lists, communicate with other computers, draw graphics, and perform a host of other functions. Some applications packages perform multiple functions by integrating word processing, database, spreadsheet, and other tasks into a single software package.

Word Processing

One of the most common applications programs on the market, word processing software allows the user to write, edit, and print text documents. To take full advantage of word processing software, the user must have a printer connected to the computer. The typical word processing program allows the user to enter text via the keyboard and edit the text for any desired format (letter, report, etc.). After the document is written or edited, it can be saved on disk and retrieved later. Word processing programs usually come on floppy disks and are easily installed on almost all personal computer systems.

In simple terms, a word processing software package allows the computer to perform as an automated typewriter—but with many more-sophisticated functions, such as moving or deleting blocks of text, sorting lists alphabetically or numerically, searching for a word or phrase and automatically replacing it with a specified insertion, and writing in newspaper-like columns. Word processing packages often include a spell checker that points out possible spelling mistakes and provides alternatives for corrections. Many word processing programs also have features that allow both text and graphics to be incorporated into a document. These packages are called desktop publishing programs. For example, WordPerfect, from WordPerfect Corporation, is a word processing package that also has some desktop publishing features. WordPerfect runs on many different computer systems, including Macintosh and IBM PC. Microsoft Word is another word processing program that runs on many different personal computers. There are also other word processing programs on the market that have various features and abilities to perform editing tasks.

Databases

Database programs may be thought of as electronic filing cabinets. With a database program the user can keep track of all manner of lists and sort the lists for specific purposes. Database programs range from the very simple to the complex, allowing the user to manage small or large quantities of data. Some databases, called flat-filing systems, are the electronic equivalent of three-by-five-inch–card boxes. More complex databases, known as relational databases, allow the user to relate or sort two databases with respect to one another and produce a third list, based on criteria provided by the user. For example, dBASE, from Borland, is a relational database program for MS-DOS personal computers. Fox Base, a product of Microsoft, is another relational database.

Spreadsheets

Spreadsheets, with their numerical columns or rows, are used primarily for performing mathematical calculations. Typically, spreadsheets are used in accounting for managing the books of a business; there are also applications in the hard sciences and statistics and for algebraic formulas. The user presses the arrow movement keys to move through the spreadsheet and enters numbers and labels through the keyboard. Lotus 1-2-3, from Lotus Development Corporation, was the first electronic spreadsheet developed, and it is still in use for both business and scientific applications. For example, Excel, from Microsoft, is a graphics-based spreadsheet. Quattro Pro, from Borland, is another spreadsheet package for both text and graphics-based systems.

Utilities

The series of applications programs known as utilities are both broad based and many; this classification of software performs many different functions for the user. Utilities help the user manage the data stored on the system and diagnose and repair potential problems with the hardware or software. For example, with utilities the user can un-delete accidentally deleted files, sort files by user-defined parameters, search for files or text within files, restore disks that have been accidentally erased, check for computer viruses, etc. Utilities generally are used by more technically minded and advanced computer users, but this is becoming less true as these powerful packages become more user friendly. For example, Norton Utilities, from Symantec Corporation, is compatible with both the IBM and Macintosh platforms. PC-Tools, from Central Point Software, is another source of software utilities.

Telecommunications

Telecommunications packages let the user send and receive information with other personal computers or with remote computerized information databanks. Once the computer has been equipped with a modem, almost any telecommunications program can be engaged to send and receive text and graphics files over the telephone lines. These programs contain dialing directories, allowing the user to select a particular remote computer system. Many telecommunications packages also allow the user to record all incoming information and save it permanently to a file. Procomm, from Datastorm Technologies, Telix, from Exis, and Qmodem, from Mustang Software, are examples of telecommunications packages on the market.

Programming Languages

Programming languages are one of the most basic tools offered by the software industry. By using programming languages the user can create new software programs and build customized software for a specific need or task. In the past, programming was not for the fainthearted because it required the skills of a systems engineer. With the user-friendly crop of programming languages on the market, a relative novice can create software packages, in many cases as polished as those of a professional programmer. BASIC, the most widely known language in the computer world, is frequently the language most users learn or teach themselves. One of the most-used computer languages currently is C, an almost universal dialect that can run on most computer systems.

Personal Computer Manufacturers

Since the evolution of the personal computer during the mid-1970s, computers are found in homes, schools, and large and small businesses in ever-growing numbers. Although there are many brands available, the majority of adaptive hardware and software is manufactured for three main brands/types of computers: the Apple IIGS, Apple Macintosh, and IBM PC (and PC-compatible).

Computer brands are not all compatible with one another. For example, software intended for an Apple will not run on an IBM because of the basic architectural differences between the different brands of CPUs. Computer purchasers should make certain that the selected software and hardware will run on their computer brand of choice.

The Apple IIGS

In the mid-1970s, the Apple computer was created by two young men who wanted to develop an affordable computer for the general public. Apple Computer, Inc., is now one of the major suppliers in the computer industry. The current Apple machine now being sold by Apple dealers, the Apple IIGS, has text, graphics, and sound capabilities.

The basic Apple IIGS system comes with 1MB of memory and a 3.5-inch floppy disk drive, color monitor, keyboard, and mouse. It can be purchased with a hard disk drive, additional floppy drives, additional memory, and other extra equipment if desired. The Apple IIGS computer can perform word processing, database management, spreadsheet functions, programming, and other applications. The Apple IIGS also has built-in adaptive functions, including a screen magnification program (see Chapter 3) and a keyboard modification program (see Chapter 5). The memory size can be expanded with memory expansion circuit cards, creating a larger work space for memory-intensive functions such as desktop publishing and drawing graphics. The Apple IIGS also can be outfitted with printers, modems, and a wide range of adaptive technologies.

The Apple has an open architecture; that is, its specifications are published in the public domain so that other vendors can create hardware and software products for that machine. Its open architecture makes the Apple relatively easy to upgrade and expand. Expansion slots also make it possible to adapt the system with assistive hardware.

The Apple II's uncomplicated disk operating system allows the user to perform many disk housekeeping functions, such as copying disks, formatting disks, moving individual files, programming in BASIC, and running applications programs from a menu-driven user interface. With the range of mainstream and adaptive hardware and software available for the Apple, the machine is useful as a platform for adaptation.

The Apple Macintosh

The Apple Macintosh, another product of Apple Computer, Inc., is a graphics-based personal computer system. The graphics-based user interface shortens the time required to understand system functions. The Macintosh computer is compatible with many adaptive hardware and software packages, making it a system of interest among the disabled community.

The typical Macintosh system has 2MB of memory and a 3.5-inch floppy disk drive, 40MB hard disk drive, black-and-white monitor, detachable keyboard, and mouse. There are several versions of the Macintosh, and Apple creates upgraded Macintosh systems with some regularity. The physical appearance of the Macintosh can vary slightly from machine to machine. Macintosh systems, such as the Macintosh Classic and Macintosh Plus, are housed in a hard plastic case containing the monitor, disk drives, and CPU. The Macintosh II series resembles the family of IBM PC computers with separate enclosures for the CPU and video monitor, each connected by interface cables. The Macintosh series also features a detachable keyboard with external connectors for attaching the mouse.

The mouse plays a major role within the Macintosh environment. For example, to view any file the user points to its icon with the mouse, then clicks the mouse button to open the file and display file contents on a window on screen. Multiple files can be open at the same time. To delete a file, the user merely points to the desired file, clicks a mouse button, and drags the icon of the file into the trash can icon. The deleted file can be recovered if the user has not "emptied the trash."

The Macintosh is a system compatible with many mainstream and adaptive hardware and software products. It also has built-in adaptive software, including a screen magnification program (see Chapter 3), a keyboard modification program (see Chapter 5) that allows the arrow keys to substitute for the mouse, and speech capability that makes it directly compatible with speech software for users who are blind, visually impaired, or speech impaired.

IBM PC and Compatibles

In the early 1980s, the IBM PC established itself as a standard among personal computers and led to a class of machines known as PC compatibles. In this section, we use the term IBM PC to stand for computers that are true IBM computers as well as computers that are IBM compatible. This hardware platform is compatible with many adaptive hardware and software products, making it a common system among persons with disabilities.

The base IBM PC system consists of 1MB of memory and a 5.25-inch floppy disk drive, 40MB hard disk, monochrome monitor, and detachable keyboard. The unit is capable of great expansion and can be augmented with additional floppy disk drives, larger hard disk drives, more memory, color monitors, etc. The IBM PC consists of several individual components built around a modular configuration. The main element is the CPU housing. The memory, main mother board, disk drives, and expansion slots and connectors are contained within this enclosure. The CPU housing has connectors for attaching a keyboard and a video monitor and for interfacing a printer and other peripheral devices.

The basic hardware configuration of the IBM PC contributes to its adaptability because the computer is built along an open-architecture format. In other words, the IBM PC has easily accessible expansion slots that allow all manner of adaptive hardware to be plugged into the machine.

Laptops and Notebooks

As personal computers became more powerful, they also grew smaller due to demands from the business community and the general public for computers that were both robust and compact. Business persons want to take their computers on trips and to conferences and meetings; therefore, the ideal personal computer for a busy executive should fit in a briefcase, be lightweight, and be capable of running word processing, database, and spreadsheet software. Persons with disabilities also require lightweight computers. In fact, portability is a desired trait in almost any adaptive or mainstream device, and it is especially important for persons with disabilities because their computers are used for more demanding tasks than writing letters or looking up phone numbers. That is, persons with disabilities often must carry their computers to communicate with friends, family, and coworkers. Many powerful computer systems are portable and can be adapted for persons with a wide range of disabilities.

Shortly after the personal computer was developed the technology began shrinking in size, leading to the development of a new class of computers called "luggables." These semiportable computers weighed about 20 pounds and were about the same general size and shape as a portable sewing machine. They were highly sought after and often called upon to perform demonstrations and other work on the road. Compaq Computer began its corporate career offering luggable IBM PC-compatible machines to the general market. These portable computers contained many features of powerful desktop-sized personal computers including video screen, full keyboard, floppy and hard disk drives, and input and output ports. Eventually, portables were equipped with battery power, thus making them more portable and useful in varying situations.

As the demand for truly lightweight and portable computers grew, a new generation of even smaller computers sprang into existence. These petite machines received the fitting name *laptop* because they were generally operated while placed on the lap. The laptop computer was a welcome innovation for persons who wanted to carry their computers on the road. The typical laptop weighed in at under 10 pounds, and its flat shape made it much easier to carry. About the same basic shape as a large, thick notebook, a typical laptop computer could easily be carried in a shoulder bag, briefcase, or backpack.

Laptop computers are almost always battery powered, thus making them ideal for performing work while in transit. The current laptop computer comes equipped with a keyboard, mouse, floppy disk drive, hard disk drive, modem, fax, and even color video display. Many models of laptop computers also contain expansion slots, making them adaptable for persons with disabilities. Today, users can purchase laptops with the same power as personal computers and enjoy the same computer power and flexibility on the road as they have in the office. For example, the Apple PowerBook, a notebook-sized computer, includes a hard disk drive, floppy drive, monitor, mouse, and full keyboard, as well as a modem and printer ports. Toshiba, IBM, Sharp, Apple, Compaq, and Tandy are some producers for the laptop market.

The development of ever smaller and lighter portable computers continues. Presently, the notebook computer is the machine of choice for busy users. These computers weigh less than 5 pounds and are about half the size of most laptops. The average notebook computer has many of the features of the larger laptops, including full keyboard, mouse, hard disk drive, floppy disk drive, modem, fax, color video display, and large disk and memory capacity. A few notebook computers also have expansion slots for adding mainstream or adaptive equipment.

As computers continue to evolve, we can say with certainty that they will grow ever smaller, lighter, and more powerful. Portable computers allow persons with disabilities to carry the equivalent of bookshelves of information on the road and to access that information with their choice of adaptive equipment. Prices for these transportable computers also are being steadily lowered, making it possible for more individuals to take advantage of this technology.

Selecting a Personal Computer

At first glance, choosing a personal computer can seem a formidable task, one requiring the skills of an electronics engineer or computer expert. There are many questions to ask: What adaptive hardware and software will be necessary? Which computers will accept those adaptive devices or programs? How much memory is needed and how many disk drives? What physical size is appropriate? What mainstream software will perform the tasks in mind? Selecting the right adaptive equipment, personal computer, and software does not have to be a hardship; it can actually be a pleasant task, so long as the goal is approached after some planning.

The first question the user should ask is "What type of adaptive technology is needed?" This is not always an easy question to answer, but Chapters 3–6 provide some basic guidelines. The important concept with any form of adaptive technology is to provide a tool to allow the user to perform independently.

Once the adaptive equipment requirements are determined, the user is ready to select the computer hardware. The hardware obviously should be compatible with the adaptive equipment. If the desired adaptive equipment is based on a circuit card, the user should determine that the card is compatible with the computer hardware. If the adaptation is software based, the user should determine what computer the software will run on. The computer should have enough CPU power, random access memory, and disk storage space to run both the mainstream and adaptive functions. In addition, the user may want to purchase the computer from a reliable local dealer for easier access to technical support and maintenance.

The next question is "What software applications programs will be used?" Make a list of the computer functions needed. For example, the list may include tasks such as writing letters and class papers, compiling mailing lists and phone numbers, keeping track of personal and business finances, or drawing blueprints, pictures, or color graphics. Such a list of intended applications will help the user select appropriate software to meet the requirements.

Next, the user should browse through software catalogs and do some judicious window shopping. To avoid impulse buying do not bring money, credit cards, or a checkbook on the first of these shopping expeditions. The user also should strongly consider visiting a local computer users group or computer club, as these organizations offer a wealth of knowledge on the world of computers. For example, the Boston Computer Society of Cambridge, Massachusetts, the largest computer organization of its kind in the country, has a demonstration center that contains nearly every computer system in existence as well as a large software library that allows users to try before buying. Of course, the user should contact the various adaptive vendors and determine if their particular adaptive hardware or software will work with the mainstream software.

Use Figure 1 to record priorities for shopping for computer software, hardware, and adaptive devices. While reading the rest of this book, take time to make notations on the checklist.

Figure 1. Personal computer checklist

Directions: Check all items required. Complete the other columns when a potential decision is reached. Then check compatibility of items across sections.

Adaptive Equipment Required	Brand	Memory/Hardware Considerations
___ 1. Speech synthesis system		
___ internal hardware	_____	_____
___ external hardware	_____	_____
___ software	_____	_____
___ screen reader	_____	_____
___ 2. Magnification system		
___ optical aid	_____	_____
___ large monitor	_____	_____
___ closed circuit television	_____	_____
___ software-based magnification	_____	_____
___ hardware-based magnification	_____	_____
___ 3. Braille system		
___ braille translation software	_____	_____
___ braille printer	_____	_____

___ refreshable braille display

___ pocket braille computer

___ 4. Optical character recognition system

___ 5. Baudot/ASCII modem

___ 6. Beep indicator software

___ 7. Computerized sign language training

___ 8. Adapted keyboard
    ___ keyguard

___ 9. Keyboard modification software
    ___ macro software
    ___ sticky key and key modifier
    software

___ 10. Alternative input systems
    ___ adapted switches and scanning
    keyboard

    ___ Morse code system

    ___ word-prediction software

___ 11. Voice recognition system
    ___ hardware

    ___ software

___ 12. Alternative communications device

System Hardware Requirements

1. CPU (clock speed) _____

2. Memory (amount) _____

3. Disk space (amount)
    ___ hard disk (size) _____
    ___ floppy disk (number, size) _____

4. Expansion slots (number) _____

5. Serial ports (number) _____

6. Parallel ports (number) _____

7. SCSI port _____

8. Keyboard (type) _____

System Hardware Requirements (cont.)

9. Monitor (graphic/text,
   color/monochrome, brand) _____

10. Printer (type, brand) _____

11. Modem
    ____ internal (speed, brand) _____
    ____ external (speed, brand) _____

12. Fax
    ____ internal (speed, brand) _____
    ____ external (speed, brand) _____

____ 13. Network (type, brand) _____

____ 14. CD-ROM
    ____ internal (brand) _____
    ____ external (brand) _____

____ 15. Other _____

Applications Needed	Brand	Memory/Hardware Considerations
____ 1. Writing letters and other documents	_____	_____
____ 2. Filing mailing lists and other information	_____	_____
____ 3. Bookkeeping and financial forecasting	_____	_____
____ 4. Electronic mail and online communications	_____	_____
____ 5. Programming and writing new applications	_____	_____
____ 6. Drawing graphics and other images	_____	_____
____ 7. Sending/receiving documents via fax	_____	_____
____ 8. Optical character recognition scanning	_____	_____
____ 9. Computer-aided design	_____	_____
____ 10. Games and role playing	_____	_____
____ 11. Other _____		

3

Technology for Persons with Vision Impairments

With the appropriate assistive technology, persons with vision impairments can operate computers, access huge databanks, and read printed books and other materials at will. Keep in mind that persons with low vision possess differing visual abilities. A technology that is useful for one person might not help another. The most reliable method to determine if a technology is suited for an individual is to try that technology in a setting similar to that of the one in which it will ultimately be used.

The major categories of adaptive technologies to assist persons with vision impairments include speech synthesis, magnification systems, braille printers, and optical character recognition. Speech synthesis systems allow computers and other devices to speak out loud, thus making them accessible to persons with vision impairments. Magnification systems enlarge the text displayed on computer screens as well as printed texts, making them much easier to read. Braille printers and displays translate printed text into braille, permitting access to personal computer screens and other forms of information. Optical character recognition systems read the printed word and speak it aloud or transmit the text into personal computers for storage and retrieval. This chapter explores each of these basic technologies and discusses some specific products in detail. The inventory of products discussed here is in no way complete, and inclusion or omission does not imply endorsement or rejection. The final section of the chapter includes names, addresses, and telephone numbers of producers of these technologies.

Speech Synthesis

Speech synthesis is the artificial generation of the spoken word through the application of computer-based hardware and software. Typically, a speech synthesizer is a dedicated computer with a single task: to run text-to-speech software that translates text into the basic building blocks of speech known as phonemes. A speech synthesizer contains many of the components found on personal computers and in many ways is a computer system in miniature with its own memory, microprocessor, and output device. The on-board memory is designed to allow the text-to-speech software a place to reside when loaded, and the synthesizer's micropro-cessor is the engine that drives the software. The output device for a speech synthesizer is a speaker driven by a digital-signal processor—a dedicated microprocessor designed to process the many calculations that are necessary to generate speech output—and a digital-to-analog converter that translates the binary code to an audio signal suitable for playback on a speaker and amplifier. The technology of speech synthesis is one of the most powerful computer applications being used to assist persons who are blind or visually impaired. It is also one of the least expensive computer adaptations available; thus, it is a widely used adaptation for per-sons who are blind or visually impaired.

To convert a standard personal computer into a talking com-puter, the user must install additional hardware and software. The speech synthesizer hardware can be either a circuit card or an external peripheral device. The software is a screen reader, a software package designed to verbalize text or graphics and to drive the speech hardware. Once these are installed, the keyboard and screen become accessible to the user. The now-talking computer system makes the large base of commercial applications software packages accessible.

Internal Speech Synthesis Hardware

Internal speech synthesizers are circuit cards that plug into the expansion slots of personal computers. A typical circuit-card–based speech synthesizer contains its own memory, microproces-sor, digital-signal processor, digital-to-analog converter, speaker, and volume and pitch controls. Some synthesizers also contain controls for altering the rate of speech, although most synthesizers handle this speed control via software. Many synthesizers also have jacks to connect headphones or external speakers, while some

The Vert Systems Speech Plus text-to-speech synthesizer circuit card for IBM PCs and compatibles plugs into the mother board of the computer. *Courtesy of TeleSensory, Inc.*

units have their own speakers attached directly to the card. If the synthesizer has a speaker attached directly to the card, it is best to use an external speaker or headphones for clearer sound reproduction so the sound is not muffled by the computer cover or external housing.

Compatibility is an issue with internal speech synthesizers, as they are designed to work with only one type of computer system. That is, a speech synthesizer circuit card designed for an IBM PC will not operate with a Macintosh computer. Installing a speech synthesizer circuit card is not difficult, but it may be intimidating to an individual who has never before opened a computer. Installers should be familiar with how to remove the cover from their computers and how to insert and remove circuit cards in general.

Internal speech units offer both advantages and disadvantages. One advantage is that once an internal synthesizer is installed, it is not easily removed; thus, it is less prone to theft or abuse. Therefore, internal models are useful in a computer-lab environment in which the same personal computer is used by various people. The internal variety also responds more quickly to software commands issued by the user than external units because the synthesizer is connected directly to the computer's circuitry.

As discussed in Chapter 2, each circuit card within a personal computer is assigned a specific address space, known as an interrupt. Every circuit card must have its own unique interrupt, or it will conflict with other cards and refuse to operate. Therefore, users must determine the interrupts of other circuit cards installed in the system before installing the speech synthesizer.

Some internal speech synthesizers also require software drivers to operate. These device drivers tell the computer how to communicate with the speech hardware and how to pass data back and forth efficiently. Software device drivers consume memory and can cause potential conflicts with other software running on the system. Such conflicts can be solved easily if the installer knows how to properly configure hardware and software from different vendors.

Following are some examples of internal speech synthesizers. See the list at the end of this chapter for names and addresses of these and other suppliers.

Artic Business Vision

Artic Technologies produces a line of internal and external voice synthesizers for desktop and laptop computers. The Artic Business Vision package comes with an internal voice synthesizer and an MS-DOS–based screen reader. The system is text based and works with most word processors, databases, spreadsheets, telecommunications packages, and other commercial software. The voice synthesizer provides the user with a verbal window on the computer, allowing access to the screen. Once the hardware is installed, screen reading software must be loaded to control the voice hardware.

DECtalk PC

The DECtalk PC, from Digital Equipment Corporation, is an unlimited vocabulary text-to-speech synthesizer. This device is used for many applications within the disabled community including speech access systems for persons with vision impairments as well as alternative communications systems for persons with speech impairments. The DECtalk PC, made especially for the family of IBM PC-compatible computers, features both male and female voices. The unit comes with installation software and an external speaker. Documentation is provided on disk, making it accessible to persons with vision impairments. The DECtalk PC is based on the earlier DCT 01 DECtalk system, which was an external serially driven synthesizer. DECtalk PC can speak at up to 500 words per minute. Digital Equipment Corporation does not provide its own screen reader software for the circuit card, but many screen reader manufacturers sell and support this synthesizer.

Echo II

Echo II, from Echo Speech Corporation, is an unlimited vocabulary text-to-speech synthesizer circuit card that plugs into an expansion slot and is compatible with Apple II and Apple IIGS personal computers. It comes with Textalker, a screen reader that allows many Apple-based computer programs to speak aloud. For the Apple IIGS, the Textalker-GS screen reader software can be purchased, making even more software speech accessible. The Echo is compatible with many software packages for both the visually impaired and the learning disabled.

Speaqualizer

A product of American Printing House for the Blind, Speaqualizer is an internal speech synthesizer for the family of IBM PC-compatible personal computers. Speaqualizer does not require any software to operate; thus, it is transparent to the applications software and operating system. Unlike other synthesizers that require a separate screen reader software package, Speaqualizer contains its own screen reader in read-only memory. The synthesizer has an unlimited vocabulary and can verbalize most word processors, databases, spreadsheets, and other commercial software. Speaqualizer is suited for a hardware engineer who is visually impaired—the synthesizer will verbalize system boot screens, which are inaccessible to screen-reader–based synthesizers that first must wait for the disk operating system to load. It constantly monitors the video memory space and uses an external keypad to read select areas of this memory region. Since Speaqualizer uses no separate disk-based software, there are several basic advantages: it does not use any system memory for its operation, it does not depend on the disk operating system, and it speaks before DOS is loaded. Speaqualizer comes bundled with a full-sized IBM-style circuit card, an interface cable, and a separate control panel.

VertPro

VertPro, from TeleSensory, is a speech system for IBM PC-compatible microcomputer systems. This speech access system comes with voice synthesizer circuit card, external speaker, headphones, and IBM PC-based screen reader software. It also comes with an audio cassette tutorial. VertPro features a natural-sounding male or female voice that is well-suited to persons who have difficulty understanding synthesized speech. The unit is based on the DECtalk PC card from Digital Equipment Corporation.

External Speech Synthesis Hardware

External speech synthesizers are similar to the internal units except that they connect to the computer through the serial or parallel port rather than through the mother board. The typical external speech synthesizer contains its own memory, microprocessor, digital-to-analog converter, speaker, and headphone jacks within a self-contained housing. The synthesizer also contains controls for adjusting volume, pitch, and speaking rates. An external speech synthesizer connects to a personal computer via an interface cable, which connects the serial port on the computer to the serial port on the synthesizer. Most synthesizers come equipped with their own interface cables suitable for most computer models. It is a relatively uncomplicated matter to connect a speech synthesizer in this fashion. An external synthesizer also requires a separate power supply for its operation—either a power pack similar to most AC adapters currently on the market or an internal battery that enables it to operate without direct household current.

External synthesizers, too, have advantages and disadvantages. One of the advantages offered by external synthesizers is the ease of installation. In many cases, the user can connect most external voice synthesizers in half an hour, not counting the time it takes to configure the software drivers and screen reader. Another advantage offered by external synthesizers is their transportability from one machine to another, making it easy to use the same hardware on a home computer and a work machine, including laptop or notebook computers. Among the disadvantages of some external synthesizers is that they may be easily tampered with. Naturally, due to their external nature, they take up extra space within the work environment. Furthermore, because the external synthesizer uses one of the computer's serial or parallel ports, a second interface port may have to be installed for a modem or printer.

Following are some examples of external speech synthesizers. See the list at the end of this chapter for names and addresses of these and other suppliers.

Accent SA

Accent SA, from Aicom Corporation, is an unlimited vocabulary external voice synthesizer that is compatible with most personal computers with serial interface ports. The system will work on most IBM PC computers as well as Apple IIGS machines. Accent SA comes with a serial interface cable and an AC adapter external power supply; therefore, the system can run on AC or battery power. Its portability makes it useful for several computer systems. It also is useful to programmers interested in developing their own voice applications because extensive software drivers are provided for those working in BASIC or other high-level programming languages. The company also manufactures a card-based speech synthesizer, the Accent PC, which plugs into most IBM PC-compatible desktop computers, and speech synthesizer circuit cards for some laptop computers.

Accent, an external text-to-speech voice synthesizer, interfaces to the host computer through the standard serial interface port and is driven by several disk-based software utilities to convert text into speech. *Courtesy of TeleSensory, Inc.*

Artic Transport

Artic Technologies, the producer of the Artic Business Vision internal voice synthesizer, also produces an external speech synthesizer called Artic Transport. This external synthesizer is designed especially for laptop computers or for desktop users who want a portable synthesizer. The unit can be powered either by batteries or standard household current and comes complete with interface cables, screen reading software, and manuals on disk and audio tape. The unit also can be driven by many other screen reader software packages.

Echo PC

The Echo PC, from Echo Speech Corporation, is an external text-to-speech synthesizer that comes equipped with an attached cable. The device is compatible with most personal computers that have a standard serial interface port. The Echo PC is battery powered by a single 9-volt battery and includes an AC adapter. This portable unit is suited for interfacing to desktop, laptop, or notebook computers.

Speech Synthesis Software

Screen readers, software programs that directly command voice synthesizers, can drive either internal or external voice hardware.

Screen reading software allows persons with vision impairments to access commercial software with an unlimited vocabulary voice and to convert the text or graphics display of personal computers into verbal output. One of the first programs to be loaded into memory upon system start, a screen reader can coexist in memory with other software packages. Screen readers link the voice hardware to the computer's operating system so the keyboard and video display become verbally interactive; thus, users can hear their keystrokes spoken aloud and can read the video display on command. Depending on the needs of the user, the typical screen reader can instruct the synthesizer to speak keystrokes as individual letters or as words. The screen reader also can command the synthesizer to verbalize the video display character-by-character, word-by-word, line-by-line, or screen-by-screen.

Most screen readers are programmable and use menus to customize the software to each mainstream application. Depending on what information is present on the computer's display, the screen reader can be programmed to automatically read select portions of the screen. In other words, if the phrase "Help Screen" appears on the video display, the screen reader can be programmed to automatically read the entire video display based on that visual trigger. Users can customize their screen readers to work with specific word processors, databases, spreadsheets, telecommunications packages, and other software.

Windows, select portions of the screen, represent segments of the screen separated by boxes or some other delineating factor. Users can program screen readers and build voice windows to be spoken at the press of a key. For example, the user can tell the screen reader to verbalize the top twelve lines of the screen when a function key is pressed. Other windows, either overlapping or not, can be set up and read aloud at the press of a different function key. Thus, when appropriately configured, the screen reader allows the user to verbally glance at any portion of the video screen.

Color is used extensively in most software, and screen readers can recognize colors and act according to user requirements. Windows also can be distinguished by their color or other video attributes, and a screen reader can be programmed to either filter them out or speak them aloud. For example, if a blue text window pops up on the video display, the screen reader can be programmed to detect the blue text and verbalize it automatically. Similarly, if a menu uses highlighted text to indicate choices or if a flashing text message appears, the screen reader can be programmed to track that precise color or attribute and speak it aloud. Such programmed reactions can be useful when the user wants to track and verbalize a highlighted menu bar that moves when the cursor is relocated with an arrow key or mouse or when tracking the highlighted cell in a worksheet. In other words, the user can define exactly what the synthesizer should speak and what it should ignore.

The term "silence is golden" also applies to screen readers, and there are commands to squelch the speech upon command. The user even can tell the screen reader what not to verbalize and set up windows of silence on the display. This can be useful when a program talks too much. For example, a program that constantly prints the time and date to the screen brings endless chatter from the voice synthesizer. The silence feature is important because a screen reader will verbalize every word present on the video display and will not stop talking until it is commanded to do so. If a user hears what he or she wants early in this verbal landslide, then a way of silencing the speech is mandatory to allow the user to quickly skim the screen for a precise bit of important information. In general, there are two ways to silence the speech of any given screen reader: permanent silence or temporary silence. Permanent silence can be useful if a sighted person takes over the machine to accomplish a task.

One of the most important features offered by contemporary screen readers is known as screen review mode. This mode freezes the current application and reads what is currently on the video display. If a screen reader did not have a review mode, there would be no way for a user to replay previously spoken information; therefore, the user would have to be constantly on alert, waiting for every syllable emanating from the synthesizer's speaker. With a screen review mode the user can temporarily silence the speech and read the screen back at leisure. Review mode is most handy for programs that do not allow the user to redisplay the current screen of information or to move through that screen with an arrow key.

During review mode a second cursor, known as the review cursor, is activated. This cursor can be moved around the screen, independent of the writing cursor, simply by striking the up, down, left, or right arrow keys. Screen review mode also allows the user to control the voice synthesizer hardware by acting as a control panel to adjust parameters such as volume, pitch, and speaking rate. The user can tell the synthesizer what punctuation marks to pronounce or filter out; how to pronounce numbers, either as full digits or as words; to weed out strings of repeating characters, such as dots and dashes or other decorative characters; and to indicate capital letters, by using a higher pitch for a capital or by speaking "capital" when a capital letter is detected.

Tiny Talk

Tiny Talk, a shareware program from OMS Development, is an MS-DOS–based screen reader that uses little memory. It is compatible with most speech synthesizers, including Sounding Board, DECtalk PC, Accent SA, Accent PC, Artic, and other synthesizers. The software will drive both internal and external voice hardware.

Vocal-Eyes

Vocal-Eyes, from GW Micro, is a screen reader software package for the family of IBM PC-compatibles. The software is menu driven, allowing the user to configure it for most word processors, databases, spreadsheets, telecommunications packages, and other commercial software. Vocal-Eyes can be purchased with its own dedicated speech synthesizer—the Sounding Board. This system contains everything the user needs to make almost any IBM PC-compatible computer fully accessible to a user who is blind or visually impaired. The system comes with a speech synthesizer, external speaker, headphones, and the Vocal-Eyes screen reader software package. There are versions of the package for desktop computers as well as for certain laptops. Vocal-Eyes is a memory-conservative screen reader, making it compatible with applications in which memory is at a premium. The manual is offered in print, on disk, and on tape. The company also provides technical support by telephone.

Screen Readers for Graphics

Screen readers also can make a graphical user interface, such as Windows, OS/2, and System 7, speak with an unlimited vocabulary. Working much like its text-based counterparts, a graphics-based screen reader can verbalize icons, windows, and small windows within windows. Such screen readers can track the cursor and the mouse, allowing the user to read any object on the screen. The next sections describe specific screen readers that work within a graphics environment.

outSPOKEN

Berkeley Systems' outSPOKEN is compatible with the Apple Macintosh and works with most word processors, databases, spreadsheets, and other software packages that run under a graphics interface. The program can verbalize the screen display and individual keystrokes. Although outSPOKEN is software only, it does not require additional hardware to make the Macintosh speak because the Macintosh computer has built-in hardware capable of

The outSPOKEN software package for the Macintosh personal computer was the first screen reader to work under a graphics environment. *Courtesy of Berkeley Systems.*

producing an unlimited vocabulary voice. Therefore, there is no need to install a speech synthesizer card or to connect an external synthesizer.

The outSPOKEN program can verbalize icons and other graphic symbols. The user can define voice labels for icons by highlighting the icons and typing in text labels that will be spoken every time the icons are highlighted. The program can verbalize text as individual letters, words, or lines. Navigation commands under the outSPOKEN environment allow the user to employ the arrow keys instead of a mouse. Whether navigating by arrow keys or mouse, the user receives a verbal confirmation of whatever is under the cursor.

Screen Reader/2

Screen Reader/2, from IBM, is a graphics-based screen reader for the OS/2 operating system and Presentation Manager. As with Microsoft Windows, graphical user interfaces often display more than one window on the screen at a time. The Screen Reader/2 system consists of both hardware and software and comes bundled with a control keypad, allowing the user who is blind or visually impaired to verbalize any window displayed on the screen.

Users program the system through the Screen Reader/2 keypad. The keypad has a dedicated Help key, allowing the user to obtain assistance on all aspects of the screen reader software. Within the help mode, the user can press any key on the keypad and get a verbal description of that key's particular function. If the user so desires, the system also can be operated without a keypad, and Alt key combinations can be programmed to replace almost any keypad function.

As with Microsoft Windows, graphical user interfaces often display more than one window on the screen at a time. One of the most important jobs that is performed by Screen Reader/2 is keeping all screen windows isolated so that the user can deal with each window individually and not become confused with overlapping text and graphics. If the user is running a word processor and then switches to an online session, Screen Reader/2 knows which one is currently active and automatically loads custom environments for the correct task.

The Screen Reader/2 programming language is PAL, which stands for *Profile Access Language*. Based on Pascal, PAL is a true computer language in its own right. Commands within PAL can read any portion of the screen. These screen-reading functions can be set up with various triggers to read windows, lines, words, or characters when a preselected portion of the screen changes. The triggers also can be activated within loops that repeat verbalization until some condition changes.

Screen Reader/2 will work with many word processors, databases, spreadsheets, and other software packages. The speech software can make MS-DOS and OS/2 applications speak with an unlimited vocabulary and can work with most commercial synthesizers.

Window Bridge

Window Bridge, from Syntha-Voice, is a screen reader that works with many DOS/windows application programs. It is the first screen reader for Microsoft Windows to enter the adaptive marketplace. Window Bridge allows persons who are blind to access Windows and Windows-based applications programs. The program requires either an internal or external voice synthesizer. Window Bridge supports the Syntha-Voice synthesizer, Audapter from Personal Data Systems, DECtalk from Digital Equipment Corporation, the Accent PC and SA from Aicom Corporation, and the Artic 215 from Artic Technologies.

The company plans to add more supported synthesizers to the list in the future.

Window Bridge comes bundled in a three-ring notebook binder containing a program disk and a printed technical manual. The manual also is provided on disk, making it accessible to users with vision impairments.

Once Window Bridge has been installed, the system begins speaking immediately, as with a text-based screen reader. The software includes a review mode that allows the user to read any portion of the screen by moving the cursor with an arrow key. About fifteen seconds after Microsoft Windows is loaded, the Window Bridge program verbalizes both Window's program manager screen (a list of programs and utilities available) and other windows each filled with various applications. Window's icons can be voice labeled, and the user can select the window to enter by pressing a menu key.

Although the program requires a mouse, Window Bridge supports the keyboard as an alternative. Moving the up or down arrow key allows the user to move the mouse pointer around the screen. A mouse locator command allows the user to find any point on the screen by typing in a text string. An audible mouse function emits tones while the mouse moves: rising tones for upward mouse movements and falling tones for downward mouse movements.

Adapting a Screen Reader for Use with Mainstream Software

Adapting an off-the-shelf software package to operate with a screen reader is an involved task that requires skill with both the mainstream and adaptive software. This section should prove a useful exercise to illustrate how to adapt mainstream software packages.

The following example assumes that the user is working on an IBM PC-compatible computer system equipped with the MS-DOS operating system, a hard disk drive, either an internal or external speech device, and an MS-DOS–based screen reading software package. The version of DOS is not important nor is the brand of the screen reader being employed. Although the example is based on using the IBM PC version of the WordPerfect word-processing software package, no product endorsement is intended. The example uses features found on most screen readers, so it will prove to be a universal one.

First, start the computer and load the disk operating system by turning on the computer and waiting for the DOS prompt. Once the DOS system has loaded, the DOS prompt appears on the screen. This prompt will not speak until the screen reader is loaded.

Next, load the screen reader software. If the screen reader is stored in a different subdirectory, change to that directory using the Change Directory command in DOS. For our purposes, let's assume that the speech program is stored in a directory called "voice."

Type: cd\voice   (then press the Enter key)

Once the user has arrived at the correct subdirectory, start the screen reader by typing its name at the command prompt. (We shall assume that this command is called "talk.")

Type: talk   (press the Enter key)

When the screen reader loads correctly, the computer will begin speaking automatically.

Now, load the word-processing program by issuing standard DOS commands. First, move to the directory containing the word-processing program by using the Change Directory command, for example:

Type: cd\wp51   (press the Enter key)
Then type: WP   (press the Enter key)

The WordPerfect title screen will appear, then quickly disappear to be replaced by a blank screen where work is performed. The screen has two basic components: the space where actual documents are shown or composed (the first 24 lines of the video display) and the status line that gives the directory and file name, page number, line number, and cursor position.

With WordPerfect on the screen, we can begin building speech windows to verbalize select portions of the display. Since Word-Perfect displays its status line at the bottom of the screen, set up a speech window confined to the bottom line of the display. Program the screen reader to define a window with coordinates at line 25 from column position 1 to column position 80 and assign a hot key to read that line when the hot key is struck. Next, configure another window to read the top 24 lines of the screen. This will be useful to read the text within the work space or to read other menus that pop up on the screen. A third speech window can be built to read the entire screen from the upper left corner to the bottom right.

WordPerfect uses the standard cursor for most operations, which makes it easy for most screen readers to interact with the program. There are instances where the standard cursor is not displayed, but these can be dealt with by most screen reading systems. For example, the WordPerfect spelling checker displays inverse video attributes to emphasize a misspelled word. Therefore, program the screen reader to track that video attribute and assign a hot key to verbalize the highlighted word on command.

Construct another speech window to read the menu choices that WordPerfect displays when spell checking a document. This menu appears in a window from line 15 to the bottom of the text window. This definition process is relatively easy. First, define a window consisting of the entire screen from line 1 to line 25. Within this full screen window, the screen reader should be instructed to read inverse video. Depending on the screen reader, this can be accomplished in a variety of ways. Some screen readers allow the user to select video tracking from a menu, while others require the user to manually key-in window coordinates for this function as well as the exact color to track within those coordinates. This can be done most effectively with the WordPerfect spell checker actually on the screen because this task is more efficient and intuitive if performed with a working program. To customize the screen reader to verbalize the WordPerfect thesaurus, set up another speech window to read the choices offered.

It also is possible to set up monitor windows with most screen readers, an efficient method for customizing commercial software. The concepts of monitoring are uncomplicated, and many screen readers are capitalizing on this powerful feature. The screen reader can be instructed to constantly watch the entire screen or a portion of the screen for any change whatsoever. If anything changes within the target region, the screen reader can be instructed to take action. For example, if the status line changes for any reason, the screen reader can be instructed to speak it aloud. If the phrase "help screen" appears on the display, the screen reader can be programmed to automatically verbalize the text. Using the many functions of commercial screen readers, off-the-shelf software packages can speak with an unlimited vocabulary voice, allowing persons with vision impairments equal access.

Other Adaptive Speech Applications

Spinoffs from computer-based voice technology also assist persons at home, school, and on the job. These include direct spinoffs that create various talking devices such as talking credit card readers, talking machines to read paper money, and talking dictionaries. Even television programming can have an additional voice that describes the visual portion of select video broadcasts and films. Following are examples of such adaptive speech applications.

Special Touch Talking Credit Card Reader

Discover Financial Services has created a talking computerized credit card reader called Special Touch designed especially for persons with visual impairments. The system is used on the job at point-of-sale registers, allowing persons with vision impairments to work alongside their sighted counterparts. This is an important system because in the past, persons with vision impairments had to rely on assistance to process credit card transactions. Now, equipped with this system, persons with vision impairments can independently process on-the-job credit card transactions. The device uses a voice synthesizer that verbally reproduces all visual information in an audio format.

The Note Teller

An age-old problem for persons with vision impairments, the task of identifying paper money can be a serious and costly obstacle for the individual managing a home or a small business. The Note Teller, from Brytech, is a portable, battery powered, paper-money identification machine about the same size and weight as a small transistor radio. The device uses a voice synthesizer, speaking in either English or Spanish, that can identify paper bank notes from $1 to $100 denominations. When the user inserts paper money into the machine in any orientation, the voice synthesizer announces the amount aloud in a digitized voice. The unit includes a three-position volume switch and an earphone jack.

The Franklin Language Master Special Edition

Printed dictionaries have long been inaccessible to persons with vision impairments, and braille dictionaries are large and cumbersome and not easily transported. A hand-held talking dictionary has become reality with the Franklin Language Master SE from Franklin Electronic Publishers. This portable talking dictionary, about the size of a paperback book, contains the *Webster's Collegiate Thesaurus* and *Webster's Dictionary*. The Language Master has a typewriter-like keyboard, a volume control, and an external speaker/headphone jack. The keyboard can be programmed to speak each keystroke, and the screen also can be read back aloud with the strike of the Read key. The unit also can display text in enlarged format for persons with vision impairments and can function as a portable communications device for persons unable to speak.

Descriptive Video

Television programming need not present a barrier during periods of silence in a broadcast. Descriptive video provides a verbal description of scenery, costumes, and facial expressions of the characters. WGBH Channel 2 in Boston has pioneered the technology of descriptive video with its descriptive video service (DVS). WGBH has produced television programs and full-length movies with rich verbal descriptions included. To hear the descriptions the user must use the SAP button (secondary audio program channel) on the VCR or television. On the secondary audio program channel the descriptions travel parallel to the standard audio and video segments of a broadcast. Descriptive video can be useful for accessing entertainment broadcasts as well as technically oriented training videotapes.

In summary, the technology of speech synthesis is providing many useful devices to increase the independence and productivity of persons with vision impairments. Speech technology continues to improve, and the price for high-quality speech is decreasing because of competition and more efficient computer hardware. We can expect speech synthesis to become more widespread over the next several years due to the mainstream demands for this technology.

Magnification Systems

One of the most widespread technologies for persons who are visually impaired, magnification systems that enlarge text and graphics empower many individuals to pursue career and educational goals. Objects that are magnified produce a larger image within the eye; thus, they are much easier to see. The technology of magnification systems can be employed to read books and other printed material and to magnify information displayed on computer screens. The following sections discuss many forms of magnification technology, including low-technology optical aids, magnification software programs, hardware-based magnification systems, and closed circuit television reading systems.

Optical Aids

One of the first magnification approaches to try is that of optical aids, often called low-vision aids. These optical aids consist of magnifying glasses and small hand-held telescopes—inexpensive low-vision technologies useful for reading text or even computer screens. Some low-vision aids are hand held; others can be mounted on eyeglass frames. Users should consult with their physicians or low-vision clinics for evaluations of the various optical aids and devices.

The fact that most low-vision aids are portable is of immense value to the user. This allows the user to carry the various devices for many different applications at work or school and at home to read daily mail, the newspaper, food containers, medicine bottles, or the occasional novel. The devices also may be useful for mobility purposes, making the individual a safer and more confident traveler.

Some low-vision optical aids can be attached to personal computers. Once these devices have been fitted to the face of the monitor, the lens provides about 2× magnification. This type of lens also provides a shield from glare, which may be a great barrier to a person with low vision.

Compu-Lenz

The Compu-Lenz, from Florida New Concepts Marketing, is an optical screen magnification system consisting of a plastic lens and mounting hardware. The Compu-Lenz is designed to fit over many standard computer monitors to provide about 2× magnification. The device has no electronic or moving parts. The unit is portable enough to be carried in a backpack or briefcase.

Large Monitors

For the user who needs computer magnification, mainstream technology often can supply the answer. A larger monitor can provide the user with a magnification environment, thus gaining access to the wealth of information stored in a personal computer. A larger monitor will provide increased character size but will not reduce any of the information content that is normally present. Although the magnification will not be as great as that of a hardware or software magnification system, many individuals find such larger monitors useful.

Closed Circuit Television Systems

The closed circuit television system (CCTV) is an efficient way for persons with low vision to read books and other printed material independently. These devices consist of a detachable video camera and a television-type screen. CCTV systems also come equipped with sliding trays or tables that hold books and other printed information beneath the video camera and that adjust for maximum visibility. These sliding trays and tables can be motorized, allowing individuals to scan books or other printed material automatically. CCTV systems can provide from 2× to about 60× magnification, depending on the system.

The typical CCTV is relatively easy to operate, and a little user training is frequently all that is required. The user merely aims the video camera at the desired reading material and focuses the image on the video display, allowing the user to read the printed material in as large a type face as necessary for clarity. These units are about the same size and weight as a small television system, but portable units are also on the market. Monitors range in size from 4 inches all the way up to 20 inches and come in color or black-and-white.

Many CCTV systems can be interfaced to a personal computer to perform double-duty reading tasks. By splitting the image, half of the screen can contain a printed book or other print material while the other half contains output from a computer video monitor. This can be extremely useful for an individual who is entering print information into a personal computer or who must interact with both computers and printed text. However, a CCTV cannot magnify the computer image without magnification software.

Magni-Cam

The Magni-Cam, from Innoventions, is a portable CCTV system used by persons with low vision to read books, magazines, newspapers, food containers, or other printed materials around the home or office. The system consists of a hand-held camera that interfaces to standard color or black-and-white television sets. The hand-held camera scans printed material and displays the information in large type on a television system. The extent of magnification depends on the size of the television screen being used. For example, the magnification range for a 12-inch screen is from 6× to 24×. For a 24-inch screen, the range is from 12× to 48×. The Magni-Cam comes equipped with a transformer, interface box, and a 7-ounce hand-held camera. A set of wooden blocks is included to adjust the height of the camera above the printed page for focusing the camera. Options include a carrying case and an adapter switch, which allows the user to switch between reading and normal television viewing without having to disconnect the unit. The unit can be carried from home to office in a briefcase or in the optional carrying case. The Magni-Cam can display in reverse video (white-on-black), which is useful for persons with certain eye conditions. In addition, the unit has a built-in contrast control adjustment that allows the user to filter out bleed-through from poor quality print. The device contains a built-in 2-inch fluorescent lighting system on the underside of the camera.

Meva ME2A

The Meva ME2A system, from TeleSensory, is a lightweight, portable, battery-powered CCTV system for persons with vision impairments. The unit consists of a hand-held camera, a 4-inch video display screen, an analog/digital processor, and a rechargeable battery pack. The Meva is suitable for use in various academic and vocational situations in which portability and battery operation are essential. The system weighs less than 8 pounds and operates on battery power for up to 3 hours. A second battery pack is available to extend battery life. The unit has a user-selectable analog and digital display mode, and its 4-inch, flat video screen display weighs about 2 pounds. The camera is a charged-couple device (CCD), which is a solid-state camera system, making for clearer images. The illumination source is built into the camera stand, making for more efficient reading for long periods. The unit contains a video-enhancement system that can display positive (black-on-white) or negative (white-on-black) images.

20/20

The 20/20, from Optelec, is a one-piece desktop CCTV system consisting of a 14-inch black-and-white video display monitor mounted above a camera system. The system is designed for educational and academic situations. Basic features include brightness and contrast controls, size and focus knobs, image reversal, and power switches. The camera system is a solid-state charged-couple device. The video display is large enough for comfortable reading and can tilt and swivel for ergonomic control of the viewing angle. The unit can display both positive and negative images with a magnification range from 3× to 60×. It also provides split-screen display from a secondary camera or magnification software. Using this split-screen technique, the individual can read paper-based printed material as well as computer-based data at the same time, greatly speeding up productivity and efficiency. The 20/20 has a remote computer input to allow split-screen display of computer output. A mount is also provided for an optional secondary camera.

Vantage CCD

Vantage, from TeleSensory, is a CCTV system that magnifies any printed text. The user positions the reading material under the adjustable camera, which magnifies the text from 3× to 45×. The printed material appears enlarged on the built-in video screen in bright, bold characters. The nonglare screen can be raised, lowered, and tilted. A split screen mode can be used to view two documents at the same time. Vantage also can work with the Vista video enhancement card from TeleSensory. The system comes with a black-and-white 14-inch nonglare screen; green screens, amber screens, and 19-inch screens are also available. Manuals are in large print format.

Voyager

The Voyager, from TeleSensory, is a one-piece desktop CCTV magnification system with a 12-inch black-and-white video display monitor mounted above a camera system. The unit is designed for vocational and academic situations, but it is suited for home applications as well. The system's features include brightness, contrast, size, and focus controls; image reversal; and power

The Vantage CCTV uses a 14-inch monitor, a video camera, and a stand to enlarge printed text for persons with low vision. *Courtesy of TeleSensory, Inc.*

switches. The camera is a charged-couple device. The Voyager has a recessed, retractable, and adjustable-height leg system and a built-in, luggage-style carrying handle for transportability. The video system can display normal and reverse video. The unit has a magnification range of 3× to 45× and weighs about 40 pounds. TeleSensory also manufactures a color CCTV, Versa Color, that comes equipped with a tilt/swivel monitor.

Software-Based Magnification Programs

Perhaps the most-used magnification adaptation currently on the market is that of magnification software. This software allows personal computer users to increase the size of the characters displayed on a computer's video screen. Magnification programs can enlarge both text and graphics, depending on the brand of magnification software chosen. The user is strongly advised to "test drive" any potential magnification software package before selecting one for purchase. This is important because not all magnification programs are exactly alike in producing the shapes of characters while in enlargement mode.

The typical magnification program is a memory-resident utility that is run immediately after the disk operating system is loaded. This is an important point to keep firmly in mind with most adaptive software. Adaptive software that is loaded immediately after the disk operating system can magnify the software that is loaded into memory later in sequence. The average magnification software program can magnify the video display from 1.4× to 16×. Most magnification software packages are compatible with EGA and VGA video monitors and video adapter cards.

Magnification programs usually employ cursor-movement keys to navigate the video screen. The following commands are typical for several magnification programs, but they may vary from program to program. The Home key automatically moves the cursor to the top of the video display, while the End key takes the cursor to the bottom. The arrow keys move the cursor around by letter, word, or line units, depending on the package. Many magnification packages can be programmed to follow the standard cursor around the screen, so the user is always certain of the exact location of the cursor within the document or other task. With magnification, fewer characters in a line and fewer lines are visible on a screen than without magnification. Therefore, the ends of lines are not visible all at a time. Some magnification packages employ a review mode, allowing the user to strike a key to navigate over to the unmagnified screen image using the cursor-control keys. Many magnification packages use a mouse instead of the cursor keys to enter review mode and to read portions of the screen that are currently off the magnification display. Then the mouse can be used to read any portion of the unmagnified display, and the user can return to the previous location by pressing any other key on the keyboard.

The current generation of magnification software programs has the advantage of being an inexpensive adaptation when compared to hardware-based magnification processors—usually about one quarter the cost of most hardware-based systems. Additional advantages of software-based magnification programs are that no additional hardware is needed and that the adaptation can be made with little or no technical assistance. Most programs have their own software installation utility, allowing the inexperienced user to load the software onto the hard or floppy disk of almost any computer. Another benefit that magnification software has over hardware-based magnification processors is that they can easily be moved from one machine to another by simply uninstalling the software from one machine, physically bringing the magnification software to another computer, and then installing it on that machine. In this manner, a magnification user can use the same magnification program on a home computer and on a computer at a work site or in a school laboratory.

The current generation of magnification programs is compatible with much off-the-shelf video hardware for most personal computers. Most magnification programs are able to work with existing VGA video cards; however, the user may be required to switch the existing video card for a compatible circuit card to make the magnification program fully compatible.

The IBM family of personal computers is compatible with many magnification programs. The magnification programs for the IBM PC are designed to magnify other commercial applications software, such as word processors, databases, and spreadsheets along with telecommunications software, programming languages, and other software. The family of Apple IIGS computers has its own built-in magnification software called CloseView. There are also many applications that generate text enlargement for the Apple IIGS.

Braille Edit Express

The Braille Edit Express program, from Raised Dot Computing, is an Apple IIGS-based word-processing program that has its own built-in magnification processor. The user can enlarge the size of the video display while within Braille Edit Express, and the software also can translate text into braille with its built-in braille translator. The software works with many speech and braille adaptive devices. It was one of the first programs of its kind to become popular among schools and the disabled community.

CloseView

The Macintosh and Apple IIGS computers come bundled with their own magnification program, known as CloseView, directly from the factory. This magnification program is available by simply moving the pointer to its icon and clicking the mouse. The CloseView program can enlarge most software and is useful with word-processing, database, spreadsheet, and other applications packages.

inLARGE

The inLARGE program, from Berkeley Systems, is a Macintosh-based screen enlargement software package that works with most off-the-shelf software programs including word processors, databases, spreadsheets, telecommunications packages, and others. The inLARGE software can be installed to automatically load each time the system is started, making it easier to operate for a user with low vision. It also can work in conjunction with the outSPOKEN Macintosh screen reader (also from Berkeley Systems) to provide large print and voice output simultaneously.

MAGic

MAGic, from Microsystems Software, is an IBM PC-based magnification software package. A mouse can be used to move around the screen, or this feature can be disabled. MAGic can magnify both MS-DOS and Microsoft Windows programs. The MAGic software can be set to automatically scroll the screen to allow the user to move through documents with fewer keystroke commands. MAGic is designed to allow users to employ their preferred word-processing, database, spreadsheet, or other software program under the umbrella of the magnification environment. MAGic is compatible with most VGA, XGA, and SVGA video systems with resolutions from 640 by 480 to 1024 by 768. It automatically senses the computer's current video resolution and self-adjusts its parameters. MAGic uses little in terms of memory resources. The company provides free technical support.

ZoomText

ZoomText, from AI Squared, is an MS-DOS– and Windows–based screen magnification software program that runs on IBM PC-compatible personal computers. The software can work with most word processors, databases, spreadsheets, telecommunications software, programming languages, and other off-the-shelf software. The user can employ the arrow keys or the mouse to move around the magnified screen. ZoomText can magnify the screen up to 16×. The company also offers a 2× magnification package called inFOCUS.

Installing and Running a Magnification Software Package

Following is a general description of how a typical magnification software package is installed and operated. Since the program is software based, the user does not need to install any additional hardware on the system provided the correct video card is already installed. Typically, installation takes only a few minutes, and this process is usually handled with a software utility provided by the manufacturer.

First, the user must insert the program disk into one of the floppy disk drives. The command to begin the installation process is usually "install" followed by the Enter key.

Once the install command is executed, the program will ask for the source drive letter (where the magnification package installation disk is currently residing). The install program will then ask for the letter of the destination drive—where the enlargement software should be copied. The install program also will ask the user to place the new files in an appropriate folder or subdirectory on the target disk drive so that it will not become confused with other files stored on the system.

Next, the install program will ask if the information is correct and will verify all information before the actual copy is made to the destination drive. The install program also will often ask if the user intends to use Microsoft Windows. Depending on the answer, the install program alters the installation process so that the software will be more compatible with the user's working environment. The next question asks if the user wants to automatically start the magnification software each time the computer is started. If so, the enlargement software will be loaded each time the system is activated.

The typical magnification program can be run in a number of ways, depending on the system on which it is installed. When an enlargement software package is loaded onto the hard disk of an IBM PC, it can be loaded into memory and activated by typing its name at the command or DOS prompt. This will load the software into memory, allowing the user to strike control keys to increase screen magnification on command. Once the software is loaded into memory, the user will see the copyright screen, indicating that the program is ready for work and that other programs can now be loaded. Then the normal DOS prompt will reappear.

Hardware-Based Magnification Systems

Hardware-based magnification systems provide an enlarged video environment similar to that of software-based enlargement packages. These magnification processors come equipped with text-enlargement software as well as a dedicated video-controller circuit card that is responsible for processing the magnification commands. Therefore, the user must remove the old video card and replace it with the new video card. These systems are an appropriate alternative for users who have video systems that are not compatible with magnification software.

Hardware-based magnification systems offer features not found on software-only enlargement programs. These dedicated hardware packages can be purchased with external camera systems that allow the user to scan text and graphics images into computer memory and to enlarge and manipulate those images on the video display. With a hardware-based magnification processor, the user can display a split-screen image, with half the display devoted to the computer's output and the other half devoted to a textbook or other printed material. These systems also come bundled with a mouse to control cursor movement.

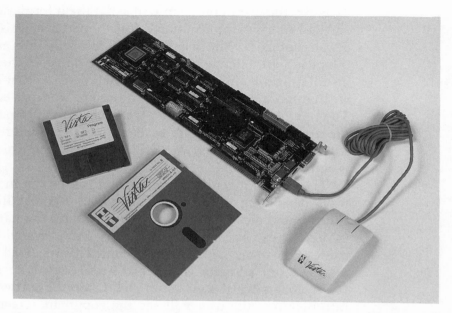

The Vista text and graphics magnification circuit card, mouse, and software disks are shown. The card plugs into most IBM PCs and compatibles to enlarge text and graphics. *Courtesy of TeleSensory, Inc.*

Display Processor 11

The Display Processor 11, a hardware-based magnification processor from TeleSensory, contains an interface card and dedicated monitor and control box. The system is compatible with most IBM PC-compatible computers and does not require any system software to operate.

Vista

Vista, from TeleSensory, is a hardware-based magnification circuit card. The system comes complete with text magnification software, mouse, and large-print documentation. The card is compatible with most IBM-compatible systems. Vista can work with most off-the-shelf word processors, databases, spreadsheets, telecommunications software, networks, and other software. The Vista system works under the MS-DOS operating system and the Microsoft Windows graphical user interface. It also can be used in conjunction with speech synthesis systems.

Vista can be programmed to track the standard cursor as well as colors and video attributes. It also can be programmed to retain vital screen information even while under high magnification. For example, the system can be instructed to retain a status line or other information regardless of the text magnification settings.

In summary, magnification systems are a cornerstone technology. The current class of magnification hardware and software packages are compatible with both text-based and graphics-based systems, a user-friendly environment for the individual with low vision. We can look forward to more magnification software in the near future because these utilities are desired by large segments of our aging population. Increasing numbers of vendors are entering this market.

Braille Systems

A version of the braille alphabet consisting of dots and dashes was originally used by French military in the field as a way to read and write messages under the cover of darkness. Louis Braille discovered this military code and decided to adapt it for use by the blind. In 1829 the braille alphabet was first published as a tactile writing system for individuals who were blind.

Today, the braille alphabet is incorporated into many adaptive hardware and software systems to assist persons with vision impairments. Braille printers can emboss braille at speeds of up to several hundred characters per second, and braille displays can provide braille output for computer access. The following sections discuss creating braille documents using a personal computer and word-processing software; using braille printers for personal, business, and mass-production applications; using braille translation software to translate word-processing text files into braille suitable for embossing on a braille printer; and refreshable braille displays, devices designed for accessing personal computers via mechanical braille output.

From Early Braille to Computer Technology

A braille character is called a cell, with each cell consisting of varying configurations of six individual dots. The dots are numbered 1 through 6, with dot 1 in the upper left corner of the cell and dots 2 and 3 just underneath. Dot 4 is in the upper right corner of the cell and dots 5 and 6 are just below. Using this combination of dots, it is possible to write letters, math symbols, music symbols, and even foreign languages. In the past, only skilled braille transcribers could convert printed text into braille because the rules for the production of braille are very strict and exacting. There are two basic forms of literary braille, Grade 1 and Grade 2. Grade 1 braille consists of the alphabet, numbers, and standard punctuation symbols, with no contractions. Grade 2 braille consists of the preceding and complex contractions to save page space.

From the early days of braille, the alphabet was embossed by hand using a wooden stylus and a slate. People still write braille using the slate-and-stylus method. The cells are written backward, from right to left, allowing the finished product to be turned over and read from left to right. The modern braille slate is hinged for inserting paper. The slate is then snapped closed to hold the document firmly in place. The slate consists of four to six lines of cell templates with guide holes to align the individual braille dots. The dots are punched by using a metal stylus through the guide cells. The pointed stylus is about an inch long. The user inserts the tip of the stylus into the appropriate aperture, pushes down with firm pressure, and forms the individual dots. The braille slate is portable and is analogous to pencil and paper.

As the technology of braille continued to advance, methods were developed to create documents in a more efficient manner. One of the first innovations was the mechanical braille writer, a device that produces braille at the speed of a typist. The braille writer contains six keys, one for each of the cell dots, and a space bar. It also has a handle for moving the carriage back to the left margin as well as a line-feed key to move the paper up line by line. The braille writer is available in electric models, making the braille production process faster and more efficient.

Perkins Brailler

The Perkins Brailler, a product of the Perkins School for the Blind, is about the size of a small portable typewriter. It can be purchased in either a manual or an electric model. The Perkins Brailler is used in employment and education settings. The device is constructed of cast metal, and it is not uncommon to encounter working units that are many decades old. Until a few years ago, the braille writer was one of the most efficient tools for producing braille. But the personal computer has taken over where the mechanical braille writer began.

Braille Translation Software

To create a personal computer capable of producing braille, the user needs to add both hardware and software to the existing system. The software is the braille translator, and the hardware is a braille printer. Braille translation software packages convert standard text into correctly formatted and contracted braille. Because of braille translation software and personal computers, braille can be produced now in quantity with limited knowledge of the discipline.

The process is one of text flowing in one end and braille flowing out the other, with the software in the middle performing the translation process. Braille translation software packages are available for many personal computers, including Apple IIGS, IBM PC, and Macintosh. The price range for these software packages is generally about a few hundred dollars, making braille translation affordable for most users.

Most braille translators work in two steps. First, they translate each print symbol in the source document into a corresponding braille computer symbol suitable for sending to a braille printer at a later stage. Second, the braille translator properly reformats the text to fit on the smaller braille page. The second step is the more complex task because the size differential between print and braille can be considerable in most cases. An example might better demonstrate the size difference: The average 8.5-inch by 11-inch print page consists of approximately 55 lines of text, with each text line containing about 70 characters (including word spaces). The average braille page, using the same sized paper, contains 25 lines per page and about 30 characters per line. This indicates that the denser print page must be compressed to fit on the braille page without losing critical formatting information.

The average book printed in braille is obviously much larger than its ink-print counterpart, several times bulkier on the average. To save space, braille uses numerous contractions for common words, such as *and*, *the*, *for*, and for common letter combinations, such as *st*, *er*, *ing*, and *ed*. In the past, the myriad braille contractions required the skills of an experienced transcriber to implement, but due to braille translation software, the personal computer can assist greatly in the production of braille.

The braille translator performs its formatting task according to precise rules of operation. Paragraphs are treated as they are laid out in the printed page, and double carriage returns are replaced with single ones to save space. The braille translator also converts paragraph indentions from five spaces to two spaces and converts every occurrence of a period and two spaces to a period and a single space to save space on the braille page. This reformatting is not a problem if standard paragraph units are used consistently on the print-source page. The braille translator performs the translation, compresses the lines to fit the shorter braille page format, and begins a new braille page after each twenty-five lines.

The difficulty begins when the translator encounters documents with more complex formatting, such as tables of figures or multiple rows and columns. These special cases must be reformatted by experienced braille transcribers after the translation process has been completed. Fine-tuning of the reformatting issue is still continuing. This has caused the industry to create sifters for specific word-processing packages that automatically translate specific word-processor formatting symbols into braille-compatible codes to fit more easily on the braille page.

Duxbury Braille Translator

The Duxbury Braille Translator, a product of Duxbury Systems, is compatible with IBM PC and Macintosh computer systems. The software works with most word-processing software packages to produce batches of braille output. One version of the translator is specifically compatible with WordPerfect, allowing native WordPerfect documents to be translated and formatted automatically. The software works with most braille printers, and the company offers technical support. The software is being used around the world for production of braille textbooks and other documents. The company also works with braille production houses on large-scale braille production techniques.

PC-Braille

The PC-Braille translation program, a product of ARTS Computer Products, works interactively with the WordPerfect word-processing package. PC-Braille can work directly with native WordPerfect text files to translate and sift for formatting. After the user creates the source document in WordPerfect, PC-Braille completes the translating and formatting tasks.

Hot Dots and Mega Dots

Hot Dots and Mega Dots, from Raised Dot Computing, are braille translation packages for the IBM PC family of personal computers. The programs are menu driven and are compatible with most commercial braille printers.

Ransley Braille Interface

The Ransley Braille Interface, from HumanWare, is a hardware-based braille translator. It is an external device that is connected to the computer's serial port before the printer is plugged into the Ransley. The Ransley translator functions similar to a memory-resident translator working with the mainstream software package. When the user wants to print a braille document, the mainstream program is merely instructed to print in its standard fashion.

The Ransley intercepts text sent to the printer, translates it into braille code, then passes the translated text on to the printer for embossing. The braille translation software is contained on a read-only memory chip inside the device, and little or no knowledge of braille is required to operate the system.

Braille Printers

Braille printers, or braille embossers, are devices that are dedicated to printing out documents in braille. The typical braille printer uses blunt pins to punch dots into 100-pound weight paper for production of braille hard copy. The pins drive the paper against a rubberized plate that absorbs the force of impact and prevents the pins from punching the dots completely through the paper.

As with print printers, there are several classes of braille printers, each designed to perform specific tasks. The basic divisions are personal, medium duty, and heavy duty.

Personal-Class Braille Printers

The personal-class braille printer, designed for light-duty applications, is the least expensive of the three classes of braille printers. This type of printer is best suited for the casual home user who wants to produce a few pages of braille per day, such as shopping lists or personal correspondence in braille. They are not intended to generate production runs of braille, as would be required by a school or public facility. The average personal-class braille printer embosses at a speed of about 20 characters per second.

Braille Blazer

The Braille Blazer, produced by Blazie Engineering, is an example of a personal-class braille printer. This unit contains both a braille printer and a speech synthesizer. Thus, the device can print braille and access personal computers with a screen reader software package. The Braille Blazer is compatible with most braille translation software packages. It interfaces to most computers through the standard serial interface port. The unit prints at a speed of about 20 characters per second, and the voice can operate simultaneously with the print mechanism. This printer is portable and can be purchased with an optional carrying case.

Juliet

Juliet, from Enabling Technologies, is a personal-class printer that also is capable of performing as a medium-weight unit. The printer is compatible with most personal computers equipped with standard serial or parallel ports and with most off-the-shelf braille translation software packages. The Juliet prints up to 40 characters per second and includes a tractor-feed mechanism. It can emboss on paper stock as well as plastic and metal, making it suitable for making braille signs.

Medium-Weight Braille Printers

Medium-weight braille printers are suited for somewhat heavier duty applications than those of personal-class braille printers.

They have a somewhat higher printing speed than personal class machines, with speeds ranging from 20 to 40 characters per second. Medium-weight printers are more solidly constructed and are suited for small-business applications or for the user with heavier braille demands than those handled by personal-class printers. Medium-class printers are frequently used for small public facilities and organizations that need to print braille for their clients on a regular basis. However, these printers are not suited for a braille publishing house or other organization that needs to print entire books in braille.

Romeo

The Romeo, from Enabling Technologies, is an example of a medium-weight braille printer capable of functioning also as a personal-class printer. The Romeo prints at either 20 or 40 characters per second and has a tractor-feed mechanism. Built-in serial or parallel ports make the Romeo compatible with most commercially available personal computer systems. It also is compatible with most braille translation software packages.

The Romeo braille printer can print incoming text without having to wait for a complete line to be received. This is useful when short text messages are received from a text telephone (see Chapter 4). The printer also has a View key that allows the user to read the last line that has been printed without having to manually advance the paper, which is useful because the print head is partially covered by a metal housing. Pressing the View key advances the paper for reading; pressing it again returns the paper to the previous position for additional printing. The Romeo printer also includes graphics capability, multicopy mode, sideways printing, and six- or eight-dot braille. (The extra two dots indicate the color or video state of the character, i.e., flashing, underlined, etc.) It has its own carrying case and weighs about 27 pounds.

VersaPoint

The VersaPoint, from TeleSensory, is an example of a medium-class braille printer that can emboss at speeds of up to 40 characters per second. This printer can interface with most personal computers through the standard serial or parallel port. VersaPoint comes equipped with a tractor-feed mechanism and produces both text and graphics with the aid of an optional graphics printing package.

Heavy-Duty Braille Printers

The heavy-duty class of braille printers is suitable for a braille production house or for organizations that need to print large quantities of braille for students or an entire staff. These heavy-duty class printers can print at speeds of up to hundreds of characters per

The VersaPoint braille printer uses a tractor-feed mechanism to move paper through the printer. *Courtesy of TeleSensory, Inc.*

second. They also can emboss interpoint braille—or print on both sides of the paper—which makes them more cost effective in terms of stock usage. Some heavy-duty printers can emboss on plastic or metal sheets, making them suitable for printing braille signs.

BookMaker, Braille Express, PED-30, and TED-600

The BookMaker printer, from Enabling Technologies, is capable of printing on both sides of the paper. It has a speed of 80 characters per second and can produce 200 pages of braille in about an hour using 100 sheets of paper. The printer also can produce text and graphics on the same page. Using the printer's built-in telephone-style keypad, the user can configure the printer to work with most personal computer systems. The current parameter settings can be printed out in braille or in a 32-character visual display. BookMaker has a built-in multicopy mode for making many copies of a document automatically.

Enabling Technologies produces several other braille printers suitable for braille production houses. The Braille Express prints at 150 characters per second and prints on both sides of the page. The Plate Embossing Device (PED-30) prints 36 plates per hour, with each plate consisting of two pages of braille. The TED-600 prints 600 lines per minute and prints on both sides of the page.

Everest

TeleSensory manufactures the Everest braille printer, a unit that prints on both sides of the pages at speeds of up to 100 characters per second. Equipped with both a serial and parallel port, the printer can interface with most personal computers. The Everest has the Duxbury Braille Translator software stored in its permanent memory, so there is no need to purchase a separate braille translation software package.

Marathon

The Marathon braille embosser, from Enabling Technologies, is suitable for producing large quantities of braille output. The unit can print about 200 characters per second. It interfaces with most personal computers through its built-in serial or parallel port and is compatible with most braille translation software packages.

Refreshable Braille Displays

Refreshable braille displays connect to personal computers and translate text displayed on the screen into instantaneous braille output. The braille display typically attaches to the computer through one of the serial ports, and software sends the device a copy of the text displayed on the screen. When the device receives the text, it automatically displays it in braille on a strip that contains mechanical braille dots that pop up and down under computer control. A refreshable braille display thus does not produce braille characters on paper but employs electro-mechanical dots. Refreshable braille displays can be of great value for users performing word processing, database management, spreadsheet functions, computer programming, etc. Different units may display 20, 40, or 80 braille characters at a time.

The refreshable braille display can be an effective access technology for persons who are deaf-blind since these devices readily attach to many brands of personal computer systems and allow the end user to read screen text in braille symbols.

As described earlier, paper-based braille consists of a six-dot code with combinations of the six dots forming precise characters and symbols. Refreshable braille displays are capable of printing more than six dots per braille cell to provide additional information about the character under the cursor. The additional dots indicate, for example, if the character is underlined or flashing. This is known as eight-dot braille. Users can program their displays to track select colors on the screen and to follow those colors faithfully through menu changes so that menu choices can be made in braille output mode. When a selected menu item is highlighted,

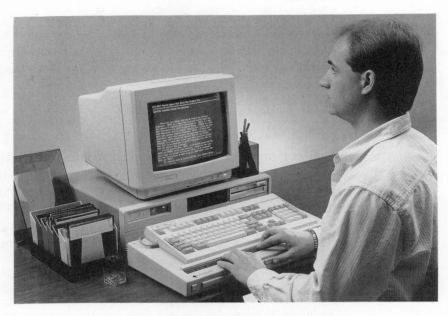

The Navigator refreshable braille display's dots pop up and down under computer software control, allowing the screen to be read by touching the braille strip on the device (shown under the keyboard). *Courtesy of TeleSensory, Inc.*

the display presents it clearly along with its exact video attribute, if required.

Most refreshable braille displays connect to personal computers through an output port, thus making the installation procedure relatively easy. Once the refreshable braille display is connected to an output port of the computer, the user must load software to control the unit from the keyboard. Some refreshable braille displays can use optional braille keyboards that allow users to enter data in a braille mode. The software locks onto the computer's cursor and tracks the cursor from within most applications packages including word processors, databases, spreadsheets, telecommunications software, programming languages, etc. The refreshable display software allows users to read text line-by-line, word-by-word, or character-by-character.

KeyBraille

KeyBraille, from HumanWare, is a refreshable display for IBM PC-compatible personal computers, including most desktop and laptop computers. It attaches to a computer through a parallel port.

Navigator

The Navigator, from TeleSensory, is a refreshable display for IBM PC-compatible personal computers, including most desktop and laptop computers. It can be purchased in 20-, 40-, or 80-cell (character) configurations, depending on the requirements of the user. The Navigator attaches to the PC via the serial port.

Pocket Braille Computers

Smaller computers are offered each passing year, and the adaptive computers on the market are no exception. For many years, persons with vision impairments have searched for portable devices that offer equal access to electronic information. This search led to the development of dedicated computer systems equipped with either voice or braille output but still revolving around the braille keyboard as an input device.

Braille 'n Speak and Type 'n Speak

The Braille 'n Speak, from Blazie Engineering, is a portable braille computer about the size and weight of a paperback book. The unit can run for 8 to 10 hours on a battery charge. Braille 'n Speak contains a standard six-dot braille keyboard, an unlimited vocabulary text-to-speech synthesizer for output, and a built-in braille translator. The device is compatible with most ink and braille printers. It can be purchased with as much as 640K of memory and with an optional 3.5-inch floppy disk drive. A user enters information into the built-in word processor through the braille keyboard in either Grade 1 or Grade 2 braille. It has a built-in serial interface port suitable for connecting a printer or modem. The device also can function as a speech synthesizer using the optional Speak-Sys software package and is compatible with many commercially available screen reader software packages. Blazie Engineering also makes a similar device, the Type 'n Speak, a portable computer with a typewriter-like keyboard and voice synthesizer.

BrailleMate

The BrailleMate, from TeleSensory, is a pocket braille computer that has two methods of output: an unlimited vocabulary speech synthesizer and an eight-dot braille cell. The system can interface with most personal computers, modems, and other office equipment and can send or receive information through its built-in serial and parallel ports. BrailleMate has a built-in magnetic card reader that can be used in place of a disk drive to store files. The unit contains built-in word-processing, telecommunications, and appointment software. As with the Braille 'n Speak, the unit also can be used as a speech synthesizer and is compatible with screen reader software.

BrailleMate pocket braille computer can handle word-processing and telecommunications functions. *Courtesy of TeleSensory, Inc.*

Optical Character Recognition Systems

Because of the inherent barriers presented by the printed word, persons who are visually impaired are sometimes referred to as "print handicapped." Books and other printed materials are virtually inaccessible in printed form. The use of optical character recognition (OCR) systems can overcome the barrier to reading printed material. These systems are used to transform inaccessible printed material into speech or machine-readable form, bringing the printed word to persons with vision impairments. OCR systems use artificial intelligence to scan the printed page and to recognize the text characters present on the page through sophisticated pattern-matching software. They can read a printed page in about one minute.

From the Kurzweil Reading Machine to Today's OCR Devices

In the 1970s a computer pioneer named Raymond Kurzweil created and marketed the first computer-based reading machine for persons with vision impairments. His Kurzweil Reading Machine was about the size of a large desktop copying machine and contained a flatbed scanner, central processing unit, and detachable keyboard. The basic system consisted of an OCR system driving an unlimited-vocabulary, text-to-speech synthesis system that read printed books and other materials aloud. The Kurzweil Reading Machine was a much sought-after technology for schools and other institutions, but at $30,000—the price of a two-bedroom house at the time—it was outside the purchasing power of most private individuals. For more than a decade, Kurzweil remained the only company offering a stand-alone reading machine to persons with vision impairments.

Since the development of the first Kurzweil Reading Machine, scanning technology has progressed a great deal. The scanners available on the market today are many times more powerful, and the prices have decreased as well. Now, through OCR technology, persons who are blind or visually impaired can enjoy equal access to the printed word. Kurzweil still remains a major producer in the scanner market, but other companies also provide products and approaches. Some are stand-alone (self-contained) systems, others are computer-based, while others can function both independently and with a computer.

Arkenstone Reader and An Open Book

The Arkenstone Reader, from Arkenstone, Inc., is a computer-based OCR system that can function as a reading machine for persons with vision impairments and other disabilities. The device is based on off-the-shelf computer hardware and software that has been modified. The Arkenstone is based on the Calera OCR circuit card and the Hewlett-Packard ScanJet Plus desktop scanner. (The Calera circuit card also drives other desktop scanners.) One version of the Arkenstone takes a different approach from that of the original Kurzweil Reading Machine in that the Arkenstone is not a dedicated reading machine with its own built-in computer system; instead, it attaches to an existing system as an external device. The Calera circuit card is compatible with IBM PC and PC-compatible computers of the 286 class or higher. Once the card is plugged into the system, the user connects an interface cable from the desktop flatbed scanner to the computer and copies the OCR software to the hard disk. The system is accessed through the user's adaptive hardware and software.

The latest version of the Arkenstone, An Open Book, is compatible with 386 platforms and does not require a Calera circuit card to operate. Arkenstone also manufactures a stand-alone version of the An Open Book scanner based on a 386 computer system. The stand-alone system can be upgraded to a 386-class personal computer by adding an optional keyboard and monitor. Consult the manufacturer for exact hardware, processor, and memory requirements.

Optacon

The Optacon, from TeleSensory, is another form of scanner used by persons with vision impairments. Consisting of a hand-held camera and a vibrating array of pins, the user can read a book with the unit by moving the camera over any printed material. The camera sends an exact (not braille) copy of the text to the vibrating pin array, which immediately raises the image so that it can be felt by the user. The Optacon can be used to read entire books, magazines, food containers, and just about anything else in printed form. The unit is battery powered, portable, and about the size of a small tape recorder. It can be interfaced to a personal computer through its built-in serial interface port, allowing the user to read graphics and text visible on a computer screen.

OsCaR

The OsCaR, from TeleSensory, is an IBM PC-based OCR system designed for persons with vision impairments. The system is based on the Calera text recognition circuit card and the Hewlett-Packard ScanJet Plus desktop scanner. The system is compatible with most IBM PC-compatible computers with a platform of 286 or higher and with speech synthesizers and screen reader software. The OsCaR can scan a document, translate it into braille, and then emboss the text directly on a braille printer connected to the computer system. The latest version of the OsCaR uses the Hewlett-Packard IIP scanner and does not require a Calera recognition circuit card.

Reading Edge

The Reading Edge, from Xerox Imaging Systems, is a stand-alone, portable OCR system that is the size of a large briefcase and that weighs about 20 pounds. The Reading Edge includes a flatbed scanner, DECtalk speech synthesizer, speaker, and an 18-button keypad. The system features automatic page orientation and a document feeder. The Reading Edge will read most printed material and speak the text aloud through the DECtalk voice synthesizer. The scanner can accommodate paper sizes as large as 8.5 inches by 17 inches. The device is a stand-alone reading machine that does not require a personal computer to drive it. Xerox also markets a software package, the Reading AdvantEDGE, that will drive Hewlett-Packard and Xerox scanners.

Scanning Text into a Word Processor

Many users employ OCR systems to read books and other documents and to save these documents on personal computers for future reading or retrieval. The user can configure a system for scanning documents into various word-processor formats and employ speech, magnification, or braille technology to read the scanned documents. Most scanners can be equipped with an automatic document feeder that allows the user to fill the scanner with stacks of pages to read. The document feeder automatically inserts one page at a time into the scanner. Thus, the scanner and its feeder can transform a job that would have taken days of hand-tended operation into an almost automatic procedure. Books are scanned by laying the opened pages face down, scanning, then turning the pages and placing that view face down, etc.

A document that has been scanned into a word-processing file format becomes immediately more useful and universal in terms of access. For example, the file can be spoken aloud by using a speech synthesizer and screen reading software. Alternately, the electronic file can be used to produce a magnified version of the document by printing with different type faces or by using a hardware- or software-based magnification system. Furthermore, the document can be translated into braille using a braille translation software package and braille printer.

Scanning systems have reached a prominent state of development. The future of this technology is extremely positive chiefly because the mainstream business world relies on scanning technology for document and image processing; this demand is driving down prices for OCR systems. Software-based OCR systems also are driving prices down as less hardware is required to configure an OCR system. All in all, this positive trend can only bring increased productivity and opportunity to persons who need this technology.

Products for Persons with Vision Impairments

The following lists give names, addresses, and phone numbers for companies serving persons who are blind or visually impaired. Separate sections list vendors of adaptive technology for speech synthesis systems, magnification systems, braille systems, and optical character recognition systems. No endorsements are intended by inclusion on this list. Similarly, lack of inclusion does not imply lack of endorsement.

Speech Synthesis Providers

Aicom Corp.
  1590 Oakland Rd., Ste. B112
  San Jose, CA 95131
  408-453-8251

American Printing House
  for the Blind
  P.O. Box 6085
  Louisville, KY 40206-0085
  502-895-2405

Artic Technologies
55 Park St.
Troy, MI 48083
313-588-7370

Berkeley Systems, Inc.
2095 Rose St.
Berkeley, CA 94709
510-540-5535

Blazie Engineering
105 E. Jarrettsville Rd.
Forest Hill, MD 20510
410-893-9333

Brytech, Inc.
P.O. Box 1357
Ogdensburg, NY 13669
613-727-5800

Computer Conversations, Inc.
6297 Worthington Rd. SW
Alexandria, OH 43001
614-924-2885

Covox, Inc.
675-D Conger St.
Eugene, OR 97402
503-342-1271

Digital Equipment Corp.
Continental Blvd.
Merrimack, NH 03054
603-884-8990

Discover Financial
Services, Inc.
2500 Lake Cook Rd.
Riverwoods, IL 60015
708-405-3892
708-405-3269

Echo Speech Corp.
6460 Via Real
Carpinteria, CA 93013
805-684-4593

Franklin Electronic
Publishers
122 Burrs Rd.
Mt. Holly, NJ 08060
800-762-5382
609-261-4800, Ext. 254

GW Micro
310 Racquet Dr.
Fort Wayne, IN 46825
219-483-3625

Henter-Joyce, Inc.
10901-C Roosevelt Blvd.,
Ste. 1200
St. Petersburg, FL 33716
813-576-5658

HumanWare, Inc.
6245 King Rd.
Loomis, CA 95650
916-652-7253

IBM Independence Series
Information Center
Building 5
P.O. Box 1328
Boca Raton, FL 33429
800-426-4832

MicroTalk Software
3375 Peterson
Louisville, KY 40206
502-897-2705

OMS Development
1921 Highland Ave.
Wilmette, IL 60091
708-251-5787

Personal Data Systems, Inc.
100 W. Rincon, Ste. 217
Campbell, CA 95008
408-866-1126

RC Systems, Inc.
121 W. Winesap Rd.
Bothell, WA 98012
206-672-6909

Syntha-Voice Computers, Inc.
125 Gailmont Dr.
Hamilton, ON L8K 4B8
CANADA
416-578-0565

TeleSensory, Inc.
455 N. Bernardo Ave.
P.O. Box 7455
Mountain View, CA 94039
415-960-0920

Magnification System Providers

AI Squared
P.O. Box 669
Manchester Center, VT
05255-0669
802-362-3612

Apple Computer, Inc.
Worldwide Disability
Solutions Group
20525 Mariani Ave.
Cupertino, CA 95014
408-996-1010

Artic Technologies
55 Park St.
Troy, MI 48083
313-588-7370

Berkeley Systems, Inc.
2095 Rose St.
Berkeley, CA 94709
510-540-5535

Computer Conversations, Inc.
6297 Worthington Rd. S.W.
Alexandria, OH 43001
614-924-2885

Florida New Concepts
Marketing, Inc.
P.O. Box 261
Port Richey, FL 34673
813-842-3231

HumanWare, Inc.
6245 King Rd.
Loomis, CA 95650
916-652-7253

Innoventions, Inc.
5921 S. Middlefield Rd.,
Ste. 102
Littleton, CO 80123-2877
800-854-6554
303-797-6554

Lyon Computer Discourse,
Ltd.
70 W. 10th Ave.
N. Vancouver, BC V5Y 11R6
CANADA
604-875-9993

Microsystems Software, Inc.
600 Worcester Rd., Ste. B2
Framingham, MA 01701
508-626-8511

Optelec USA Inc.
4 Lyberty Way
P.O. Box 729
Westford, MA 01886
508-392-0707

Syntha-Voice Computers, Inc.
125 Gailmont Dr.
Hamilton, ON L8K 4B8
CANADA
416-578-0565

TeleSensory, Inc.
455 North Bernardo Ave.
P.O. Box 7455
Mountain View, CA 94039
415-960-0920

Braille Printer and Display Providers

American Printing House for
the Blind
P.O. Box 6085
Louisville, KY 40206-0085
502-895-2405

American Thermoform Corp.
2311 Travers Ave.
City of Commerce, CA
90040
213-723-9021

ARTS Computer
Products, Inc.
33 Richdale Ave.
Cambridge, MA 02140
617-547-5320

Blazie Engineering
105 E. Jarrettsville Rd.
Forest Hill, MD 20510
410-893-9333

Densitron Corp.
2039 Hwy. 1 S.
Camden, SC 29020
803-842-5008

Duxbury Systems, Inc.
435 King St.
P.O. Box 1504
Littleton, MA 01460
508-486-9766

Enabling Technologies Co.
3102 S.E. Jay St.
Stuart, FL 34997
407-283-4817

HumanWare, Inc.
6245 King Rd.
Loomis, CA 95650
916-652-7253

MicroTalk Software
3375 Peterson
Louisville, KY 40206
502-897-2705

Perkins School for the Blind
175 N. Beacon St.
Watertown, MA 02172
617-924-3434

Raised Dot Computing, Inc.
408 S. Baldwin St.
Madison, WI 53703
608-257-9595

TeleSensory, Inc.
455 N. Bernardo Ave.
P.O. Box 7455
Mountain View, CA 94039
415-960-0920

Optical Character Recognition System Providers

Adhoc Reading Systems, Inc.
28 Brunswick Woods Dr.
East Brunswick, NJ 08816
908-254-7300

Olduvai Corp.
7520 Red Rd., Ste. A
South Miami, FL 33143
800-822-0772

Arkenstone, Inc.
1390 Borregas Ave.
Sunnyvale, CA 94089
800-444-4443
408-752-2200

TeleSensory
455 N. Bernardo Ave.
P.O. Box 7455
Mountain View, CA 94039
415-960-0920

DEST Corp.
1015 E. Brokaw Rd.
San Jose, CA 95131
408-436-2700

Visuaide 2000, Inc.
955 rue D'Assigny
Longueuil, PQ J4K 5C3
CANADA
514-463-1717

OCR Systems, Inc.
1800 Byberry Rd., Ste. 1405
Huntingdon   Valley,   PA
16652
800-233-4627
215-938-7460

Xerox Imaging Systems, Inc.
9 Centennial Dr.
Peabody, MA 01960
800-343-0311
508-977-2000

Technology for Persons with Hearing Impairments

Instant access to data has become an important part of our society. To fully compete, persons with hearing impairments must have access to this vast storehouse of information. For persons who are deaf or hearing impaired, adaptive technology can convert audible information into a visual format. For those who are both deaf and blind, assistive systems can translate information into braille.

The adaptive technologies for persons with hearing impairments presented in this chapter include text telephones and relay services; computer-assisted access systems for text telephones, facsimile communication, computer-assisted access, and sign language training; signaling systems; captioning devices; and electronic amplification systems. Text telephones and relay services provide persons who are deaf or hearing impaired the ability to communicate with friends, family, and coworkers over the telephone. Baudot/ASCII modems linked to personal computers allow communication with both text telephones and other personal computers, providing for a wider range of communications alternatives. Computer-aided transcription provides hard-copy printouts of meetings and other group gatherings in either a print or braille format. Personal computers equipped with training software can be used to teach American Sign Language or to reinforce existing skills. Signaling systems offer a way to monitor the environment for important sound sources. Captioning systems translate the spoken word into text, making television programming and other media more accessible. Electronic amplification systems provide sound amplification and filtering for face-to-face communication and group communication. Telephone amplification systems boost the sound signal of the telephone, making for increased access. The following sections describe how these technologies

The Superprint text telephone uses a standard telephone with the handset placed in the acoustic coupler and a keyboard for typing and receiving messages over the telephone. *Courtesy of Ultratec, Inc., Madison, Wisconsin.*

function and offer specific examples. Lists at the end of the chapter include names and addresses of providers of these technologies.

Text Telephones

Text telephones, often known as TDDs (Telecommunications Devices for the Deaf) or as TTYs (teletypewriters), are used to send typed messages back and forth over telephone lines. Text telephones are often used by persons unable to benefit from amplification technology as well as by persons with speech impairments. Most units, about the size of a small briefcase, are portable and run on battery power. Their main components consist of a keyboard, a visual display, and telephone connectors. The keyboard contains most of the symbols available on a typewriter, arranged in either a three- or four-row configuration. The visual display usually is like that of a digital clock or calculator, employing light-emitting diodes rather than a cathode ray tube. Text telephones connect to the telephone system in one of two ways: by using a direct connect modular jack, as on most telephones, or by inserting the telephone handset into a rubberized acoustic coupler.

In the early 1960s Robert Weitbrecht, an engineer at Stanford Research Institute who was deaf, produced the basic research that led to the text telephones of today. Weitbrecht produced a modem that could link a teletype with the telephone system. At the time, teletypes were widely used to print out text messages from computers and wire services for the government, the military, and businesses. The technology proved to be of great benefit to individuals with hearing impairments and opened up a world of increased communications. As a result of Weitbrecht's ground-breaking work, surplus teletypes were donated to persons with hearing impairments, leading to the text telephone networks of today.

Text telephones speak a language known as Baudot. The Baudot code was brought into use in 1874 when it was used to increase traffic on telegraph systems. Baudot is a 5-bit binary language that is transmitted at a fixed speed of 45.5 bits per second, about 60 words per minute. The Baudot code is almost totally out of use except for text telephones. Newer text telephones often have the capability to speak the language known as ASCII, which is also used by personal computers. Baudot and ASCII are fundamentally incompatible with one another (see the discussion on Baudot/ASCII modems later in this chapter). Text telephone conversations can only take place if both participants agree beforehand to communicate in either Baudot or ASCII code. Fortunately, newer text telephones can select between Baudot and ASCII code at the flick of a switch.

Talking on a Text Telephone

A text telephone is relatively simple to operate. The individual types messages on the keyboard that transmit over the telephone lines and appear on the video display of the remote text telephone. Once a call has been established, the individuals can communicate with one another by typing messages back and forth. The two-way message traffic appears on both video displays in real time as the messages are flashed over the telephone lines.

When communicating over a text telephone, some basic guidelines should be observed. Since most text telephones can display only one line of text at a time, there is no need to press the Enter or Return key after each line. When talking over a text telephone, it is important to let the other person know that it is his or her turn to speak by typing *GA*, which stands for "go ahead." When the conversation is over, type *SK* for "stop keying."

Compact

The Compact, from Ultratec, is a portable text telephone unit that can be carried in a coat pocket. The unit features a memory storage area suitable for storing text of conversations, telephone numbers, memos, or other text material. The Compact also features a built-in recorded voice that announces that an incoming text telephone call is being placed and alerts hearing persons to activate their text telephones. The system includes acoustic couplers that are compatible with newer telephone handsets. The user can adjust the visual display, which has a 2-line, 80-character output. The Compact has a 57-key keyboard with typewriter-style keys for touch typing. The unit features a built-in rechargeable battery pack and an AC adapter plug. The Compact can be purchased with a number of options, such as ASCII-code capability, memory expansion, a carrying case, and an extended warranty.

Memory Printer

The Memory Printer text telephone, from KRI, comes equipped with a standard keyboard, 20-character display, and a built-in printer. The printer can print 20 characters per line, with 24 characters per line in condensed mode or 12 characters per line in wide mode. The unit runs on either batteries or household current. Memory Printer options include direct connect, ASCII code, clock calendar, and a flashing strobe call-indicator.

Minicom and Superprint

The Minicom IV text telephone, from Ultratec, features a 20-character display and a 4-row, typewriter-style keyboard. The unit can connect to external printers through its built-in printer interface port. The Minicom cannot be adapted or upgraded to talk to ASCII-based systems.

The Superprint 100 text telephone, from Ultratec, features a 20-character display and a 4-row, typewriter-style keyboard. The unit has a built-in printer port capable of interfacing to most external printers, a user-replaceable rechargeable battery pack, and a heavy-duty plastic case. The Superprint 200 includes a built-in 24-character printer, and the Superprint 400 comes complete with an auto-answer mode capable of taking messages while the user is absent. Options available include ASCII-code capability and a digitized voice to announce to hearing persons that an incoming text telephone call is being placed. The system also includes 8 kilobytes of memory to store the text of messages, phone numbers, or other text information.

For users who are visually impaired, Ultratec also features an enlarged display that connects to its products. The Large Visual Display is an oversized rectangular screen that displays letters about ten times the size of a standard text telephone display.

Portaview

The Portaview, from KRI, is a nonprinting text telephone that contains a standard keyboard and 20-character display. The device can be powered by either AC or battery. The options available for the line of Portaview text telephones include direct-connect jacks, additional memory, auto-answer feature, and ASCII code.

Supercom

The Supercom text telephone, from Ultratec, features a printer interface. The unit comes equipped with a 20-character display and a 4-row, typewriter-style keyboard. The device features an 8-kilobyte memory storage area suitable for holding text of conversations, notes, or other information and up to ten telephone numbers and auto-answer messages. Supercom comes with a direct-connect telephone jack, thus reducing errors caused by background noise. This unit has a built-in voice that can announce a call to a hearing person. It can function as a text-telephone–based answering machine, taking messages while the user is elsewhere. Supercom comes equipped with an AC power adapter and replaceable batteries. It can be purchased with an ASCII-code option, allowing the unit to communicate with personal computers as well as text telephones.

Text Telephones and the ADA

According to the Americans with Disabilities Act, "One text telephone must be provided inside any building that has four or more public pay telephones, counting both interior and exterior phones. In addition, one text telephone must be provided whenever there is an interior public pay phone in a stadium or arena; convention center; hotel with a convention center; covered shopping mall; or hospital emergency, recovery, or waiting room. One accessible public phone must be provided for each floor unless the floor has two or more banks of phones, in which case there must be one accessible phone for each bank."

Pay Phone Text Telephone

The Pay Phone Text Telephone, from Ultratec, is a device that can be attached to any public pay telephone. The keyboard unit is housed in a metal drawer that is bolted underneath the phone. When the user places the phone receiver on a special hook on the side of the phone casing, the drawer opens and exposes the text telephone controls. The text telephone feature does not interfere with standard use of the pay phone. The Pay Phone text telephone can store a conversation in a 2,000-character memory so the user can scroll through the conversation. When the call is completed, the memory is cleared. The unit weighs about 30 pounds.

Braille Text Telephones

Not all text telephones are confined to visual output methods; some provide braille output so that persons who are both blind and deaf can interact with others in employment, social, and educational settings. It should not be assumed that all persons who are deaf-blind are totally blind and totally deaf. It is always more accurate to evaluate persons with disabilities as individuals with different capabilities. Individuals who have some remaining hearing and vision can employ the standard access technology

When a caller places a call to a text telephone, the Pay Phone Text Telephone drawer automatically slides open to access the unit. *Courtesy of Ultratec, Inc., Madison, Wisconsin.*

that applies to persons with vision impairments, such as speech synthesis, magnification systems, braille printers and displays, and optical character recognition systems. If the person is totally blind and totally deaf, then braille access technology may be most appropriate. As discussed in Chapter 3, braille printers and refreshable braille displays allow computers and other communications devices to be readily accessed.

InfoTouch

InfoTouch, from Enabling Technologies Company, is a text telephone system designed especially for persons who are deaf-blind. The system uses a Romeo braille printer (see Chapter 3), a vibrating braille display to provide tactile output, and a modified Ultratec Superprint text telephone. The tactile display alerts the user to the presence of an incoming call by converting the audible ring to a tactile format. The tactile signal vibrates at the same frequency as a ring, dial tone, or busy signal.

InfoTouch contains two basic keyboard modes to allow the user to enter commands and text into the system. The device can emulate a 6-key braille keyboard, which is similar to a standard Perkins Braillwriter. This is appropriate

The TeleBraille II braille text telephone for persons who are deaf-blind uses a standard telephone handset that is inserted into an acoustic coupler. The refreshable braille display beneath the unit allows the user to read incoming messages in braille. *Courtesy of TeleSensory, Inc.*

for an individual more familiar with the braille keyboard than with the standard computer-style keyboard. The other keyboard mode emulates a typewriter-style keyboard similar to that found with most personal computer systems.

The system is equipped with both American and international text telephone codes, making it compatible with both American and European telephone systems, and includes both Baudot and ASCII codes. InfoTouch features a stored digitized voice that announces outgoing calls with a verbal message until it is answered by another text telephone. The unit also has an external printer port for interfacing to letter-quality or dot-matrix printers.

TeleBraille

The TeleBraille, from TeleSensory, is a braille-output communications device for persons who are deaf-blind. The TeleBraille consists of an Ultratec text telephone equipped with a refreshable braille display for tactile output. It is similar in function to the InfoTouch system, but TeleBraille uses a refreshable braille display based on the TeleSensory Navigator (see Chapter 3) rather than a hard-copy braille printer as its output device. The Navigator employed in this system is capable of presenting twenty braille characters at a time on its refreshable display.

The TeleBraille can function with either a braille keyboard or a standard typewriter-style keyboard, depending on the requirements of the user. The incoming and outgoing messages appear on the refreshable braille display. The last cell of the braille display functions as a telephone line-status indicator and vibrates at the same frequency as a dial tone, ring, or busy signal. The system has internal memory for storing conversations and other text, automatic dialing for up to twenty-six phone numbers, and answering machine capabilities. The TeleBraille can connect to either a print or braille printer, allowing for both print or braille hard copy. The unit also comes equipped with a user-replaceable battery pack and a carrying case.

Relay Services

Although the text telephone is an efficient instrument for allowing persons with hearing impairments to communicate independently with the community in general, it has a basic built-in limitation: it cannot allow a person to call another person who does not also have a text telephone. However, communications services can fill that need. Relay bureaus are dedicated to placing telephone calls for persons who are deaf or hearing impaired or who have other disabilities. These services are most useful for calling persons who do not have a text telephone. A person who is deaf or hearing impaired uses the service by calling the relay bureau from a text telephone, and a hearing person places the call over standard voice lines. A hearing person at the relay bureau functions as a translator, relaying messages between the persons at both ends of the conversation. The Americans with Disabilities Act mandates that a national relay network be established by July 26, 1993.

Facsimile Communication

Persons who are deaf or hearing impaired may find it easier to communicate by facsimile (or fax) machines than by using relay networks. This important communications technology has become a standard part of almost every office and retail business and of many homes. Fax machines can transmit almost any image to another fax machine over standard telephone lines at a rate of about two pages per minute.

Short messages, long documents, and detailed pictures and drawings can be sent by fax. In addition, fax machines can be used to alert an individual that a telephone call is coming from a text telephone. A fax can be used to ask for information, such as the times of classes or meetings, or to order food or other products over the telephone.

However, with all their benefits, fax machines are of little use for rapid, two-way conversation because information currently can be faxed in only one direction at a time.

Fax machines can be purchased as stand-alone devices that are about the same size as a small desktop photocopier. They are also available on circuit cards for computers, allowing documents created on a personal computer to be transmitted to any destination under control of disk-based software. (See Chapter 6 for additional information in accessing online information via fax.)

Computer-Assisted Access

Computers can be used as text telephones and for general information access, empowering persons with hearing impairments at school and on the job. With their personal computers, persons with hearing impairments also can access electronic mail, local area networks, bulletin boards, and online services to send and receive information in an accessible environment. (See Chapter 6 for an in-depth discussion of each of these means of communicating.)

In general, the personal computer does not present a barrier for those who are deaf or hearing impaired. In fact, it can provide a valuable means of access to the telephone system and stored online information. The personal computer can readily be adapted to talk with both text telephones and personal computers by adding a Baudot/ASCII modem to the system. For persons who are deaf-blind, further adaptations such as braille systems or those described in Chapter 3 may be desirable. The following sections describe hardware and software to make the computer more accessible to persons with hearing impairments.

Baudot/ASCII Modems

Offering a world of communications possibilities, Baudot/ASCII modems can communicate with text telephones as well as with personal computers. These modems connect to a personal computer in the same manner as standard modems; they can be internal, circuit-card–based devices or external devices that attach to a serial port. As with standard modems, Baudot/ASCII modems require software to operate. With a Baudot/ASCII-modem–equipped personal computer, an individual can send and receive calls from both text telephones and personal computers, allowing persons to talk by typing messages back and forth as on a standard text telephone. Because Baudot/ASCII modems speak the language of the text telephone (Baudot) and the language of the personal computer (ASCII), these modems can span the gulf of the electronic language incompatibility barrier. However, only Baudot or only ASCII must be used at each end of the communication.

With the growing number of computers, there is a strong need for text telephone users to communicate with personal computers. Fortunately, text telephones can often be made ASCII-compatible by adding an ASCII-code module to the unit. Following are brief descriptions of several commercially available Baudot/ASCII modems.

CM-4

The CM-4, from Phone TTY, is an external Baudot/ASCII modem. The CM-4 operates at speeds of 45.5 baud in Baudot up to 300 baud in ASCII. The modem connects to IBM PC-compatible computers through the serial interface port.

Intele-Modem

The Intele-Modem, from Ultratec, is an external modem that can speak both Baudot and ASCII. The modem can interface to most personal computers through a standard serial port with either 25-pin or 9-pin interface cables. Intele-modem sends and receives data at either 45 or 300 bits per second and automatically converts the incoming Baudot code to ASCII. This internal conversion makes the modem compatible with commercial communications software. Thus, the user can employ almost any standard telecommunications software to send and receive text telephone calls. The system has a modular jack for direct connection to the phone system, making for static-free calls in both directions. The front panel lamps indicate the line status of the modem, that is, whether a number is busy or a connection has been established. The lamps also indicate if an incoming call is coming from a computer or another text telephone. The modem also can be used to communicate with bulletin boards and online services. It comes bundled with a telephone cable and power supply.

MIC300I

The MIC300I, from Microflip, is an internal text telephone modem for IBM PC-compatible computers. The unit is a circuit card that plugs into standard expansion slots. Because of its size, the modem can fit into select laptop computers that have standard IBM expansion slots. The modem comes with disk-based software and can talk to both text telephones and ASCII-based computers. The speed is 300 baud for ASCII communications and 45.5 baud for Baudot. The modem can detect automatically if incoming calls are from a text telephone or from a personal computer, and the modem can adjust

The Intele-Modem from Ultratec connects to most personal computers through a serial interface. The unit can communicate with text telephones and personal computers. *Courtesy of Ultratec, Inc., Madison, Wisconsin.*

automatically when calling either text telephones or computers. The software works with both MS-DOS and Microsoft Windows. The modem can function as an answering machine, allowing it to receive calls while the user is away. The software is memory resident, taking about 40 kilobytes of memory. Other applications can run in the foreground, such as word processors, databases, and spreadsheets. When an incoming call arrives, the user activates the modem software by pressing an activation key. The software is compatible with several magnification programs and refreshable braille output systems.

PhoneCommunicator

The PhoneCommunicator, from IBM, is a circuit card that plugs into IBM PC-compatible personal computers. The device permits persons who are deaf or hard of hearing to communicate over the telephone system with its built-in speech synthesizer, text telephone, modem, and touch-tone decoder. The system consists of a modem that is capable of talking with text telephones as well as personal computers. The modem can send and receive data at 45.5, 300, and 1200 baud. Using the synthesizer and touch-tone decoder, the device can communicate with individuals who have neither text telephones nor personal computers. Once connected, the user who is hearing impaired can type messages on the computer keyboard that are spoken aloud by the voice synthesizer. The hearing person then can respond via a touch-tone telephone keypad. The device converts these touch-tone signals into standard text, which is displayed on the user's video screen. The PhoneCommunicator also comes with software on disk to control system functions.

Smart Modem 85

The Smart Modem 85 (SM-85), a product of KRI, is an external modem capable of communicating with both personal computers and text telephones. The modem connects to most personal computers through any standard serial port. The SM-85 can communicate with personal computer systems in ASCII and with text telephones operating under Baudot. The modem automatically detects if it is in communication with an ASCII or text telephone host and adjusts its data transmission and reception accordingly. It can dial in either pulse or standard tone and can hold up to ten phone numbers in memory. The system can automatically answer the telephone with a preprogrammed welcome message and has memory for storing text messages. A built-in lithium battery backs up the system's memory and powers the optional time and date clock calendar.

Text Telephone Software

Just as standard modems require software, the same holds true for Baudot/ASCII modems. Text Telephone software permits standard modems to function as text telephones. Some Baudot/ASCII modems have their own dedicated software; other software programs are memory resident and can work with many hardware configurations. The following describes several telecommunications software packages.

ASCII-TDD Software

The ASCII-TDD Software, produced by the Technology Assessment Program at Gallaudet University, is an MS-DOS–based software package that allows personal computers equipped with Hayes-compatible modems to talk to text telephone users. (A Hayes-compatible modem is a 300-baud modem that is a standard in the computer industry and is commonly available.) The software uses standard ASCII and communicates with text telephones in ASCII mode. The text telephone being called thus must be able to communicate in ASCII as well. The software, compatible with other forms of adaptive hardware and software, includes disk-based documentation. The ASCII-TDD Software is freeware and is not sold for commercial profit. The user can freely copy and distribute the software, and no fee is charged for its use. Technical support and assistance are available by calling the Technology Assessment Program bulletin board. (See the list at the end of Chapter 6 for the telephone number for this bulletin board.)

The ASCII-TDD software can be installed to either a hard or floppy disk and copied to an appropriate subdirectory on the hard disk. Once the software has been installed, it can be started by typing "ASCII-TDD," followed by the Enter key. The program will load into memory, and the title screen will appear. Press the Enter key again to go to the next screen and set up the software for communications. The software first attempts to communicate with any modem hardware installed in the system. If this is successful, a setup file is created so communications can begin.

If the software has been configured properly, the main menu screen will appear. The main menu offers five basic options: answer the phone, dial the phone, set up the software, read the documentation, and exit to the operating system. With the answer option, the software automatically answers the telephone and broadcasts a carrier signal. The dial option asks the user for a telephone number to dial. The setup option allows the user to reconfigure the program for a new system if necessary. The information option displays the contents of the documentation on screen, one page at a time. The exit option returns to the disk operating system and the software is unloaded from main memory.

Futura-TDD

Futura-TDD, from Phone TTY, is a general-purpose telecommunications pro-gram for persons who use the CM-4 text telephone modem. The software allows CM-4 owners to place calls to text telephones, computers, or bulletin boards. The program has a graphical user interface. The Futura software allows computer users equipped with Hayes-compatible modems to talk to persons with a text telephone as long as the text telephone has a 300-baud ASCII mode built in.

Phone TTY Multi Bulletin Board

Phone TTY Multi Bulletin Board software, from Phone TTY, is a bulletin board package written for the CM-4 Baudot/ASCII modem. The software allows up to eight callers to access one PC if the callers each have a telephone line and a modem. Multi Bulletin Board software is being used by both public and private organizations to set up text-telephone–accessible bulletin boards for customers and clients.

Pop-up-TDD

Pop-up-TDD, from Phone TTY, allows persons to communicate in both Baudot and ASCII using the CM-4 modem. As its name implies, Pop-up-TDD is a memory-resident software package in which the user presses a function key to start the program. The program is loaded into memory, where it resides until an incoming call is detected. The user then can activate the program and begin communications. This is a useful feature because the user can work on another software application while waiting for incoming calls.

Talking on a Baudot/ASCII Modem

Baudot/ASCII modems are relatively simple to operate. Text telephones and Baudot/ASCII modems can communicate with each other, provided they agree beforehand which language—Baudot or ASCII—they will both use. The following example assumes that both persons are using personal computers equipped with Baudot/ASCII modems. The individuals merely type messages back and forth to one another on the computer keyboard and the messages appear on the computer screens in real time as the messages are flashed over the telephone lines.

As with using text telephones, some basic guidelines should be observed when communicating over a personal computer equipped with a Baudot/ASCII modem. Since the typical computer screen displays about 25 lines of text, the user must press the Enter or Return key after each line. It is important to let the other person know that it is his or her turn to speak by typing *GA*, which stands for "go ahead." When the conversation is over, type *SK* for "stop keying."

Visual Beep Indicator Software

The primary exception to the lack of barriers presented by personal computers for persons with hearing impairments is the "beep" tone. This is a signal that computers use when an error condition has occurred or when the user needs to provide more information. Since the speaker beep may be inaudible to persons with hearing impairments, software can provide a visual rendering of the speakers beeping. Following are some examples of commercially available applications that make the beep indicator visual.

AccessDOS ShowSounds

AccessDOS, from IBM, offers a set of keyboard utilities to assist persons with disabilities. (See Chapter 5 for a complete description of AccessDOS.) Among the utility programs offered by AccessDOS, ShowSounds is intended to assist persons with hearing impairments as they operate the personal computer. ShowSounds displays a small musical note in the upper left corner of the screen when the computer beeps. The program also can flash the screen when the speaker beeps.

The Macintosh Speaker

As part of the Macintosh operating system, by using the control panel screen the user can set the volume of the internal speaker to any desired level. If the user sets the level of the speaker to zero, then the screen will flash every time the speaker audibly beeps.

SeeBEEP

SeeBEEP, from Microsystems Software, is a memory-resident software program for IBM PC users who are deaf or hearing impaired. Whenever the computer beeps, SeeBEEP provides a visual indication in one of two ways. The entire screen can flash and change color, or the word "beep" can appear where the cursor is positioned. The flash time may be adjusted from 0.2 to 2 seconds. SeeBEEP can be turned on and off with predefined hot keys. A shareware version that is not compatible with graphics mode is available on the manufacturer's bulletin board.

Computer-Aided Transcription

Computer-aided transcription serves persons who are deaf or hearing impaired who attend public gatherings, such as group assemblies, town meetings, classroom sessions, and courtroom proceedings. These services increase accessibility to the public functions by providing a real-time visual transcript of the proceedings. Computer-aided transcription is relatively simple in concept, requiring a skilled typist who can type 60 to 90 words per minute, a personal computer, a large display monitor, and word-processing software.

Another form of transcription service, computer-aided real-time transcription (CART), requires a trained court stenographer and a computer program that converts the stenographic symbols into standard printed text. Although this system provides real-time text of public gatherings, it may be more expensive than computer-aided transcription because trained stenographers cost more per hour than trained typists. The stenographic method provides a real-time verbatim transcript of the proceedings, while computer-aided transcription provides summaries or partial transcripts of a meeting or gathering.

While the typist or stenographer is keying in the audio portion of the presentation, the text of the speech scrolls onto the display monitor or video output screen. The entire text can also be saved to the hard disk or to the floppy disk of the transcription computer, allowing a printed or braille copy to be generated upon request. Information about obtaining transcription services can be found by contacting a local state rehabilitation commission or commission for the deaf.

In computer-aided transcription, a laptop computer is connected to a large screen display, allowing those present to read a printed transcript of a speech or lecture. *Courtesy of Gallaudet University, Washington, D.C.*

RAPIDTEXT

RAPIDTEXT, from Rapidtext, Inc., is a software program that allows the user to perform computer-assisted real-time transcription. The software interprets stenographic notes from a steno machine, translates them into English text, and sends it to a computer screen for viewing. Proper names of individual speakers may be preprogrammed and recalled by the stenographer. RAPID-TEXT requires a desktop or laptop IBM computer with at least 640K of memory and a 20MB hard drive, WordPerfect word processing software (version 5.0 or higher), and a steno machine. The software comes with a printed manual.

Computerized Sign Language Training

Persons who are deaf or hearing impaired use several visual languages to communicate: American Sign Language (ASL), Signed English, and Finger Spelling. ASL is a visual language that uses hand, arm, and body movements to relate words and concepts. ASL has its own syntax that does not resemble the English language. Signed English, another visual form of sign language, corresponds with the spoken form of the English language. Signed English also uses visual hand, arm, and body movements to construct words and phrases. Finger Spelling, a less complex form of sign language, uses the hands and fingers to spell out words one letter at a time. Finger Spelling thus has a one-to-one correspondence with the English alphabet.

A personal computer can be a valuable tool for teaching or reinforcing ASL or Finger Spelling. A variety of software programs to teach and reinforce ASL are available for Apple II, Macintosh, and IBM PC computer systems. These software programs use graphics representations of sign symbols.

Computerized Animated Vocabulary of American Sign Language

The Computerized Animated Vocabulary of American Sign Language, from E & IS Signware, is a software program that allows persons to practice their receptive skills in ASL. English words selected by the user from the 2,600-word vocabulary are translated into animated displays of the equivalent ASL. Signs on the computer screen are seen from the perspective of one viewing a human signer. Motion of the signs can be speeded up, slowed down, or frozen. English captions can be turned on and off. A series of words selected from any of the sixteen data diskettes can be stored on a work disk by the user and played back in sequence.

Elementary Signer

Elementary Signer, from E & IS Signware, is designed to introduce elementary school students to ASL. Words selected by the student are translated into the equivalent ASL and displayed on the screen in computer animation. The 160-word vocabulary allows students to converse in simple sentences. Signs can be displayed with or without captions. Motions of the signs can be slowed down, speeded up, frozen, or repeated. The learning comprehension mode tests students' knowledge of signs and keeps score. The software is available for the Apple II, Macintosh, and IBM PC.

Fingerspeller and Fingernumbers

Fingerspeller, from Specialsoft, is an Apple II-compatible software program designed to teach the Finger Spelling alphabet. The program can generate a line drawing on the computer screen of each letter of the alphabet. Fingerspeller displays the signs with their meaning one at a time and provides practice drills. The software can develop students' reading rates by projecting sequences of up to 120 signs at an adjustable rate. Fingernumbers teaches the manual numbers from 0 to 999,999. It is included with Fingerspeller, or it may be purchased separately.

FingerZoids

The FingerZoids program, from E & IS Signware, is an arcade-type interactive game that teaches the Finger Spelling alphabet. The software is compatible with Apple II and Macintosh personal computers. Invaders in the shape of letters from the ASL alphabet descend from the top of the screen. The object of the game is to shoot them down by pressing the corresponding English letter key. The program keeps score and posts high scores. The software comes with a printed instruction manual.

Micro-Interpreter I Fingerspeller

Micro-Interpreter I Fingerspeller, from E & IS Signware, is a program that teaches Finger Spelling. The program displays line graphics of a hand forming the letter shapes. Letters on the computer screen are seen from the perspective of one viewing a human signer. Individual letters or words (which are spelled out one letter at a time) of up to thirty letters can be displayed at four user-selected speeds. Words can be captioned or noncaptioned. The learning comprehension mode allows users to test their skills from a preprogrammed list of words stored on disk or from their own word lists while the program keeps score. The software is available for the Apple II, Macintosh, and IBM PC computers.

PC-Fingers

PC-Fingers, from Midwest Health Programs, is a program for teaching and drilling Finger Spelling. Each alphabetic character appears on the screen as a line graphic of a hand posed for that letter. Various levels of instructional difficulty are available. The advanced level displays whole words and phrases. The program can be run at speeds from 1.3 to 11.8 signs per second.

Talking Hands

Talking Hands, from Ebsco Curriculum Materials, is a Finger Spelling drill and practice program. The program will display finger signs for the letters as typed. The program also can display hand signs serially or at random for drill. Up to 36 messages of 10 lines and 80 characters in length can be stored on disk and played back for practice. The speed of sign presentation (from 1 to 40 signs per minute) can be user-specified. The software runs on Apple II personal computers.

Signaling Systems

As with other forms of assistive technology, the goal of many adaptive systems is to transform one type of signal into another. Signaling systems monitor sound in the environment and convert the sound energy to a visible, tactile, or vibrating signal, allowing persons with severe hearing impairments to live more independently. These systems are more often employed by persons who are totally deaf than by those with minimal hearing impairments. For the person who is deaf or who has a severe hearing impairment and must manage a home or business, many sound sources in the environment must be monitored on a daily basis. Signaling systems constantly monitor select sound sources, listening for specific frequencies and durations. When the signaler detects a desired sound, it alerts the person.

The doorbell is an ordinary audio-signaling system that alerts hearing persons to the presence of a visitor. For the person who is deaf, the doorbell is not useful as a signaling device. For a person who is hearing impaired, the doorbell may be audible only when the person is in the same room with the ringer and may be totally inaudible some distance from the doorbell. Doorbell signalers are perhaps the most common type of sound-monitoring equipment for persons with hearing impairments. There are three basic types of doorbell signalers: hard-wired, acoustic, or magnetic. Hard-wired doorbell signalers interface electrically to the power leads within the doorbell itself and are activated by the electrical energy that is sent to the doorbell when the doorbell button is pressed. Acoustic doorbell signalers monitor the doorbell by using a microphone and are activated by sound waves moving through the air. Magnetic signalers attach to the doorbell housing with a suction cup and are activated by the magnetic pulse that is created when the doorbell rings.

Hard-wired, acoustic, and magnetic signalers operate in much the same manner despite their differing approaches to monitoring the doorbell system. When any of these signalers detects a ringing doorbell, it immediately alerts the user by transmitting a code signal to a receiver by sending a signal through the standard electrical system of the building. When the transmitter sends an alert signal to a remote receiver, the receiver flashes a room lamp under its jurisdiction, for example. The receiver includes a built-in electrical outlet to accept the power plug of a room lamp or other appliance. Multiple receivers may be used to flash every lamp in the house when the doorbell is pressed.

Each system has advantages and disadvantages. Hard-wired signalers are less prone to false signals because they are not activated by sound energy; however, they require a professional to install. On the other hand, acoustic signalers are more prone to false positive incidents, but they can be installed more readily by nonprofessionals. In contrast, magnetic signalers offer the reliability of a hard-wired system with the ease of installation of an acoustic system.

Using the same basic technology, other important sounds in the environment can be monitored. For example, parents need to listen for the sound of a crying baby. A baby signaler placed close to the child constantly monitors for crying. Because the baby's cry is unique, the signaler simply listens for a specific duration and pitch. When it detects the target pitch and intensity, it transmits an alert signal to a remote receiver to flash lamps in the vicinity of the parents.

Similarly, but perhaps not as critical, a buzzing alarm clock is another important sound that also must be monitored. Persons with hearing impairments can monitor this vital sound and be alerted to its presence through visual or tactile output. Adapted alarm clocks allow persons with hearing impairments to trigger a lamp or vibrating signaler. When the alarm rings, it activates power to the built-in outlet, which turns on lamps or vibrators connected to the clock. The following examples of signalers provide some insight into devices that are available. See the list at the end of this chapter for vendors that supply signal systems.

Super Signal

The Super Signal, from Ultratec, is a signaling system for persons with hearing impairments. The system can alert the user to various sounds around the home, school, or office by flashing lamps or by turning on select appliances. It can detect ringing doorbells, telephones, crying babies, and other sound sources. The Super Signal can be installed by a nonprofessional. The system is modular, consisting of separate transmitters and receivers. The transmitter monitors a particular sound source and transmits to one or more receivers stationed around the home or office when the sound is perceived. The system connects to as many room lamps or appliances as needed. When the doorbell rings, the wireless transmitter sends a signal to a receiver, which then flashes specific lights on and off. The telephone signaler plugs into the telephone, and sends signals to a wireless receiver connected to various room lamps to flash when a call is present. When a baby cries, the wireless transmitter sends signals to receivers, instructing them to flash lamps in another room.

The Super Signal System can be purchased with an optional wireless pager. When the pager is activated, signals are sent to a remote receiver module. The module then turns on the lamp or appliance under its jurisdiction. The device also has an optional paging system. The pager can be used to announce dinner, a telephone call, or a group meeting. When the pager button is depressed, selected room lamps flash, signaling the event.

Super Signal Clock

The Super Signal Clock, from Ultratec, is an adapted alarm clock that can transmit to a receiver module. When the alarm sounds, the remote receiver can trigger a room lamp or vibrating pad.

Watchman

The Watchman signaling system, from Ultratec, is an adjustable sound-signaling system that turns sounds in the environment into visual signals.

The system consists of a series of transmitters and receivers that work together to monitor selected sounds in the environment. The Watchman can monitor a telephone, alarm clock, doorbell, crying baby, and almost any other sound. Readily installed by a nonprofessional, the Watchman uses transmitters and receivers plugged into existing electrical outlets. Lamps plugged into the receivers act as the visual signalers. The Watchman features an adjustable sound signal control as well as an adjustable signal-lamp flash rate.

Signaling systems are relatively inexpensive. They provide valuable assistance around the home, school, and office. Future signalers based on microprocessor technology will be capable of distinguishing selected sounds from background noise. This technology probably will develop significantly in the future.

Captioning Systems

Captioning systems make television programs more accessible to persons with hearing impairments by providing text messages of dialogue at the bottom (usually the lower third) of the video screen. Not unlike subtitles found on foreign films, captioning offers a visual record of the spoken word.

There are two basic types of captioning: closed and open. Both closed and open captioning provide the user with a text message on screen. Closed captions require a decoder for the caption to be visible, while open captions do not need a decoder. As dictated by the "Television Decoder Circuitry Act of 1990," television sets larger than 13 inches that are sold in the United States beginning in 1993 must come equipped with a microchip to decode closed captioning.

TELECAPTION 4000 and VR 100

The National Captioning Institute, a nonprofit organization that performs research and development on captioning technology for persons with hearing impairments, distributes two caption decoders through a network of national dealers: the TELECAPTION 4000 and the VR 100. These decoders allow the individual who is hearing impaired to decode the closed-caption signal contained within selected programming. The decoders are similar to a cable box and are installed between the television and the antenna or cable source.

Closed caption text messages shown at the bottom of a standard television screen allow persons who are deaf or hearing impaired to read a transcript of the audio portion of selected programming. *Courtesy of Gallaudet University.*

Making Captioned Videotapes

Numerous companies that provide training videotapes also are incorporating captioning into their products to assist persons with disabilities as well as to sell their products to persons with hearing impairments. By using a personal computer and two videocassette recorders, the open or closed captions can be added to existing videotapes.

First, the user creates the text captions on a word-processing program or with the built-in text editor of the software. The system requires two videocassette recorders—one to play back the original and another to record the captioned version. Then the computer mixes the original videotape frames with the captioned text and transfers the newly captioned video image to the second videorecorder.

Caption Maker and Caption Maker Plus

The Caption Maker and Caption Maker Plus, from Computer Prompting & Captioning, can produce either open or closed captions. The system has been used by various corporations, government agencies, educational institutions, and video-production houses to assist people with hearing impairments. The system is compatible with IBM PC computers and consists of a software package and circuit card.

Electronic Amplification Systems

Amplification devices are among the most common adaptive technology for persons who are hearing impaired. These devices boost sound energy allowing persons with limited hearing to more easily perceive the spoken word, music, and other sound sources. Electronic amplification systems can be used to access face-to-face communication, public gatherings, telephone calls, and television or radio programs.

One of the earliest attempts at amplification technology was the ear trumpet, a horn-shaped apparatus designed to concentrate acoustic energy and project it directly into the ear. The device usually was made of thin metal and was held up to the ear by hand. In the early 1900s Alexander Graham Bell built one of the first electrically based amplification systems—a large device powered by giant storage batteries that used a carbon microphone to amplify sound energy. By no means was this system portable or inconspicuous. In contrast, modern amplification systems can fit in a pocket or purse or can be worn almost invisibly in the ear.

Today's tiny amplification devices are designed to collect sound energy, amplify the signal, filter out unwanted frequencies, and focus the boosted and clarified signal directly into the ear. These systems also compensate for hearing losses at different frequencies. That is, if an individual has a hearing loss confined to higher frequencies, the higher frequencies can be amplified to a greater extent than the lower frequencies, thus compensating more equally for the specific hearing loss.

Amplification systems contain three basic components: a microphone, amplifier, and speaker. The microphone collects sound energy through the use of a moving diaphragm. When the diaphragm is distorted by sound waves moving through the air, electrical pulses are created that produce an analog signal of the incoming sound wave. This electrical wave is then routed to the amplifier and the signal is increased. Next, the amplified signal is sent to the speaker, which directs the boosted sound energy directly into the ear. The net effect of this process is to make most sounds louder, thus easier to perceive. Two of the most common types of amplification systems in use today are hearing aids and assistive listening devices. Another system frequently employed by persons who are hearing impaired is the telephone amplification system.

Hearing Aids

Among the most common forms of adaptive technologies are hearing aids. These electronic amplification devices amplify sound energy and direct the boosted signal directly into the ear. Most hearing aids consist of a tiny molded plastic shell that is customized to fit inside the ear of the wearer. A microphone, speaker, and amplifier are all contained within the shell. Users can adjust the volume level by turning a small control. Hearing aids can be used to amplify face-to-face conversations, telephone calls, and even public meetings and gatherings. Some hearing aids come equipped with a telecoil, permitting them to tune into assistive listening systems (described in the next section) in auditoriums or public facilities.

Audiotone A-526

The A-526, from Audiotone, is a behind-the-ear hearing aid designed for individuals with moderate to severe hearing losses. The unit features an electret microphone and continuously adjustable frequency response and output control. The unit also includes a telecoil, making it compatible with assistive listening systems found in public facilities. The aid also has an audio input capability for use with portable assistive listening devices. As with most hearing aids, the A-526 is available from local distributors and must be custom fitted to the user.

HSI Model P, PLP, EP, EC, EZ

HSI, Hearing Services International, offers a line of in-the-ear and canal hearing aids that are custom-built according to the specific hearing loss. Typical units feature raised-rib volume controls, automatic signal processors for reduction of background noise, output and tone control switches, telecoil switches, nonallergic shells, and windscreens for outdoor use. The hearing aids are available in tan, brown, pink, and dark brown.

Panasonic WHO1

The WHO1, from Panasonic, is a hearing aid styled similarly to a fountain pen. It is designed to provide amplification for people who are hesitant about wearing the standard styles of hearing aids. The device comes with universal ear pieces and a cord, receiver, battery, and carrying case. The WHO1 has a top-mounted unidirectional microphone and separate controls for volume output and tone. A fold-out pedestal allows the unit to sit on a desk or table for use as a personal amplifier.

Siemens 408 W-H

The 408 W-H, from Siemens Hearing Instruments, is a behind-the-ear hearing aid designed for individuals with mild hearing impairments. The unit has an electret microphone, gain control, tone control, and a telecoil.

Assistive Listening Devices

Assistive listening devices, based on the technology used in hearing aids, are used chiefly in public situations such as in meetings or conferences. Like hearing aids, assistive listening devices amplify sound energy and contain a microphone, amplifier, and speaker. In contrast to hearing aids, assistive listening devices consist of two separate units: a microphone-transmitter and a speaker-receiver, each about the size of a pack of playing cards. The transmitter and receiver communicate with one another through radio waves or infrared light. An assistive listening device permits the user to filter out background noise within an auditorium by focusing the microphone on the speaker. A microphone placed in front of a speaker or worn on the speaker's clothing does a more efficient job of amplifying a speaker's words and overcoming background noise than a microphone placed in the middle of the same room as the speaker. Similarly, the microphone-transmitter of an assistive listening device on or near a speaker is better at picking up the speaker's words and overcoming background noise than a microphone within a hearing aid worn by someone in the audience who is seated farther away from the speaker.

Assistive listening devices can use a number of broadcast techniques to achieve their purpose. Some systems use infrared signals; others use some form of radio waves. The infrared waves that communicate between the transmitter and the receiver are similar to those of a television remote control and are invisible to the unaided eye. Infrared systems are useful in auditoriums where multiple performances take place because infrared broadcasts are stopped by walls, unlike radio signals that bleed through floors, ceilings, and walls. Radio-based systems are useful both indoors and out of doors, while infrared systems can receive interference from direct sunlight, which also contains infrared energy.

Easy Listener

The Easy Listener, from Phonic Ear, is an FM amplification system for use in classrooms and in smaller or larger groups. The teacher-worn microphone transmits sound to the student-worn receiver. The receiver units resemble a wearable cassette player. Students can choose between small, lightweight headsets or hearing-aid–style earphones. Microphones may be directional, omnidirectional, or boom microphones.

Personal FM System

The Personal FM System, from Phonic Ear, is a wireless FM amplification system with independent microphone and FM volume controls designed for students or adults. The unit comes equipped with a modular battery pack and separate microphone and FM gain controls. Its estimated battery life is 25 hours with a rechargeable battery pack. The transmitter includes a lapel nondirectional microphone, a rechargeable battery pack, and a wire belt clip. The receiver includes a battery pack, volume control, and belt clip.

Pocketalker

The Pocketalker, from William Sound Corporation, is a portable assistive listening device. The unit can amplify voice, television, radio, and other sounds. The system contains circuitry to reduce the level of background noise, thus producing a clearer signal. It has a variable volume control for user adjustment.

Sound Enhancement System

The Sound Enhancement System, from Telex Communications, is an FM-based assistive listening device. The unit can be used indoors or outdoors. The base-station transmitter reaches up to 500 feet and can interface with a public address system. The unit operates on 120-volt household current and has a peak-reading audio-level meter for audio monitoring. This portable, battery-operated unit can be clipped onto a belt or carried in a pocket, or it can be mounted permanently in a component rack.

Telex TW 3

The TW 3, from Telex Communications, is a wireless amplification system. The device consists of a microphone-transmitter in one unit, designed primarily for classroom use with hearing impaired students. The unit can transmit speech or the output from audiovisual devices such as videocassette recorders, televisions, or other audio outputs. It can be either hand-held or worn around the neck. The device comes equipped with a battery-status light and audio-limiter circuitry to prevent overmodulation without overamplification and distortion of background sounds. The TW 3 also includes an auxiliary input jack with voice-over capability, allowing the instructor to speak to the group at any time. The microphone-transmitter has a rechargeable battery and a lavaliere neck strap.

Telephone Amplification Systems

For persons who are hearing impaired, the telephone need not present a barrier due to electronic amplification systems that attach to the telephone. For those who have limited but functional hearing, telephone amplification systems allow greater access to the telephone. Amplified telephone handsets attach to most telephones and have variable volume-adjustment controls that allow the user to modify the sound level for comfortable listening.

Volume Control Handset

The Volume Control Handset, from AT&T, can increase the volume level up to 30 percent. The unit has an adjustable volume control built into the handset and includes a standard modular telephone interface jack. The handset can be attached to almost any telephone by unplugging the old handset and installing the new one. The unit is compatible with hearing aids equipped with standard telephone coils. Made of solid plastic, the device is portable and can be carried in briefcase or purse.

Walker Clarity

The Walker Clarity, from Walker Equipment, is an adapted telephone made especially for persons with hearing impairments. The telephone amplifies the audio signal but also makes it clearer through select-frequency filtering and adjustment. The phone has a visual ringer suitable for persons with limited hearing. The ringer has an adjustable volume control, useful for persons who have difficulty detecting an incoming call. The phone can hold up to three emergency telephone numbers in its memory and a programmable ten-number memory for speed dialing. The phone can also dial in either pulse or tone formats. It also includes last-number redial and a mute button.

Products for Persons Who Are Deaf or Hearing Impaired*

The following lists include vendors that manufacture and distribute technology to assist persons who are deaf or hearing impaired. The lists are divided into vendors of the following types of adaptive devices: text telephones, computer-based access products, sign language training software, signaling systems, captioning systems, electronic amplification systems, and products for persons who are deaf-blind.

Text Telephone Providers

AT&T Special Needs Center
2001 Rte. 46, Ste. 310
Parsippany, NJ 07054
800-233-1222
800-833-3232 (TDD)

Audiotone
P.O. Box 2905
Phoenix, AZ 85062
800-528-5424
602-254-5886

*Text telephone numbers are indicated by TDD.

Deafworks Co.
P.O. Box 1614
South Gate, CA 90280
310-637-1929

Integrated Microcomputer
Systems Inc.
#2 Research Pl.
Rockville, MD 20850
301-948-4790
301-869-6391 (TDD)

Microlog Corp.
20270 Goldenrod Lane
Germantown, MD 20876
800-926-3227
301-428-3227

Phone TTY, Inc.
202 Lexington Ave.
Hackensack, NJ 07601
201-489-7889
201-489-7890

Potomac Technology
1 Church St., Ste. 402
Rockville, MD 20850
800-433-2838
301-762-4005

Sound Resources, Inc.
201 E. Ogden Ave.
Hinsdale, IL 60521
708-325-6133

Technology Assessment
Program
Gallaudet University
800 Florida Ave. N.E.
Washington, DC 20002
202-651-5257 (Voice or
TDD)

Trident Technologies
1200 Summer St.
Stamford, CT 06805
203-325-2500
212-645-5656

Ultratec, Inc.
450 Science Dr.
Madison, WI 53711
608-238-5400

Computer-Based Access Product Providers

IBM Independence Series
Information Center
Bldg. 5
P.O. Box 1328
Boca Raton, FL 33429
800-426-4832

KRI, Inc.
129 Sheldon St.
El Segundo, CA 90245
800-833-4968
310-322-3202

Microflip, Inc.
11211 Petworth Lane
Glenn Dale, MD 20769
301-262-6020
301-262-1629 (TDD)

MicroSystems Software, Inc.
600 Worcester Rd.
Framingham, MA 01701
508-626-8511

Phone TTY, Inc.
  202 Lexington Ave.
  Hackensack, NJ 07601
  201-489-7889
  201-489-7890 (TDD)

Rapidtext, Inc.
  18013 Sky Park Cir.
  Irvine, CA 92714
  714-261-6333

Ultratec, Inc.
  450 Science Dr.
  Madison, WI 53711
  608-238-5400

Sign Language Training Software Providers

E & IS Signware
  206 Angie Dr.
  P.O. Box 521
  Cedar Falls, IA 50613
  (number not available)

Ebsco Curriculum Materials
  P.O. Box 1943
  Birmingham, AL 35201
  800-633-8623
  205-991-1208

Midwest Health
  Programs, Inc.
  P.O. Box 3023
  Urbana, IL 61801
  217-367-5293

Specialsoft
  P.O. Box 41058
  Santa Barbara, CA 93140
  800-421-6534

Signaling System Providers

AT&T Special Needs Center
  2001 Rte. 46, Ste. 310
  Parsippany, NJ 07054
  800-233-1222
  800-833-3232 (TDD)

Hal Hen Co.
  35-53 24th St
  Long Island City, NY 11106
  800-242-5436

Maxi Signal Products
  Div. of Mill Specialties
  5 E. 49th St.
  P.O. Box 398
  La Grange, IL 60525
  708-354-4730

Nationwide Flashing Signal
  Systems
  8120 Fenton St., Rm. 200
  Silver Spring, MD 20910
  301-589-6671
  301-589-6670

Omni Hearing Systems
  3201 Skylane Dr.
  Carrollton, TX 75006
  800-527-0872

Phone TTY, Inc.
  202 Lexington Ave.
  Hackensack, NJ 07601
  201-489-7889
  201-489-7890

Sonic Alert, Inc.
  1750 W. Hamlin Rd.
  Rochester Hills, MI 48309
  313-656-3110

Sound Resources, Inc.
  201 E. Ogden Ave.
  Hinsdale, IL 60521
  708-325-6133

Ultratec, Inc.
  450 Science Dr.
  Madison, WI 53711
  608-238-5400

Captioning System Providers

Computer Prompting &
  Captioning Co.
  3408 Wisconsin Ave. N.W.
  Washington, DC 20016
  202-966-0980

National Captioning Institute
  5203 Leesburg Pike
  Falls Church, VA 22041
  703-998-2461

Electronic Amplification System Providers

American Phone Products, Inc.
  5192 Bolsa Ave., Rm. 5
  Huntington Beach, CA
    92649
  714-897-0808

AT&T Special Needs Center
  2001 Rte. 46, Ste. 310
  Parsippany, NJ 07054
  800-233-1222
  800-833-3232 (TDD)

Audiotone
  P.O. Box 2905
  Phoenix, AZ 85062
  800-528-5424
  602-254-5886

Earmark
  1125 Dixwell Ave.
  Hamden, CT 06514
  203-777-2130

Electone, Inc.
  P.O. Box 910
  Winter Park, FL 32790
  800-432-7483

Exceptional Hearing Services
  515 Northgate Dr., Ste. D
  San Rafael, CA 94903-3639
  415-499-7766

G N Netcom
  5600 Rowland Rd., Ste. 285
  Minnetonka, MN 55343
  612-932-2992

Hal Hen Co.
  35-53 24th St.
  Long Island City, NY 11106
  800-242-5436

HSI Hearing Services Intnl.
  7480 Washington Ave. S.
  Eden Prairie, MN 55344
  800-328-3832
  612-829-5757

Jay L Warren, Inc.
  P.O. Box 25413
  Chicago, IL 60625
  312-275-1525

Luminaud
8688 Tyler Blvd.
Mentor, OH 44060
216-255-9082

Panasonic Co.
1 Panasonic Way
Mail Stop 2F3
Secaucus, NJ 07094
800-447-4700
201-348-7000

Phonic Ear, Inc.
250 Camino Alto
Mill Valley, CA 94941
415-383-4000

Potomac Technology
1 Church St., Ste. 402
Rockville, MD 20850
800-433-2838
301-762-4005

Precision Acoustics
501 Fifth Ave., Ste. 704
New York, NY 10017
212-986-6470

Qualitone Hearing Aids &
Audiometers
4931 W. 35th St.
Minneapolis, MN 55416
800-328-3897
612-927-7161

Radio Shack
Div. of Tandy Corp.
1500 One Tandy Ctr.
Fort Worth, TX 76102
817-390-3011

Siemens Hearing
Instruments, Inc.
10 Constitution Ave.
Piscataway, NJ 08855
800-345-0183
201-562-6600

Sound Resources, Inc.
201 E. Ogden Ave.
Hinsdale, IL 60521
708-325-6133

Starkey Laboratories, Inc.
P.O. Box 9457
Minneapolis, MN 55440
612-941-6401

Telex Communications, Inc.
9600 Aldrich Ave. S.
Minneapolis, MN 55420
800-328-3771
612-884-4051

Walker Equipment Corp.
P.O. Box 829
Hwy. 151 S.
Ringgold, GA 30736
800-426-3738

Williams Sound Corp.
5929 Baker Rd.
Minnetonka, MN 55345
800-328-6190
612-931-0291

Products for Persons Who Are Deaf-Blind

American Foundation for
the Blind
15 W. 16th St.
New York, NY 10011
201-862-8838

Enabling Technologies Co.
3102 S.E. Jay St.
Stuart, FL 34997
407-283-4817

Page Net
1121 Industrial Rd.
San Carlos, CA 94070-4106
415-591-7900

Quest Electronics
510 S. Worthington St.
Oconomowoc, WI 53066
800-558-9526
414-567-9157

Sonic Alert, Inc.
1750 W. Hamlin Rd.
Rochester Hills, MI 48309
313-656-3110

TeleSensory Corp.
455 N. Bernardo Ave.
P.O. Box 7455
Mountain View, CA 94039
800-227-8418
415-960-0920

5

Technology for Persons with Motor and/or Speech Impairments

For persons with motor and/or speech impairments, the personal computer is used both as a means of accessing information and as a primary communications device. The term *motor impairment* is used in this chapter to describe a variety of physical disabilities that result in a restriction in an individual's freedom of movement. The focus here is not on the specific disability but rather on its effect on the individual. Examples of disabilities that affect motor ability are multiple sclerosis, muscular dystrophy, and spinal-cord injuries. Many disabilities in this classification prevent the use of or impair the voluntary muscles. Some also affect the speech center, thus preventing individuals from using their spoken language ability.

Personal computers fitted with adaptive technology allow individuals to communicate and to pursue education and career goals and to control the environment, including electronic equipment and electrical appliances. This chapter discusses adapted keyboards, alternative input devices, voice recognition systems, alternative communications devices, and environmental control systems. Adapted keyboards provide a modified working environment for persons unable to work with standard keyboards. Keyboards can be adapted through either hardware or software. Hardware alternatives include templates for existing keyboards or entirely different keyboards from those usually supplied with personal computers. Software alternatives include macro programs, sticky key programs, and other programs that alter the keyboard so it is more accessible. Alternative input devices allow the user to point at select commands or objects on the screen and select an option with a blink of an eye or an adapted switch. Other adapted input devices include systems that use Morse code or word prediction for operating a personal computer. Voice recognition systems permit the user to control a personal computer through verbal command syntax. Alternative communications devices can speak for individuals who cannot speak. Environmental control systems are used to activate electronic devices in the workplace or at home.

Adapted Keyboards

For persons unable to use the traditional computer keyboard, adapted keyboard hardware allows individuals access to personal computers. Adapted keyboards are input devices created especially for users who are motor or physically disabled. These keyboards can be used by persons who have control over one hand or control of just one finger. Adapted keyboards are programmable, permitting users to define how they are most comfortable using the system. An adapted keyboard can be used with one hand, a mouthstick, or even with the feet, depending on the exact nature of the keyboard. It may be either large or small in size.

To get an overview of both the inherent advantages of using a computer keyboard and the potential barriers an unadapted keyboard might present, a look at specific keyboard operations is in order: The keys on a computer keyboard are merely mechanical switches that make electrical contact when pressed. Depending on their open or closed state, tiny switches imbedded in the keyboard send signals to the computer. To operate a keyboard effectively, the user must have significant coordination and finger control. The user must be able to strike the desired key without accidentally striking others and also must be able to release the key quickly enough to prevent the key from repeating.

Installation can be performed in a few minutes with little advanced technical experience because many adapted keyboards plug into a standard keyboard socket. Since many adapted keyboards attach directly to the computer, they do not use up system memory. Once the adapted keyboard is installed, the user's keystrokes are sent electronically to the computer just as if they had been sent there by an original equipment keyboard.

Numerous adapted keyboard products are currently available from a variety of vendors. See the list at the end of this chapter for vendors that offer adaptive keyboards and related products.

The King Keyboard from TASH has recessed keys and a built-in keyguard to separate the keys. *Courtesy of TASH, Inc.*

King Keyboard

The King Keyboard, from Technical Aids and Systems for the Handicapped (TASH), is a large adaptive keyboard, measuring 23.5 inches by 12 inches. The unit plugs into a standard PC keyboard socket. The King contains alphabetic, numeric, and programmable function keys with the most-used keys located in the center of the keyboard. The keys respond to low pressure.

PC Mini Keyboard

The PC Mini, from TASH, is a small keyboard that is useful for an individual employing one-handed input or a typing stick. The keyboard measures 7.5 inches by 4.5 inches. The Mini keyboard is appropriate for people who have a small range of movement with some finger dexterity. It has closely spaced membrane keys with the space bar in the center.

Unicorn Membrane Keyboards

Unicorn Membrane Keyboards, from Unicorn Engineering, are programmable membrane keyboards with touch-sensitive areas ("keys") for the Macintosh and Apple II computers. The keyboards have 128 keys that may be grouped together to form larger keys. Each key, when touched, can output a predefined character or message to the computer. These messages, or "setups,"

When a keyguard is fitted over a keyboard, the user must insert a finger into a hole to activate a key and to prevent accidental keystrokes. *Courtesy of Prentke Romich.*

can be saved on disk. When used with a speech synthesizer, each key can be used to output setups in spoken form. The keyboards have a clear plastic cover; overlay sheets may be placed between the keyboard and this cover to indicate the setups associated with each key. Two models are available: Model II measures approximately 14 inches by 21 inches with an active area of 10 inches by 20 inches and weighs 3.7 pounds. Model 510 measures approximately 7.5 inches by 12 inches with an active area of 5 inches by 10 inches and weighs 1.4 pounds.

Unicorn Smart Keyboard

The Unicorn Smart Keyboard, from Unicorn Engineering, is an adapted computer keyboard that plugs directly into the keyboard port. A standard keyboard can be plugged into the Unicorn and the two can be used together. This feature permits the computer to be used by persons with different abilities without the need to plug and unplug system hardware repeatedly. The Smart keyboard has 576 individual keys. The keypad is arranged in columns of 24 by 24 rows. To type on this keyboard, the user places overlays on the keyboard and adjusts keyboard functions by using a SetUp Overlay. This product comes with seven overlays: alphabet, alphabet and numbers, numbers, arrows, QWERTY for IBM, QWERTY for Apple/Macintosh, and SetUp. The keyboard is compatible with IBM and Apple/Macintosh computer systems.

Keyboard Keyguards

Keyguards are plastic or metal templates that fit over a standard computer keyboard with a hole for each key. This keyboard adaptation helps prevent accidental keystrokes and provides a place for users to rest their hands for stability while typing. Some keyguards have key latches—levers that can hold down keys such as Shift and Control—to eliminate the need to press two keys at once. Keyguards are made for individual models of computers and often are not interchangeable across specific brands of keyboards.

Keyguard

The Keyguard, from IBM, is a molded plastic cover for the standard PC computer keyboard. The guard allows the user to strike only one key at a time.

Keyboard Modification Software

Software packages can make the original equipment keyboard more accessible to persons with motor impairments. Among these are macro software that saves many keystrokes and sticky key software that addresses the requirement of having to depress two keys simultaneously. Some assistive software can allow the arrow keys to be used instead of the mouse, while others can filter out unwanted keystrokes. See the list at the end of this chapter for vendors that offer keyboard modification software.

Macro Software

The mainstream world of personal computers contains numerous software utilities that are useful to persons with disabilities even though many of these software applications were never designed with the disabled user in mind. Macro software programs clearly fit into this category. Macros are inexpensive and efficient ways to make select software packages more accessible. These programs are readily available, and they are almost limitlessly customizable.

In basic terms, a macro program types keystrokes for the user based on a stored file of user-definable commands. The user assigns a macro to a key to start a sequence of commands and then defines the individual keystrokes contained within the macro. For example, the F1 function key could be programmed to enter the name and address of an individual, saving dozens of keystrokes in the process. The F2 key could be programmed to enter a user password sequence, further saving keystrokes for a user with a motor impairment. The macro can be stored on disk to be used over and over again when necessary. The ability to define hundreds of keystrokes for a single key press can assist the user for word processing, database management, spreadsheets, telecommunications, bookkeeping, programming, and even for games.

Macro software also allows the user to redefine the keyboard by rearranging the keys into any pattern that is most convenient. By redefining a keyboard, complex key strokes can be turned into easier ones. For example, if a user who is motor disabled cannot strike a particular key on the keyboard because of the key's position, a macro can be written to electronically strike that key when another key is pressed. If a user is more familiar with a particular keyboard than with the one currently in use, a macro package can rearrange the entire keyboard to suit the individual's needs. Then, the new keyboard layout definitions can be stored to a file and loaded into memory when the rearrangement is needed. If the time comes to restore the keyboard to the original configuration, that particular keyboard definition file can be loaded back into memory.

Many mainstream software programs come packaged from the factory with their own built-in macro software. Unlike the macro programs that can control other software packages, these built-in macro programs are active only when the specific application is running in the computer's memory and is visible on screen. Two examples of mainstream software packages that contain their own built-in macro languages are WordPerfect and Lotus 1-2-3. Several commercially available macro programs can be purchased from mail order outlets or from local computer stores. These programs are relatively inexpensive and are compatible with most commercial software packages. Software catalogs are an appropriate place to look for macro software.

Since macro programs are stored on floppy disks, they are relatively simple to install. The process consists of creating a subdirectory on the hard disk and copying the software onto the main system drive. Remember, however, that the actual macro program and its set of configuration files for each application will consume disk space.

A word of caution is in order: Prior to purchasing a macro program, users should test the program with their adaptive equipment because not all macro programs are fully compatible with some forms of adaptive technology. Users may also have to experiment with various macro programs before finding one that is compatible. Sometimes loading the macro program in a different sequence can make the software more compatible with adaptive equipment. If the user needs the macro program to control the adaptive software as well, the macro program should be loaded immediately after the disk operating system has loaded so the macro program can operate with the adaptive software running in memory.

ProKey Plus

ProKey Plus, from RoseSoft, is a macro program that allows the user to type long character sequences or groups of commands by entering a two-keystroke combination such as Alt-A. ProKey allows the user to include fixed or variable-length pauses in macros. Up to 300 macros may be defined, storing a total of 30,000 characters. Macros are called up by a multiple-character name and may be created and edited while another program is running. The program includes a one-key feature for single-finger operation of Shift, Alt, and Control keys. ProKey Plus version 5.1 contains features such as menus, display messages, event scheduling, and alarm. The software runs on IBM PC-compatible computers and comes with a printed manual.

QuicKeys 2

QuicKeys 2, from CE Software, for the Apple Macintosh allows the user to customize keys so that complicated functions can be performed with a single keystroke. The number of keys that can be customized is limited only by the amount of disk space. After the program has been installed, it can be accessed from the Control Panel. QuicKeys 2 can emulate all mouse functions. Other features include "smart" sequences that permit complicated procedures to be recorded and recalled, and Real Time Recording that can be used to "teach" the program to perform routine tasks on the Macintosh. A Macintosh Plus or later model with 1MB of RAM running System 6.02 is the minimum required configuration to run QuicKeys 2. A hard drive is recommended.

Sticky Keys and Key Modifier Software

Some keyboard key-striking sequences needed for input or control of a computer can present a barrier for persons with motor disabilities. As with a typewriter, using the Shift key to capitalize a letter or insert a symbol can present a barrier to users with motor disabilities because it requires two hands to execute. For example, to write a dollar sign the user must hold down a Shift key with one finger while simultaneously pressing the 4 key—an operation that requires the use of two fingers and both hands. If this operation could be transformed into two *individual* keystrokes, the process would be much more accessible to persons with motor disabilities.

Keys for performing command and control functions also can present barriers to users with motor disabilities. These keys redefine the meaning of other keys on the keyboard. Depending on the computer brand, these keys can be called Control (Ctrl), Alternate

(Alt), Command, or Open-Apple. Such keys send commands to the computer—they do not print letters or numbers. For example, the Control-P combination (in which the Control key is held down while the *P* key is depressed) tells some computers to print the current document; Control-Q tells many programs to quit and return to the disk operating system. The meaning of these keys can change according to the particular software application program being used. However, virtually all software packages incorporate these special command keys, and there is no way to avoid their use. Sticky key software addresses the keyboard barrier of commands that require two hands to execute. Because Shift, Control, and Alt keys must be used in combination with other keys and because they return to their up position when released, these keys can be difficult to operate by persons with motor disabilities. Sticky key software can lock down such keys for users with limited hand control.

Other forms of keyboard modification utilities can emulate the mouse or slow down the effects of keys that repeat when accidentally struck. As with some electric typewriters, computer keys repeat if they are held down for a certain length of time. For some persons with motor disabilities this feature could present a barrier. Adaptive software can address this issue by turning off or modifying the repeating functions of the keyboard.

Sticky key and key modification software packages are compatible with most computer systems and are a relatively inexpensive adaptation. Most sticky key software can be purchased for around fifty dollars, and many are shareware or freeware programs. Sticky key and key modification packages are memory-resident utilities, referred to as terminate-and-stay-resident (TSR) utilities. When a sticky key program is loaded, the software takes inventory of all the keys on the keyboard, especially the status of Shift, Control, and Alt keys. When the Shift, Control, or Alt key is struck, the sticky key program locks it down as if the key were being held down by finger pressure. For example, with some sticky key software, the user can lock down the Shift key by striking it twice to type words in all capital letters. This locks down the Shift key until it is struck again to release it.

AccessDOS

AccessDOS, developed by the Trace Research and Development Center and available from IBM, is a set of keyboard utilities for persons with motor disabilities. The software is in the public domain, available free of charge and copyable. This memory-resident program is compatible with most MS-

DOS applications software. The utilities are menu driven, and documentation is available in text-file format on disk. In addition to sticky key software, the AccessDOS utilities contain other programs appropriate for users with motor impairments:

AccessDOS BounceKeys is an appropriate utility for persons who have a tendency to strike the same key multiple times. The program will not accept two presses for the same key unless the keystrokes are spaced apart by a certain time interval that was selected by the user.

AccessDOS MouseKeys is a memory resident software utility that works in concert with commercial applications software such as word processors, databases, spreadsheets, and other applications. With this program the arrow keys located on the numeric keypad and the mathematical operator keys mimic the standard functions of the mouse. The arrow keys emulate the movement of the mouse, and the mathematical operator keys mimic the clicking of the mouse buttons.

AccessDOS RepeatKeys is a utility that turns off or adjusts the automatic-repeat feature found on most keyboards. For persons with motor disabilities, sufficient fine-motor control may not be present to avoid the automatic repeat feature, resulting in long strings of unwanted characters in a document or many erroneous key commands issued to an application program.

AccessDOS SlowKeys slows down the response time for a key to become active. Some persons with motor disabilities accidentally strike unwanted keys on the way to a desired keystroke. These accidental keystrokes are typically of short duration, so they can be filtered out by the SlowKeys program. For a keystroke to take effect, it must be held down for a longer period of time than that of an accidental keystroke. The user can define the most appropriate time interval.

AccessDOS Serial Keys controls the keyboard and mouse functions using an adapted switch connected to the serial port.

AccessDOS Toggle Keys uses a beep to indicate when the caps lock, number lock, or scroll lock has been activated.

Filch

Filch, from Kinetic Designs, is a utility that alters the auto-repeat function of the standard keyboard. If necessary, the auto-repeat function can be reactivated by a single keystroke. The delay may be set at up to 13.2 seconds. Filch turns the Control, Alt, and right Shift keys into toggles, permitting one-finger operation. These keys may be latching, may latch until the release of the next non-Shift key is pressed, or both. Filch also allows each keystroke to generate an audible beep to indicate that a key has been struck successfully.

Visual feedback is also possible with the program. Audio/visual feedback can be useful to a user who may have limited finger sensitivity.

HandiSHIFT

The HandiSHIFT program, from Microsystems, is an MS-DOS–based sticky key program. The memory resident utility is compatible with most commercial word processors, databases, spreadsheets, communications packages, programming languages, and other commercial software. The program loads into memory immediately after the disk operating system and allows the user to load another application into memory. HandiSHIFT can lock and hold the Shift, Control, and Alt keys for the user.

Alternative Input Systems

When a user types on the keyboard, characters automatically are sent to the keyboard buffer, a storage area (or holding tank) within main memory. However, a keyboard is not the only device capable of inserting data into this electronic storage area. An alternative input device can feed information into a computer by using a pathway that mimics the standard operation of an original equipment computer keyboard.

Alternative input technologies interface to the computer via circuit cards or through the serial interface port and use assistive software in their operation. These devices include adapted switches, scanning keyboards, and Morse code systems. See the list at the end of this chapter for vendors that offer alternative input hardware and software products.

Adapted Switches and Scanning Keyboards

Alternative input devices often consist of both hardware and software. The hardware may consist of switches that interface to the computer, often through the serial port or through an interface circuit card. The software convinces the computer that the keystrokes are coming from the original keyboard rather than the adapted switch.

Adapted switches come in a number of different configurations. They may be controlled by hand or foot movements, breath control, spoken commands, or even the wink of an eye. In fact, any reliable muscle movement can be used to flip an adapted switch. Thus, adapted switches are custom fitted to the needs of the individual, depending on the person's abilities and the individual's stamina for depressing a switch a number of times before becoming fatigued. Single switches can be purchased in a number of configurations, such as a pillow or a flexible rubber cylinder that activates when squeezed. Other styles and configurations of switches can be employed: chin switches activated by jaw movements, sip-and-puff switches activated by breath control, and eye-gaze switches activated by eye movements.

Head mounted adapted switches allow users to control the computer by pointing at a scanning keyboard—a pictorial keyboard displayed on the screen. The scanning keyboard is displayed by software that accompanies the adapted switch. Each key is illuminated one at a time, and the user can select the desired key by using an adapted switch attached to the headset. The keyboard displayed on the screen can be programmed to scan by lighting letters one at a time at rates chosen by the user. When the desired letter or item is illuminated, the user can select that letter or item by closing the adapted switch. This process can be speeded up by using word prediction, described later in this chapter.

Freewheel

Freewheel, from Pointer Systems, is a head-mounted device that allows the user to move the cursor around the screen by moving his or her head back and forth. The unit is cordless and comes with a headset and screen-keyboard software, Freeboard for Macintosh or IBM-compatibles, that provides a visual image of the physical keyboard that can be rearranged at will by the user. After the user selects the desired "key" through head movement, he or she uses an adapted switch, such as a breath switch or other adapted switch, to "strike" that key. Commands permit switching between several active keyboard images. The Macintosh version of the system includes a sip-and-puff switch (available at additional cost for the IBM system).

HeadMaster

The HeadMaster, from Prentke Romich, is an alternative input device for Apple II, Apple Macintosh, and IBM PC-compatible personal computers. The device, consisting of a headset and assistive software, replaces the keyboard and mouse. The system also can be purchased with a remote option that allows a wireless connection between the headset and the personal computer and frees the user from having to remove the headset when away from the computer. The headset and control unit work together to measure the rotation of the head and translate these movements into accurate cursor movements on the video display. The user can click mouse buttons or pull down menus onto the screen by puffing into a special switch mounted on the headset. The HeadMaster is compatible with various scanning keyboard programs that display a picture of the keyboard on screen, allowing the user to select keys from a scanning array.

The HeadMaster consists of a head-mounted mouse and sip-and-puff switch. *Courtesy of Prentke Romich Company.*

☰ TetraScan Keyboard

The TetraScan keyboard, from Zygo Industries, contains a visual array of the standard keys found on a computer keyboard. The keyboard displays a pictorial representation of the keyboard on its illuminated display panel and is operated by a single-switch mechanism, allowing the user to send a keystroke for any key displayed on the visual display. The keyboard works with almost any type of single-switch mechanism, such as a switch that can be activated by the chin, breath control, eye movements, or any other reliable muscle movement.

The TetraScan has 4K of user-programmable memory allowing the user to program information into 156 locations so that selection of a single key can send a long series of characters to the computer automatically. Audible feedback is provided for each "key" activation. Because it is a hardware approach, the Zygo TetraScan keyboard requires no system memory to operate.

Morse Code Systems

Another type of alternative input device is based on Morse code. These relatively inexpensive systems rely on the two-level binary code of dots and dashes for a simple, but often effective, method of data entry. Morse code can be employed to enter text into computers for most word processors, databases, spreadsheets, telecommunications packages, and other software. Morse code systems are readily interfaced to most personal computers through the standard serial or parallel ports. The systems consist of adapted switches and software. For the user able to take advantage of this technology, Morse code can be a fast and efficient method for entering data and issuing commands to the computer. These systems can also be used for person-to-person communication because many Morse systems can translate the dots and dashes into standard text or voice output; therefore, only the sender needs to learn Morse code.

Adaptive Firmware Card

The Adaptive Firmware Card, from Don Johnston Development Equipment, can accept Morse code commands. The card offers several adapted input methods including scanning and single switch. It is compatible with the Apple IIGS line of personal computers.

HandiCODE

The HandiCODE program, from Microsystems Software, is a Morse code command and control system for MS-DOS–based personal computers. The software consists of a memory-resident utility that converts Morse code signals into ASCII code, permitting the user to control the computer with an adapted switch. The hardware consists of a Morse code switch that can be attached easily to the arm of a wheelchair or mounted on a desktop. This switch interfaces with the personal computer through a standard serial port. The software also can allow users to set up two user-definable keys on the keyboard as the Morse code keys, allowing users with finger dexterity to operate the system without the need of an external switch.

Morse Code WSKE

Morse Code WSKE, from Words +, is a RAM-resident program that allows IBM PC-compatible personal computers to be used as an alternative communication/computer access system. The system provides dual word prediction (see next section) along with automatic word endings, punctuation, spacing, and capitalization. The system also can provide voice output. The voice output will work with most serial port or text-to-speech voice synthesizers. The system is compatible with applications software, including some graphics programs. The Bank Street Writer word-processing program is included with Morse Code WSKE. Documentation is available on disk.

Morsek

Morsek, from Kinetic Designs, is a keyboard-emulating software package for IBM PC-compatible personal computers and select laptop computers. It interfaces with the computer through the standard serial or parallel port and uses from one to three switches to command the system in Morse code key sequences. Alternatively, the user can define dedicated keys on the keyboard to send the Morse code signals to the computer. A hard disk is recommended for running Morsek, particularly if the user has severe disabilities. The unit comes with documentation in print and on disk.

Word-Prediction Software

Word-prediction software, also called abbreviation-expansion software, can speed up the data-entry process for an individual using a keyboard, an adapted switch, or another form of alternative input device. The aim is to obtain the maximum data entry for the fewest number of keystrokes. As discussed with macro software, single keystrokes under the proper software control can be programmed to perform multiple keystrokes.

Word-prediction software monitors the keyboard input and watches for select characters in sequence. When the software recognizes an appropriate series of characters, the word predictor displays a menu of word choices on the video screen. Then, the user selects one of the menu choices to complete the text-entry process. For example, if the user enters the letter *a*, the word predictor might display a menu that looks something like the following:

A. apple

B. about

C. able

The user then selects from the possible word choices by keying the letter of the desired option. Word predictors typically use a disk-based dictionary to index the word choices and cross reference the words with the abbreviations that trigger the menu choices. Many word predictors also contain a user-definable dictionary, allowing individuals to add their own custom words and phrases. These programs work in a similar manner to spell checking programs available on most commercial word processing packages. Word-prediction software is intelligent and learns the user's vocabulary over time. Based on the frequency of certain words, the word predictor moves commonly used words to the top of the menu choices, permitting the user to select words and phrases with increased speed.

A person using a head stick for keyboard access can use HandiWORD to help increase input rate at the keyboard. *Courtesy of Microsystems Software, Inc.*

HandiWORD

The HandiWORD program, from Microsystems Software, is a word-prediction software package for MS-DOS computer systems. The memory-resident software is compatible with most commercial word processors, databases, spreadsheets, telecommunications, and other software. The program contains a user-definable dictionary, and the user can determine where the pop-up menu will appear. HandiWORD can be installed on either a floppy or hard disk system and can be automatically loaded into memory each time the computer is started. With an optional command-line switch, the software also can be deactivated if necessary.

MindReader

MindReader, from Brown Bag Software, is another word-prediction software package for persons with disabilities. The software is compatible with MS-DOS computers and works with most word processors, databases, spreadsheets, telecommunications programs, and other application software packages. The software resides in the background, monitoring keystrokes entered by the user. When it detects a familiar series of characters and the user selects one of the choices from a menu, the software automatically finishes typing the word for the user.

Voice Recognition Systems

Computers that comprehend the spoken word conjure up images from science fiction, but such machines are a solid reality with today's technology. Although personal computers come equipped with keyboards for data entry, microphones rapidly are becoming standard equipment for some systems. Apple Computer currently is shipping Macintosh computers with built-in microphones to allow developers to create voice applications, and this trend is obvious on other systems. IBM-compatible computers readily accept circuit cards that permit voice recognition. The Apple IIGS also can work with voice recognition hardware and software for both mainstream and disabled applications.

Simply put, voice recognition systems "listen" to spoken commands, process the verbal input, and send the commands to the computer as if they had been typed at the original keyboard. These systems are compatible with commercial software to create an interactive voice-response system for individuals with motor disabilities. That is, individuals can speak to their computers to enter commands and data. Most voice recognition systems require training before they can work, a process that can take a few hours on most systems. Due to great interest in this technology on the part of the business community, many hardware and software voice products currently are available to serve both mainstream and disabled applications. See the list at the end of this chapter for vendors that offer voice recognition hardware and software.

Voice Recognition Hardware

Parallel to speech synthesis systems, two basic types of voice recognition products are available: internal and external systems. The two types perform the same functions, but they install differently, depending on the vendor and the application. Internal circuit cards plug into the main mother board of most personal computer systems; external devices connect to serial or parallel interface ports. In either case, voice recognizers translate the spoken word into text or computer commands.

Voice recognizer circuit cards contain memory and microprocessor chips. The cards also contain an edge connector for interfacing to the main mother board of the computer. This may be a somewhat complex adaptation for a nontechnical person: As is the case with standard circuit cards, the installer must open the computer housing, locate an empty expansion slot, and plug the circuit card into the mother board. Voice recognition system circuit cards have external jacks to connect microphones for voice input. If the circuit card also has voice output capability, the unit also will have an external speaker jack for connecting headphones or speakers.

External voice recognition systems are self-contained devices, about the size and general shape of an external modem, and have interface jacks to attach to the computer. The hardware installation process for an external voice recognition system is similar to that of most external devices. The typical voice recognition system connects to a computer through an interface cable to one of the serial or parallel interface ports. External voice recognizers also contain jacks for connecting microphones, which allow the input of sound energy. For the Macintosh computer, a voice recognition system can be interfaced to the SCSI port, which typically is used to connect external disk drives and other devices.

Installing and Training Voice Recognition Software

After the internal or external voice recognition hardware is installed, the voice recognition software must be installed on the computer system by copying the disks to the computer's hard disk drive. The voice recognition software should be stored in an appropriate directory on the hard disk.

Voice recognizers are classified as speaker dependent or speaker independent. The term *speaker dependent* refers to a voice recognizer that must be trained to perform work. Speaker-dependent systems can work with multiple users at different times if the individuals have each trained the software to recognize their voices. If a voice recognition system is speaker independent, it can understand the voice of almost any speaker and does not have to be trained to perform work with an individual. Generally, speaker-independent systems are confined to small vocabularies that drastically reduce the recognition task and permit more computing power to be concentrated on the small vocabulary at hand. Speaker-independent recognition systems are appropriate for applications in which a small vocabulary is not a disadvantage, such as when only numbers must be recognized.

Voice recognition products also are grouped according to how they recognize words, either as separate units or as blocks of words. Continuous-utterance voice recognizers can understand uninterrupted bursts of speech. These systems are becoming commercially viable. Most voice recognition systems currently available are of the speaker-dependent, discrete-utterance variety. The term *discrete utterance* refers to a voice recognizer that requires a slight pause between each word, usually less than 0.1 second. This pause is crucial so the system more accurately can determine word boundaries.

For a speaker-dependent voice recognition system the user must train it to recognize his or her voice before the system can be used—a process that takes about an hour with most systems. The training process stores files of voice patterns onto the hard disk. These recorded patterns are then compared to later audio input from the microphone.

The training process for most systems is easily accomplished by speaking select words and phrases into a microphone. The process builds a memory map, or template, of the speaker's individual voice for later use when the system performs cross matches on incoming data. To accomplish the cross checking, the microphone input is converted to standard computer code. Then, this code is compared against the template files stored on disk to perform pattern matching.

The software also must be trained to work within the individual environment. The user should decide what software programs the voice recognizer will control, keeping in mind that the purpose of the voice recognition system is to replace the keyboard. To provide complete independence for the user, the voice recognizer must control all software programs, including word processing, database, spreadsheet, and the disk operating system.

Furthermore, the user must train the voice system to translate all voice commands into typed commands to control all system functions. That involves building voice commands for every key on the system, including Shift, Control, Alt, and other command-oriented keys; alphabet keys; arrow keys; and function keys. The system must be configured so that every key can be "struck" by speaking into the system.

Voice recognition products currently range in price from several hundred dollars to five thousand dollars. They can be purchased for Apple II, IBM PC, and Macintosh personal computer platforms, making this technology available on a wide variety of systems. Some voice recognition systems are designed for portable computers, allowing users to take their access technology to school or on the road for some applications. Following are some examples of voice recognition systems.

DragonDictate

DragonDictate, from Dragon Systems, is an IBM PC-based internal voice recognition system. The unit requires an IBM 386 PC or compatible, 8 megabytes of random-access-memory, 10 megabytes free space on the hard disk drive, and a CPU clock speed of 20 MHz or higher. DragonDictate consists of an IBM-style circuit card and a microphone. The system is controlled through MS-DOS–compatible software that contains the vocabulary and other voice utilities.

Once installed and properly configured, DragonDictate can control the operations of a personal computer including word processors, databases, spreadsheets, telecommunications, and other software applications and adaptive equipment connected to the computer system including speech synthesizers such as GW Micro's Vocal-Eyes for persons with vision impairments. It also can control the arrow keys, enabling the user to move around a document letter by letter, word by word, or line by line. The unit can be programmed to respond to commands such as "Read the screen" or "Silence the speech." Verbal commands can delete or insert text. Dragon Systems manufactures several voice recognition products for IBM personal computers.

Voice Navigator II

The Voice Navigator II, from Articulate Systems, works with Macintosh computer systems. The unit is an external voice recognition device that connects to the computer through the standard SCSI interface port. Voice Navigator can hold up to 200 voice commands in a single voice-template storage file. An upgrade can increase the number of commands to 1,000. The device is speaker dependent and must be trained by the user before it can be operated. The system is compatible with most Macintosh-based word processors, databases, spreadsheets, telecommunications packages, and other software. It requires a Macintosh with at least 2 megabytes of RAM, a hard disk, and SCSI cables. A desktop microphone is included. Other options include a voice recognition telephone dialing and answering package.

Voice Navigator SW

Voice Navigator SW, from Articulate Systems, is a software-only voice recognition product. The software uses the built-in sound-processing chips in newer Macintosh models to perform the voice recognition process. It is compatible with Macintosh LC, LC II, IISI, Classic II, PowerBook 140, PowerBook 170, and the Quadra 700 and 900. The program requires 4 megabytes of memory and System 6.7 or greater. The software-only approach is a practical one for Macintosh computers that have enough memory and disk space to process the voice templates. The user also should install additional

Voice Navigator II connects to Macintosh computers through a SCSI interface port. A microphone accepts voice commands. *Courtesy of Articulate Systems, Inc.*

memory into the computer to enable other applications to be processed concurrently.

VoiceType

VoiceType, from Dragon Systems, is an external voice recognition system for IBM PC-compatible personal computers. The system has a 7,000-word vocabulary consisting of a 5,000-word speaker-independent vocabulary and 2,000 words that can be defined by the user. The software drivers are memory resident and are compatible with MS-DOS and most word processors, databases, spreadsheets, and other applications packages. With a single utterance, VoiceType can send as many as 1,000 keystrokes to an application. The system uses an adaptive model to increase voice recognition accuracy by modifying its voice models of the user's voice pattern, thus constantly perfecting these models and increasing accuracy over time. VoiceType is shipped with voice recognition software, reference-guide disks, an introductory videotape, and a headset-mounted microphone.

Voice recognition is a powerful adaptive technology for persons with motor impairments. The technology was formerly one of the most expensive, but prices are rapidly decreasing. Voice recognition is appropriate for many users because it emulates natural language. When properly trained and configured, voice recognition

systems can replace the traditional computer key]
the user to operate computers and other devices ir

Alternative Communications Devices

Spoken language is perhaps the most basic form of information exchange and of communication. Due to various physical disabilities, many persons who are motor impaired also have difficulty communicating, resulting in the complete inability to speak, the inability to speak for long periods, or the inability to speak understandably. In the past, persons unable to speak had to rely on gestures to communicate with others, but modern communications devices allow persons to speak with an unlimited vocabulary voice.

An alternative communications device is essentially an electronic voice box. Some are stand-alone products; others are computer peripherals. One type of alternative communications device uses unlimited vocabulary text-to-speech synthesis, another type uses digitally recorded voices that are played back at the touch of a button, and others are a combination of the two approaches. Depending on the exact nature of the disability, alternative communications devices can be controlled by a number of methods. If the individual has no physical disability, the device can be operated through a standard computer-type keyboard. The user merely keys in the words and phrases that need to be spoken, and the device verbalizes them according to keyed-in command sequences. If the person has a disability that prevents using a standard keyboard, alternative methods for accessing the communications device must be explored. Adapted switches and scanning keyboards can be used as an alternative to control these devices. See the list at the end of this chapter for names and addresses of vendors that offer alternative communication devices.

Dynavox

The Dynavox, from Adaptive Communications Systems, is a programmable alternative communications device for persons unable to speak. The unit contains a touch screen that can display a visual representation of the keyboard layout. Because the keys are not physical, they can be arranged into any configuration for the specific requirements of the user. Thus, multiple keyboards can be accessed from a single keystroke. When the user selects an option, a submenu appears that offers a series of choices under that category. To produce the desired voice output, the user touches the specific area on the screen representing that verbalization. The Dynavox contains a memory card

The IntroTalker allows persons unable to speak on their own the ability to communicate with friends, family, classmates, and coworkers. The unit can store short or long speech sequences and play them back on command. *Courtesy of Prentke Romich Company.*

reader, similar to a disk drive, that stores vocabularies and setup sequences. It also comes with the unlimited vocabulary DECtalk speech (see Chapter 3), allowing the user to select from multiple voices and to verbalize sequences not stored in memory.

IntroTalker

The IntroTalker, from Prentke Romich, is an alternative communications device for persons who are nonverbal. The battery-powered device contains a limited vocabulary from digitized speech processing. The user presses one or a combination of IntroTalker's thirty-two keys and a stored word or phrase is spoken. The words and phrases are stored in the IntroTalker by a speaking person who recites them into the device's microphone. The unit's memory can hold up to two minutes of speech, and memory can be expanded to hold eight minutes.

Liberator

The Liberator, from Prentke Romich, is an alternative communications device for persons with speech impairments. The unit, about the size of a small laptop computer, contains many features found on most personal computers: a keyboard, video display, disk drive, and random-access-memory space. The device can speak any word, phrase, or sentence upon the press of a single key. It contains the DECtalk speech synthesizer from Digital Equipment Corporation (see Chapter 3). The unit has multiple voices, including male, female, child, and adult voices. The voice rate, pitch, and characteristics can be adjusted to suit the user's taste. The device can be used for face-to-face communication and for delivering speeches or public presentations. Capable of accepting a text file created on a computer, the Liberator can speak the file under control of the user.

Polycom

Polycom, from Zygo Industries, is a battery-operated electronic communication aid that has simple word processing functions and telecommunication capabilities. Polycom can act as a simple word processor and as an electric writing pad. The device can store short phrases and sentences that can be recalled using two keys. By using an optional telephone coupling device, Polycom also can be used as a portable text telephone. The device has a keyboard that requires only one hand for input. A display screen, which has five lines and can show up to 100 characters simultaneously, allows the user to make choices from a menu.

RealVoice

The RealVoice, from Adaptive Communications Systems, is an alternative communications device that can speak in either a male or female voice. RealVoice can speak any word or phrase and can automatically translate text into speech.

Environmental Control Systems

Access to information is critical for persons with disabilities. If a disabled person cannot activate office equipment, radios, televisions, and other devices, then access to information is limited. For persons with physical disabilities, controlling electronic devices around the home, school, or office can be difficult unless the proper adaptive technology is applied. In the past, individuals with disabilities were forced to rely on friends, family, and coworkers to operate electrical appliances.

Environmental control systems consist of two basic components. The first segment consists of a control panel, which has been adapted with appropriate switches, pointer devices, or voice input, to permit persons with motor disabilities access. The second component is a receiver station, which the appliance plugs into. The receiver can turn on the desired appliance when it receives a signal from the master control panel. These signals can be transmitted to the receivers in several ways: through existing electrical wiring, through infrared signals, or through ultrasonic signals.

Numerous environmental control systems that allow persons with disabilities to control a single appliance or to control an entire home or office are available commercially. See the list at the end of this chapter for vendor names and addresses.

Butler in a Box

Voice recognition technology is also employed for environmental control systems, allowing individuals with motor impairments to operate appliances and other devices. Butler in a Box, from Mastervoice, is a voice-activated environmental control system with speech output. The device allows hands-free operation of lights, appliances, and telephones. The system's built-in voice recognition system allows the user to activate and deactivate electrical appliances through verbal commands. Its speech synthesis system communicates with the user and verbalizes the status of various appliances under control. The unit can control televisions, radios, air conditioners, lamps, and most household and office electrical equipment. Butler in a Box uses transmitters and receivers that plug into standard household electrical outlets.

CCT Environmental Control

The CCT Environmental Control, from Consultants for Communication Technology, consists of both hardware and software that allows the user to control up to sixteen appliances or outlets with a single switch. The control system sends signals over existing house wiring using computer commands. Since the system uses existing household electrical circuits, there is no need for professional installation. The package is designed to work with IBM PC-compatible personal computer systems.

Environmental Control System

The Environmental Control System, from Fortress, is a wheelchair-mounted device that remotely controls electrical appliances using ultrasonic waves. Four color-coded buttons trigger the unit to send to each of four receiver units. The four color-coded modules can be purchased separately. The receiver units plug into standard household electrical outlets, and appliances and other electrical devices plug into the receiver units. A variety of receivers can be used with the Environmental Control System. This particular environmental control system is available as a part of Fortress's power wheelchair control systems or from TASH.

Ez-Control

The Ez-Control, from Regenesis Development, is an environmental control unit for persons with motor impairments. The device can be expanded with add-on modules that control specific household or office devices. The basic receiver of the control unit can control five devices and is activated by either single or dual switch commands. In addition to the basic unit, expansion modules can be added on as desired. Available modules include telephone, television, and VCR units and an X-10 unit that can control up to five additional devices. A remote transmitter and computer-control software for IBM systems are options for the basic control unit.

HandiPHONE

HandiPHONE, from Microsystems Software, is a computer controlled, hands-free telephone control system. The unit allows the user of IBM-compatible computers to access any standard telephone system via a speaker phone or headset without the need of manual intervention. Users can access their telephone systems using such devices as voice recognition products, switch access, track ball, mice, joystick, etc., from within any software application. When the phone rings, the user can flip an adapted switch or give voice commands and instruct the computer to answer the call electronically by sending commands to the modem. A headset or speaker phone is used to talk back and forth. The system is compatible with MS-DOS and Windows. In addition to call answering and originating, the system allows access to voice mail, paging, call transferring, call waiting, and associated features of standard telephones.

The PopDIAL software, included with HandiPHONE, provides access to up to 9,999 user-defined directory entries, each of which may have three associated telephone numbers. The HandiPHONE system includes PopDIAL software, a 2400-baud external modem, hands-free speaker phone or headset with power pack, serial modem cable, 6-foot telephone cord with standard RJ-11 connector, and a telephone line splitter.

In summary, numerous forms of adaptive technology exist to assist persons with motor and/or speech impairments. The bulk of this adaptive technology is directed at personal computer access, bringing the world of computers within reach of persons with disabilities. Once the computer is made accessible, the individual can access an expanded world of work, school, and play. The natural state of the computer is change, and can be altered through software to compensate for any disability.

Products for Persons with Motor and/or Speech Impairments

Adapted Keyboard Providers

Ability Systems Corp.
1422 Arnold Ave.
Roslyn, PA 19001
215-657-4338

Accu-Back, Inc.
1475 E. Del Amo Blvd.
Carson, CA 90746
800-272-8888
213-639-7992

William K. Bradford Publ.
Co., Inc.
310 School St.
Acton, MA 01720
508-263-6996

Cacti Computer Services
130 9th St. SW
Portage La Prairie, MB
R1N 2N4
CANADA
204-857-8675

ComputAbility Corp.
40000 Grand River, Ste. 109
Novi, MI 48375
800-433-8872
313-477-6720

Designing Aids for Disabled
Adults
249 Concord Ave., Rm. 2
Toronto, ON M6H 2P4
CANADA
416-530-0038

Dunamis, Inc.
3620 Hwy. 317
Suwanee, GA 30174
800-828-2443
404-932-0485

Ekeg Electronics Co., Ltd.
P.O. Box 46199 Station 'G'
Vancouver, BC V6R 4G5
CANADA
604-273-4358

Hach Associates
P.O. Box 11754
Winston-Salem, NC 27116
919-744-7280

J. Jordan & Associates
1127 Oxford Ct.
Neenah, WI 54956
414-725-9046

Kennedy Day School
Franciscan Children's
Hospital
Rehabilitation Hospital
30 Warren St.
Brighton, MA 02135
617-254-3800

Polytel Computer Products
Corp.
1287 Hammerwood Ave.
Sunnyville, CA 94089
408-745-1540

Psychological Corp.
555 Academic Ct.
San Antonio, TX 78204
512-299-1061

Regenesis Development Corp.
1046 Deep Cove Rd.
North Vancouver, BC
V7G 1S3
CANADA
604-929-6663

TASH, Inc.
91 Station St., Unit 1
Ajax, ON L1S 3H2
CANADA
219-462-8086
416-686-4129

Unicorn Engineering, Inc.
5221 Central Ave., Ste. 205
Richmond, CA 94704
800-899-6687
415-528-0670

WesTest Engineering Corp.
1470 N. Main St.
Bountiful, UT 84010
801-298-7100
801-292-7379

Words +, Inc.
44421 10th St. W., Ste. L
P.O. Box 1229
Lancaster, CA 93535
800-869-8521
805-949-8331

Zygo Industries, Inc.
P.O. Box 1008
Portland, OR 97207-1008
800-234-6006
503-684-6006

Keyboard Modification Software Providers

Ability Systems Corp.
1422 Arnold Ave.
Roslyn, PA 19001
215-657-4338

Apple Computer, Inc.
Worldwide Disability
Solutions Group
20525 Mariani Ave.
Cupertino, CA 95014
408-996-1010

Applied Technology for
Physically Impaired Persons
P.O. Box 110310
Campbell, CA 95011
408-378-8006

Avenue Software, Inc.
2162 Charest W. Blvd.
Sainte-Foy, PQ G1N 2G3
CANADA
418-682-3088

Beagle Bros., Inc.
6215 Ferris Square, Ste. 100
San Diego, CA 92121
619-452-5500

Borland Intnl.
1800 Green Hills Dr.
Scotts Valley, CA 95060
408-439-1604

William K. Bradford Publ.
Co., Inc.
310 School St.
Acton, MA 01720
508-263-6996

Brown Bag Software
2155 S. Bascom Ave.,
Ste. 114
Campbell, CA 95008
800-523-0764
800-323-5335

CE Software, Inc.
1801 Industrial Cir.
P.O. Box 65580
West Des Moines, IA 50265
515-224-1995

Compute Able Network, Inc.
P.O. Box 1706
Portland, OR 97207
503-645-0009
503-645-8580

Computers to Help People,
Inc.
1221 W. Johnson St.
Madison, WI 53715
608-257-5917
608-257-1270

Covington Group
4519 Perry Ave. N.
Minneapolis, MN 55422
612-537-4910

Dunamis, Inc.
3620 Hwy. 317
Suwanee, GA 30174
800-828-2443
404-932-0485

IBM Independence Series
Information Center
Bldg. 5
P.O. Box 1328
Boca Raton, FL 33429
800-426-4832

J. Jordan & Associates
1127 Oxford Ct.
Neenah, WI 54956
414-725-9046

Kinetic Designs, Inc.
14231 Anatevka Lane S.E.
Olalla, WA 98466
800-453-0330
206-857-7943

Microsoft Corp.
One Microsoft Way
Redmond, WA 98052
800-876-4726
206-454-2030

Microsystems Software, Inc.
600 Worcester Rd.
Framingham, MA 01701
508-626-8511

National Institute for
Rehabilitation Engineering
P.O. Box T
Hewitt, NJ 07421
800-736-2216
201-853-6585

Paragon Concepts, Inc.
990 Highland Dr., Ste. 312
Solana Beach, CA 92075
800-922-2993
619-481-1477

Productivity Software
International
211 E. 43rd St., Ste. 2202
New York, NY 10017
800-533-7587
212-818-1144

Regenesis Development Corp.
1046 Deep Cove Rd.
North Vancouver, BC
V7G IS3
CANADA
604-929-6663

RoseSoft, Inc.
P.O. Box 70337
Bellevue, WA 98007
206-562-0225

Sigea Systems, Inc.
19 Pelham Rd.
Weston, MA 02193
617-647-1099

Trace Center
University of Wisconsin
1500 Highland Ave.
Madison, WI 53705
608-262-6966

Unicorn Engineering, Inc.
5221 Central Ave., Ste. 205
Richmond, CA 94704
800-899-6687
415-528-0670

Words +, Inc.
44421 10th St. W., Ste. L
P.O. Box 1229
Lancaster, CA 93535
800-869-8521
805-949-8331

World Communications
245 Tonopah Dr.
Fremont, CA 94539
415-656-0911

Xpert Software
8865 Polland Ave.
San Diego, CA 92123
619-268-0112

Alternative Input Hardware and Software Providers

Ability Research, Inc.
P.O. Box 1721
Minnetonka, MN 55345
612-939-0121

Ablenet
1081 10th Ave. S.E.
Minneapolis, MN 55414
800-322-0956
612-379-0956

Adaptive Aids, Inc.
P.O. Box 57640
Tucson, AZ 85732-7640
800-223-5369
602-745-8112

Adaptive Communication
Systems, Inc.
1400 Lee Rd.
Coraopolis, PA 15108
800-227-2922

Arroyo & Associates, Inc.
2549 Rockville Centre
Pkwy.
Oceanside, NY 11572
516-763-1407

Cleo, Inc.
3957 Mayfield Rd.
Cleveland, OH 44121
216-382-9700
800-321-0595

ComputAbility Corp.
40000 Grand River, Ste. 109
Novi, MI 48375
800-433-8872
313-477-6720

Creative Switch Industries
P.O. Box 5256
Des Moines, IA 50306
515-287-5748

Crestwood Co.
6625 N. Sidney Pl.
Milwaukee, WI 53209
414-352-5678

Dickey Engineering
3 Angel Rd.
North Reading, MA 01864
508-664-2010

DU-IT Control Systems
Group, Inc.
8765 Township Rd.,
Rm. 513
Shreve, OH 44676
216-567-2906

Dunamis, Inc.
3620 Hwy. 317
Suwanee, GA 30174
800-828-2443
404-932-0485

ENCOR
P.O. Box 190
Mystic, CT 06365
203-536-4643

Extensions for Independence
555 Saturn Blvd., B-368
San Diego, CA 92032
619-423-7709
619-423-1748

Flanagan and Co. Adaptive
Devices
6832 Mokelumne Ave.
Oakland, CA 94605
415-638-3898

Handicapped Children's
Technological Services, Inc.
P.O. Box 7
Foster, RI 02825
401-861-3444

Don Johnston Developmental
Equip.
  1000 N. Rand Rd., Bldg. 115
  P.O. Box 639
  Wauconda, IL 60084
  800-999-4660
  708-526-2682

Luminaud, Inc.
  8688 Tyler Blvd.
  Mentor, OH 44060
  216-255-9082

Hugh MacMillan Rehabilitation
Centre
  350 Rumsey Rd.
  Toronto, ON M4G 1R8
  CANADA
  416-425-6220

Maddak, Inc.
  6 Industrial Ave.
  Pequannock, NJ 07440
  800-443-4926
  201-628-7600

Medical Equip. Distr., Inc.
  Medical Services Dept.
  3223 S. Loop 289, Ste. 150
  Lubbock, TX 79423
  806-793-8421
  800-253-4134

Pointer Systems, Inc.
  One Mill St.
  Burlington, VT 05401
  800-537-1562
  802-658-3260

Prentke Romich Co.
  1022 Heyl Rd.
  Wooster, OH 44691
  800-262-1984
  216-262-1984

J. A. Preston Corp.
  60 Page Rd.
  Clifton, NJ 07012
  800-631-7277
  201-777-2700

Regenesis Development Corp.
  1046 Deep Cove Rd.
  North Vancouver, BC
  V7G IS3
  CANADA
  604-929-6663

Fred Sammons, Inc.
  P.O. Box 32
  Brookfield, IL 60513
  800-323-5547

TASH, Inc.
  91 Station St., Unit 1
  Ajax, ON L1S 3H2
  CANADA
  416-686-4129

Toys for Special Children, Inc.
  385 Warburton Ave.
  Hastings, NY 10706
  914-478-0960

Words +, Inc.
  44421 10th St. W., Ste. L
  P.O. Box 1229
  Lancaster, CA 93535
  800-869-8521
  805-949-8331

Zygo Industries, Inc.
  P.O. Box 1008
  Portland, OR 97207
  800-234-6006
  503-684-6006

Voice Recognition System Providers

Animated Voice Corp.
P.O. Box 819
San Marcos, CA 92069
800-942-3699
619-744-8190

Applications Express Inc.
179 Avenue at the Common
Shrewsbury, NJ 07702
908-389-3366
614-747-2670

Applied Technology for
Physically Impaired Persons
P.O. Box 110310
Campbell, CA 95011
408-378-8006

Articulate Systems, Inc.
600 W. Cummings Park,
Ste. 4500
Woburn, MA 01801
800-443-7077
617-935-5656

Cadkey, Inc.
440 Oakland St.
Manchester, CT 06040-
2100
203-647-0220

Chatterbox Voice Learning
Systems
2265 Westwood Blvd.,
Ste. 907
Los Angeles, CA 90064
213-623-8755

Command Corp., Inc.
3675 Crestwood Pkwy.
P.O. Box 956099
Duluth, GA 30136-9502
404-925-7950

Communications Applied
Technology
11250-14 Roger Bacon Dr.
Reston, VA 22090
703-481-0068

Consultants for Communication
Technology
508 Bellevue Ter.
Pittsburgh, PA 15202
412-761-6062

R. J. Cooper & Assoc.
24843 Del Prado, Ste. 283
Dana Point, CA 92629
714-240-1912

Covox, Inc.
675-D Conger St.
Eugene, OR 97402
503-342-1271

Dragon Systems, Inc.
90 Bridge St.
Newton, MA 02158
617-965-5200

Equal Access Technologies,
Inc.
10775 S. Saginaw St., Ste. D
Grand Blanc, MI 48439
313-694-3755

GW Instruments
35 Medford
Somerville, MA 02143
617-625-4096

Hy Tek Mfg.
412 Bucktail Lane
Sugar Grove, IL 60554
312-466-7664

IBM Entry System Div.
11400 Burnet Rd.
Austin, TX 78758
512-823-5178

Interstate Electronics
1001 E. Fall Rd.
P.O. Box 3117
Anaheim, CA 92803
714-758-0500

Kempf
P.O. Box 61103
Sunnyvale, CA 94086
408-773-0219

MacSema
29383 Lamb Dr.
Albany, OR 97321
800-344-7228
503-757-1520

Power Translation Co.
11500 Statesville Rd.
Huntersville, NC 28078
704-875-2138

PRAB Command, Inc.
P.O. Box 2121
Kalamazoo, MI 49003
616-382-8200

Quartet Technology, Inc.
52 Davis Rd.
Tyngsboro, MA 01879
508-692-9313

Regenesis Development Corp.
1046 Deep Cove Rd.
North Vancouver, BC
V7G 1S3
CANADA
604-929-6663

Speller Teller Communications
3234 S. Villa Cir.
West Allis, WI 53227
414-327-4051

TASH, Inc.
91 Station St., Unit 1
Ajax, ON L1S 3H2
CANADA
219-462-8086
416-686-4129

Texas Instruments, Inc.
P.O. Box 202230
Austin, TX 78720
800-527-3500

Voice Connection
17835 Skypark Cir., Ste. C
Irvine, CA 92714
714-261-2366

Voice Recognition Technologies,
Inc.
Computer Voice Systems
Div.
220 Henley Rd.
Woodmere, NY 11598
516-295-3632
516-295-3230

Voice Technologies
120 Village Square, Ste. 143
Orinda, CA 94563
415-283-7586

Votan
4487 Technology Dr.
Fremont, CA 94538
415-490-7600

Alternative Communication System Providers

Adaptive Communication
Systems, Inc.
1400 Lee Rd.
Coraopolis, PA 15108
800-227-2922

Aids Unlimited, Inc.
Alternative Independence
Devices Services
1101 N. Calvert St., Ste. 405
Baltimore, MD 21202
301-659-0232

Attainment Co.
504 Commerce Pkwy.
Verona, WI 53593
800-327-4269

Canon U.S.A., Inc.
One Canon Plaza
Lake Success, NY 11042
516-488-6700

Communication & Therapy
Skill Builders
3830 E. Bellevue
P.O. Box 42050-P91
Tucson, AZ 85733
800-866-4446
602-323-7500

Compeer, Inc.
1409 Graywood Dr.
San Jose, CA 95129
408-255-3950

Consultants for Communication
Technology
508 Bellevue Terr.
Pittsburgh, PA 15202
412-761-6062

Crestwood Co.
6625 N. Sidney Pl.
Milwaukee, WI 53209
414-352-5678

Innovative Computer
Applications
33195 Wagon Wheel
Solon, OH 44139
216-248-6206

Jesana, Ltd.
P.O. Box 17
Irvington, NY 10533
800-443-4728

Don Johnston Development
Equip.
1000 N. Rand Rd., Bldg. 115
P.O. Box 639
Wauconda, IL 60084
800-999-4660
708-526-2682

LC Technologies, Inc.
4415 Glenn Rose St.
Fairfax, VA 22032
703-425-7509

MacLaboratory, Inc.
314 Exeter Rd.
Devon, PA 19333
215-688-3114
215-590-8629

Med Labs, Inc.
28 Vereda Cordillera
Goleta, CA 93117
805-968-2486

Mosier Mtls.
61328 Yakwahtin Ct.
Bend, OR 97702
503-388-4494

Phonic Ear, Inc.
250 Camino Alto
Mill Valley, CA 94941
800-227-0735
415-383-4000

Pointer Systems, Inc.
One Mill St.
Burlington, VT 05401
800-537-1562
802-658-3260

Prentke Romich Co.
1022 Heyl Rd.
Wooster, OH 44691
800-262-1984
216-262-1984

Rx Design, Inc.
124 Gray Rd.
Falmouth, ME 04105
207-797-2778

Sentient Systems Technology, Inc.
5001 Baum Blvd.
Pittsburgh, PA 15213
412-682-0144

Shea Products, Inc.
1721 W. Hamlin St.
Rochester Hills, MI 48309
313-852-4940

TASH, Inc.
91 Station St., Unit 1
Ajax, ON L1S 3H2
CANADA
416-686-4129

Texas Instruments, Inc.
Accessory Department
P.O. Box 53
Lubbock, TX 79408
800-842-2737

TIGER Communication System, Inc.
155 E. Broad St., Ste. 325
Rochester, NY 14604
716-454-5134

Tolfa Corp.
01860 Embarcadero Rd., Ste. 210
Palo Alto, CA 94303
415-494-3220

Words +, Inc.
44421 10th St. W., Ste. L
P.O. Box 1229
Lancaster, CA 93535
800-869-8521
805-949-8331

World Communications
245 Tonopah Dr.
Fremont, CA 94539
415-656-0911

Zygo Industries, Inc.
P.O. Box 1008
Portland, OR 97207
800-234-6006
503-684-6006

Environmental Control System Providers

Ablenet
AccessAbility
1081 10th Ave. S.E.
Minneapolis, MN 55414
800-322-0956
612-379-0956

Adaptive Communication Systems, Inc.
1400 Lee Rd.
Coraopolis, PA 15108
800-227-2922

Arroyo & Associates, Inc.
2549 Rockville Centre
Pkwy.
Oceanside, NY 11572
516-763-1407

Baylor Biomedical Services
3707 Gaston Ave., Ste. 216
Dallas, TX 75246
800-365-1890

Besam, Inc.
171 Twin Rivers Dr.
East Windsor, NJ 08520
800-752-9290
609-443-5800

Cepco
21515 Parthenia St.
Canoga Park, CA 91304
818-998-7315

Consultants for Communication
Technology
508 Bellevue Terr.
Pittsburgh, PA 15202
412-761-6062

CRT, Inc.
490 Tenth St. N.W.
Georgia Tech.
Atlanta, GA 30332-0156
800-457-9555
404-876-8580

CyberLYNX Computer
Products, Inc.
2885 E. Aurora, Ste. 13
Boulder, CO 80303
303-444-7733

DU-IT Control Systems
Group
8765 Township Rd.,
Ste. 513
Shreve, OH 44676
216-567-2906
216-567-2001

Environtrol Company, Inc.
6575 Burger Dr. S.E.
Grand Rapids, MI 49546-
7209
616-940-0122

Fortress, Inc.
827 Jefferson
Clovis, CA 93612
209-323-0292

High Tech Intelligence, Inc.
1602 S. Parker Rd., Ste. 312
Denver, CO 80231
303-695-0609

Hypertek
Rte. 22 E.
P.O. Box 137
Whitehouse, NJ 08888
908-534-9700

Don Johnston Development
Equip.
1000 N. Rand Rd., Bldg. 115
P.O. Box 639
Wauconda, IL 60084
800-999-4660
708-526-2682

Kenwood USA
P.O. Box 22745
Long Beach, CA 90801
213-639-4200

KY Enterprises
Custom Computer Solutions
3039 E. 2nd St.
Long Beach, CA 90803
213-433-5244

Mastervoice
10523 Humbolt St.
Los Alamitos, CA 90720
213-594-6581

Medical Equip. Distr.
Medical Services Dept.
3223 S. Loop 289, Ste. 150
Lubbock, TX 79423
800-253-4134
806-793-8421

Microsystems Software, Inc.
600 Worcester Rd., Ste. B-2
Framingham, MA 01701
508-626-8511

NanoPac, Inc.
4833 S. Sheridan Rd.,
Ste. 402
Tulsa, OK 74145
918-665-0329

Power Translation Co.
11500 Statesville Rd.
Huntersville, NC 28078
704-875-2138

PRAB Command, Inc.
P.O. Box 2121
Kalamazoo, MI 49003
616-382-8200

Prentke Romich Co.
1022 Heyl Rd.
Wooster, OH 44691
800-262-1984
216-262-1984

Quartet Technology, Inc.
52 Davis Rd.
Tyngsboro, MA 01879
508-692-9313

Regenesis Development Corp.
1046 Deep Cove Rd.
North Vancouver, BC
V7G 1S3
CANADA
604-929-6663

Safko International, Inc.
3140 N. Arizona Ave.,
Ste. 111
Chandler, AZ 85224
602-497-1987

TASH, Inc.
91 Station St., Unit 1
Ajax, ON L1S 3H2
CANADA
219-462-8086
416-686-4129

Voice Connection
17835 Skypark Cir., Ste. C
Irvine, CA 92714
714-261-2366

X-10 (USA), Inc.
91 Ruckman Rd.
P.O. Box 420
Closter, NJ 07624-0420
201-784-9700
800-526-0027

Zofcom, Inc.
3962 Nelson Ct.
Palo Alto, CA 94306
415-858-2003

6

Applications for Adaptive Technology

The personal computer and adaptive technology form a platform of independence for persons with disabilities. The power and capability of the typical desktop computer can be expanded further through many powerful applications that increase productivity and the rate of information exchange. The focus of this chapter is upon networking, telecommunications, and CD-ROM—peripherals that increase the amount of information available to the user. Networks of computers allow users to share data with fellow students or workers. The online world offers vast information resources waiting to be tapped with a personal computer and a modem. CD-ROM systems can provide vast libraries of information on almost any subject. The next sections explore these three empowering technologies in detail and discuss how they relate to adaptive technology.

Local Area Networks

At the onset of the personal computer revolution, microcomputers were generally not linked together and were able to share files only by sharing disks or printouts of data files—a crude and cumbersome method for data exchange, especially for large amounts of information. With the advent of networking hardware and software, clusters of personal computers can now be joined for fast and accurate interchange of information. For persons with disabilities, local area networks (LANs) create an environment in which all participants can interact as equals.

A local area network consists of several computer systems linked via interface cables to exchange data with one another in any direction. A memory-resident software utility known as the network operating system controls the local area network. A network can be as small as two computers in the same room or as large as hundreds of computers separated by thousands of miles. Nearly every large corporation has a network of computers containing the complete records of the organization, not to mention the financial records of the institution. Most colleges and universities have vast computer networks that can be accessed for information processing. Many colleges and other institutions also are linked together via an international network to exchange information. This giant computer network, which spans the globe, is known as the Internet. Networks can be accessed with a large variety of adaptive equipment, including speech synthesizers, magnification software, braille printers, voice recognizers, adapted keyboards, and alternative input devices. The task of planning and adapting a network is a complex job, one that requires a systems engineer or systems analyst.

Network Hardware

Basic network hardware consists of a circuit card that plugs into an expansion slot on a personal computer. (See Chapter 2 for an explanation of the installation.) The network interface circuit card controls information flow in and out of each computer on the network and contains interface jacks for connecting cables that run from machine to machine. A computer system connected to a network is called a workstation. Setting up a network consists of plugging the network interface circuit cards into the individual computer workstations and running interface cables to connect them. Network interface cards from different vendors perform the same basic function and differ chiefly in their data transmission rates.

Although there are several ways to configure a local area network, the two most common types are peer-to-peer and file server. With a peer-to-peer network, computers are linked together as equals. The simplest network of this type consists of two computers linked via a single interface cable. With the peer-to-peer relationship, each computer can send files to and receive files from its counterpart, and a single printer can serve the network by connecting the printer to one of the peer machines. The other peers can access the printer just as if they were connected physically to that machine.

A server-based network consists of a master computer, called a file server, that is connected to remote computers. (See the

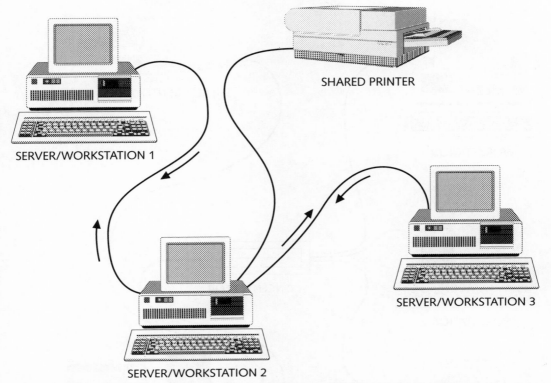

SHARED PRINTER

SERVER/WORKSTATION 1

SERVER/WORKSTATION 3

SERVER/WORKSTATION 2

A typical peer-to-peer local area network has several workstations that share information with one another. They also can share a printer, modem, or other device. *Courtesy of Cynthia E. Tumilty Lazzaro.*

drawing on page 160.) This configuration resembles a mainframe installation in which a centralized computer is accessed via remote terminals. However, a local area network using personal computers differs greatly from a mainframe setup because the computers connected to a network can function on their own if they are not logged onto the network. A file-server–based network is often called a client/server network because of the relationship between the master server and the client workstations. The file server stores in its central location all the data created by users of the network. The network can be wired together with several different forms of cable, but descriptions of these are beyond the scope of this book.

Mainstream Hardware Considerations

When creating a network workstation, whether for a peer-to-peer or file-server network, selecting the right machine for the job is critical. The most efficient computer for networking is one with numerous circuit card slots, hefty random-access memory, ample interface ports, and robust central processing unit power. Because

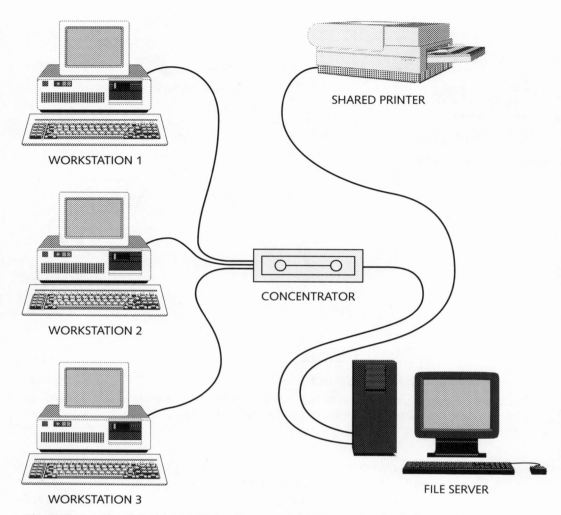

The illustration shows the basic topology of a typical local area network, with its centralized file server and workstations. The individual workstations connect to a concentrator (traffic director) that is connected to the file server. All workstations can share printer resources. *Courtesy of Cynthia E. Tumilty Lazzaro.*

workstations fitted with adaptive hardware and software will be called upon to perform a great deal of work, they will require sufficient resources to run both mainstream and adaptive applications while also possessing sufficient resources to interact with the network operating system.

The number of expansion slots on a network workstation is very important because many adaptive devices will use one or more of these slots when it is installed. The adaptive equipment is always added to the individual workstations, never the file server itself. For a peer-to-peer network, the adaptive equipment is loaded on each peer. For a file-server–based network, the adaptive equipment is loaded on one of the workstations, not the server. As an extreme example, an internal speech synthesizer added to the system uses at least one expansion slot. Add to this a hardware-based magnification system, and two slots will be occupied. A voice recognition system, alternative input device, and an adapted keyboard requiring an emulator card each use an expansion slot. Therefore, users should select computers with as many expansion slots as possible to allow for future expansion and capability.

For an adaptive workstation the number of input and output ports also is critical. More ports provide increased flexibility for expanding the system. An adaptive workstation should have at least two serial ports in addition to the standard modem port because many forms of adaptive equipment communicate with the personal computer through these communications links.

Another prime consideration for network workstations is that they have sufficient memory. The computer must have enough memory to run the adaptive software and the mainstream software, as well as the network operating system software—a tall order for many machines. (Any computer attached to the network must run the network operating system software in order to communicate with the network.) For most systems, 1 or 2 megabytes of memory is often sufficient, but the various mainstream and adaptive hardware vendors can supply exact figures. If users plan to run a graphics-based operating system in addition to the network and adaptive technology, a computer with 8 to 12 megabytes of memory may be required.

The video system required for a network workstation must be based on the print requirements of the user. For a user who is visually impaired using a magnification program, a video system compatible with magnification software must be selected. If the user is employing an IBM PC-compatible computer system, a VGA video adapter card and monitor are required for most network or stand-alone magnification software applications.

Network Software

After the network interface cards have been plugged into the individual computers and the cables have been strung together, the software for each of the network workstations must be installed. This software, the network operating system, consists of a memory-resident utility that controls the network circuit card. The network software sends information back and forth across the network, organizes users into groups, and assigns security privileges to individual users and groups of users. The network operating system behaves much like a telephone exchange, routing information packets back and forth to individual personal computers.

Network security, to prevent unauthorized use of files, and network resources are major functions of the network operating system. The network operating system knows the location of every personal computer on the network and controls access to all files stored on the system. Users can have super privileges, that is, the ability to control the entire system, or they can be granted read-only privileges, that is, no ability to create or change files on the system. The system administrator controls the network operating system and is responsible for maintaining the network on a daily basis.

The network operating system loads after typing its name at the DOS prompt or after highlighting its name with a mouse and clicking twice to activate the software. When the network software runs, users have access to software programs, printers, and data files stored on the network just as if these programs and devices resided on their local computers. With a central file server the user also has access to shared modems and the world of telecommunications services discussed later in this chapter.

File Sharing

A standard feature of most networks, file sharing allows multiple users to share data files and information. This can be useful for mainstream users and is very helpful for users with disabilities. For example, dozens of users can share a single database, allowing all in an organization to have an accurate listing of company financial or client information. Because all users access a single database, there is no possibility of confusion that would exist if multiple databases were used. The network operating system manages data flow across a network, keeping track of all stored and transmitted information and preventing data collisions and loss of data. For a disabled user, the network files represent equal access to information. Documents stored on the network can be spoken aloud using a speech synthesizer, displayed in enlarged type using a magnification package, printed in braille using a braille printer, or accessed via a voice recognition device, adapted keyboard, or special switch. In other words, the information can be accessed by all users, disabled and nondisabled alike, according to their individual wants and needs.

Printer Sharing on Local Area Networks

Printer sharing is an important feature of most networks, allowing many users to share single or multiple printers. Once users are logged onto the network, they can share printers just as if the printers were connected to their own individual personal computers. The network operating system controls the various printers connected to the system and directs print jobs to any desired printer.

The network may have several different types of printers, depending on the exact natures of the frequently needed print jobs. For example, a draft-quality dot matrix printer may be used to print internal material that does not have to be of presentation quality. A high-quality laser printer interfaced to the network allows sharp text and graphics documents to be generated in quantity, and a braille printer interfaced to the system produces braille documents at the touch of a key. Each printer has a unique name on the network, allowing the users to know the function of each printer. Users needing to print braille documents would simply direct their print output to the printer called "braille" to get a hard copy in braille.

Electronic Mail on Local Area Networks

A typical component of most local area networks, electronic mail allows all users to send text messages back and forth to one another. Electronic mail is software-controlled, with each user on the system having his or her own "mailbox." A message can be sent to any user on the system simply by sending it to the appropriate mailbox. When a new mail message arrives, the user is alerted and has the option of reading it at that time or later.

Electronic mail is an equalizing force for persons who find the printed or spoken word a barrier. For example, persons who are blind or visually impaired can read electronic mail using speech synthesis, magnification systems, or braille displays and printers; persons who are deaf or hearing impaired can interact with others by sending and receiving text-based mail messages; and persons with motor impairments can send and receive electronic mail without having to physically type on the keyboard. Electronic mail often can be sent to others who are not on the physical network by using modem hardware and software, described later in this chapter in "The Online World."

Installing Adaptive Technologies on a Local Area Network

Many adaptive hardware and software products capable of working with network workstations are currently on the market. Often products that work on stand-alone personal computers also can be used on a network. When setting up an adapted workstation, technical considerations relating to interrupts and memory address conflicts should be focused upon, particularly if the adaptive device is based on a circuit card. As stated earlier, the amount of memory a workstation has is also of prime consideration.

Troubleshooting

If the network system fails to operate properly, there are three potential problem spots to consider. First, the system hardware may be conflicting with the adaptive hardware. This can be resolved by changing interrupts and/or addresses on either the adaptive or mainstream circuit cards. As explained in Chapter 2, the interrupts and addresses can be changed either by flipping switches or changing jumpers on the appropriate circuit cards.

Second, the adaptive software may be in conflict with the network operating system software. This can be resolved by loading programs in a different order, such as loading the adaptive software after the network operating system has been loaded.

Third, memory limitations must be checked to assess potential problems. A common theme in network installations is that memory is usually at a premium and must be conserved. Users must be certain the computers have enough memory to run all applications: the adaptive software and the network operating system. The memory problem can be a serious one; however, it usually is possible to add memory to most systems by installing more memory chips on the mother board or installing a circuit card loaded with memory chips. If the memory resources of a given computer cannot be expanded, the only available option may be to limit the number of programs loaded into the computer. If so, certain programs must be used in a stand-alone mode of operation, that is, used when the computer is not logged onto the network.

All in all, networks provide an accessible environment where all can interact as equals. Many forms of adaptive technology can be interfaced to local area networks, allowing persons with disabilities increased access to information.

The Online World

Telecommunications technology links computer systems together via standard telephone lines and permits the sharing of data and information files across town or across the globe. This is referred to as "going online"—one of the most powerful applications for personal computers. In simple terms, online information is accessible to anyone who has a telephone, a computer, either an external or internal modem (see Chapter 2), and communications software. Much of the online world is compatible with existing adaptive technology. The online world offers much to persons with disabilities, providing access to vast storehouses of information as well as professional and social contacts.

Online Services

Online services consist of giant computer systems packed with information that the general public can access with a personal computer and a modem. Dozens of online services span the globe, containing information on almost every subject. These commercial databanks permit users to search online databases of information and to send and receive electronic mail with one another. Some of the more familiar of such services are CompuServe, GEnie, BIX, Prodigy, and Delphi. Online services use large computer systems that allow hundreds of users at a time to access the system.

Online services offer electronic mail, live chatting, and conferences on a wide variety of subjects. These services are solidly planted in the business of selling information—everything from abstracts of articles to technical support on computer hardware and software. Many online services offer databases that can be searched, allowing the user to quickly locate information on almost any subject. Online services also offer electronic mail, fax facilities, live chatting, and electronic conferencing. Many online services offer information for persons with disabilities, allowing disabled and nondisabled alike to interact and exchange information. See the list at the end of this chapter for commercial online service providers.

Bulletin Boards

A bulletin board (or BBS), a smaller version of an online service, consists of a personal computer equipped with communications software that allows users to call into the system to send and receive information. The typical bulletin board can accommodate one or more users at a time, but single-user bulletin boards are the most common. Literally thousands of bulletin boards are operated privately by computer clubs, small businesses, and hobbyists. Bulletin boards have much in common with their larger cousins the online services—offering many of the same services on a smaller scale. There are numerous disability-related bulletin boards across the country. An extensive list of disability-oriented bulletin boards is included at the end of this chapter.

Electronic Mail

Electronic mail is one of the most productive services offered by online services and bulletin boards. Through it, users on the system can send mail messages electronically to other system users. Unlike paper-based mail, electronic mail arrives virtually instantly, regardless of the distances involved. Some systems can deliver electronic mail completely across the country or around the world in a matter of a few seconds. (The Internet is such a system, described later in this chapter.) Electronic mail also can be used to send files such as spreadsheets, databases, graphics, and computer programs as attachments to text-mail messages.

Electronic mail is relatively easy to operate. The user composes a letter with a text editor or word-processing program, saves it on a floppy disk or hard disk, and then uses a modem to dial the telephone number of an online service or bulletin board that provides electronic mail services. The user then types in his or her name and password, which permits entry into the databank. Next, the file containing the letter is transmitted to the remote system with a mailing address attached to the document to route the letter to its destination.

Most electronic mail programs are operated through simple menus that prompt users for a destination address and title of the message and allow users to certify their mail messages. With a certified mail message, the sender receives confirmation that the recipient has read the message. As with paper-based mail, "carbon copies" can be sent by adding names to the Send list.

The chief benefit of electronic mail is its high degree of accessibility. An electronic mail message can be read easily by many forms of adaptive equipment, permitting persons with a wide range of disabilities equal access. For individuals using adaptive equipment, electronic mail is a convenient method for sending text or graphics messages without having to journey to the post office to mail a letter.

Fax

Fax (short for facsimile) also is used extensively by online services and some bulletin boards, allowing subscribers to send hard-copy messages to any remote location equipped with a fax machine. In simple terms, a fax machine uses the telephone lines to transmit a duplicate of any document by reducing the original document into regions of light and dark and reassembling the light and dark regions in their exact configuration at the remote location. Using a fax service is similar to sending electronic mail. Users merely log onto an online service by typing their name and password. Then they compose a message and transmit via the online service to a remote fax machine. The service repeats the transmission until the fax is successfully received at the remote location. The user also can choose to compose the fax or electronic mail message while offline to save money that would be spent in connect-time charges. For persons with disabilities, fax services can be a force for equality, allowing persons to send hard-copy messages from their adapted computers.

Live Chatting Online

Online chatting is a popular service offered by online networks and bulletin boards. In contrast to electronic mail and fax, online chatting allows users to communicate with one another live by typing messages back and forth. These "conversations" can be private, or they can be conducted in a fashion similar to that of a large public gathering or citizens band radio with everyone being able to "hear" one another. Through online chatting, individuals unable to travel easily from place to place can meet, make friends, and increase social contacts. Online systems sponsoring such chat facilities generally offer nightly chats on a number of topics ranging from science fiction to arts and entertainment. Some systems hold regular chats on a general topic, allowing individuals spontaneously to set the tone of the conversation.

Calling an Online Service or Bulletin Board

Placing a modem call to an online service or bulletin board is uncomplicated if the modem hardware and software are properly installed and configured. The first step is to match exactly the dial-in parameters, such as baud rate and other settings, to those of the online system. If the parameters are not matched correctly, the user will send and receive garbled information. Then, manually enter the telephone number, or select it from a menu and strike the enter key to confirm the selection. Modems with speakers will emit a dial tone as the modem begins dialing. When the connection is established, the screen will begin to fill with information from the remote system. Following are examples of what might appear on a user's video display after connecting to the BIX, Delphi, and GEnie online services. The main menu shows the options the user can select. By selecting an option and striking the Enter key, users can interact with the remote computer just as if they were sitting at that computer's keyboard. All keystrokes are sent through the telephone lines as if users were running the online service by remote control.

```
Welcome to BIX
Copyright (c) 1993
General Videotex Corporation


CoSy Conferencing System, Copyright (c) 1984 University of Guelph


Need BIX voice help...
In the US call 800-695-4775 and elsewhere call 617-354-4137,
12:00 p.m. to 11:00 p.m. EST (-5 GMT) weekdays.

name: lazzaro

password: password

Last on: Sun Feb 14 12:21:14 1993

You have 48 mail messages in your in-basket.

You are a member of 112 conferences.


    BIX Main Menu

  1  Electronic Mail
  2  Conference Subsystem
  3  Listings (file upload/download areas)
  4  NewsBytes - Industry News Briefs
  5  Subscriber Information
  6  Individual Options
  7  Quick Download
  8  Command Mode (abandon menus)
  9  Logoff (bye)

Enter a menu option or ? for help:
```

```
Welcome to DELPHI
Copyright (c) 1993
General Videotex Corporation


Logon at   : 26-FEB-1993 23:04:30
Last Logon : 25-JAN-1993 13:41:12


MAIN Menu:

Business and Finance        News, Weather, and Sports
Computing Groups            Reference and Education
Conference                  Shopping
DELPHI/Regional             Travel and Leisure
Entertainment and Games     Using DELPHI
Groups and Clubs            Workspace
Internet Services           HELP
Mail                        EXIT
Member Directory

MAIN>What do you want to do?  Go Group Widnet

Providing Comprehensive Telecommunications & Information Services
To Disability Advocates & Professionals Everywhere --

WIDNet is provided by WID --

      The World Institute on Disability
      of Oakland, California USA

WIDNET Menu:

Announcements               News and Weather Services
Coffee Shop                 Travel
Communication Services      Set Preferences
Conference                  Username Directory
Databases                   Using WIDNet
Entry Log                   Who's Here
Forums & SIGs               Workspace
MAIL (Electronic)           Help
Member Profiles             Exit

WIDNET>What do you want to do?
```

```
** Thank you for choosing GEnie **

  The Consumer Information Service
        from General Electric
        Copyright (C), 1993
GEnie Logon at: 23:12 EST on: 930226
Last Access at: 17:41 EST on: 930220

You have 1 LETTER WAITING.

GEnie                                TOP
  Page      1                        GE Information Services

  1.[*]GEnie*Basic Services          2.[*]GEnie Information
  3.[*]Billing and Setting Information  4.  Communications (GE
                                              Mail & Chat)
  5.   Computing Services            6.   Travel Services
  7.   Finance & Investing Services  8.   Online Shopping
                                             Services
  9.   News, Sports & Features       10.  Multi-Player Games
  11.  Career/Professional Services  12.  Business Services
  13.  Leisure Pursuits & Hobbies    14.  Education Services
  15.  Entertainment Services        16.  Symposiums on Global
                                             Issues
  17.  Research & Reference Services 18.  Leave GEnie (Logoff)

Enter #, <H>elp? Mail

GEnie                                MAIL
Page  200                            GE Mail
  1.[*]Display Queue of GE Mail Letters
  2.[*]Read GE Mail
  3.[*]Read (List) All Letters in your Mailbox
  4.[*]Read (List) Letters From Specific User
  5.[*]Read (List) Letters From Specific Date
  6.[*]Compose and Send GE Mail Online
  7.[*]Upload a Text Letter
  8.[*]Search GE Mail Directory
  9.[*]GE Mail Command Mode
 10.[*]About Attached Files
 11.   Send (Upload) Attached Files
 12.   Receive (Download) Attached Files
 13.[*]Send FEEDBACK to GEnie

Enter #, <P>revious, or <H>elp?
```

Electronic Conferencing

Electronic conferencing, offered by many online services and bulletin boards, allows users to post messages on almost any topic. This is not to be confused with live chatting. Online conferencing is similar to an old-fashioned message board where all can post news and comment on the messages posted by others. Conferencing systems present messages in threads or groups, allowing the user to follow the subject theme. Messages also can be read in chronological order, depending on the specific needs of the user. Users of these systems can conduct a search for a given text string to locate messages or message threads on a particular subject. Conference systems are divided by subject, with subtopics attached to each main subject area. A conference on science fiction, for example, would have subtopics such as books, movies, fantasy, horror, etc. For persons with disabilities, online conferencing represents increased independence, allowing individuals to share knowledge and communicate with those knowledgeable about or interested in a given subject.

The Internet

The Internet is a vast electronic superhighway that spans the globe, connecting corporations, universities, military installations, research facilities, government agencies, and other public and private entities. The Internet network can be accessed with a modem and personal computer, gaining admission to electronic mail and vast libraries of computer software. Most persons gain access to the Internet as students at a university or as workers for a government organization, but public-access Internet sites are now becoming available. The Internet allows individuals to connect to other computers on the network and transfer files and information at high speeds. With Internet access, a user can log onto a computer in Boston and access a computer in London.

In keeping with its theme as a storehouse of information, the Internet also offers USENET news groups on a variety of subjects. Numerous news groups exist for everything from model rocketry to cooking. Disability-oriented news groups also exist, resembling a conference in which users post messages to each other. Among them are ALT.EDUCATION.DISABLED and MISC.HANDICAP. With an Internet account, the user can read these newsgroups and share technical information on adaptive equipment and special issues relating to disabilities.

Another Internet service is Gopher, an automated document delivery service. The Gopher server displays a menu of document titles, and the user can select by moving arrow keys to the desired title. The document can be read on screen and mailed to an electronic mailbox on that system or another system if desired. One option is access to the "cornucopia of disabilities" with information from worldwide sources.

The Internet also provides a live chat area called IRC for Internet Relay Chat. IRC permits individuals around the globe to speak in real time on almost any topic imaginable. The opportunity to network electronically with others is valuable, allowing persons separated by thousands of miles to communicate quickly and easily. See the list at the end of this chapter for public-access Internet sites.

Interfacing Adaptive Technology for Online Services

Using current commercially available adaptive equipment, most personal computers can be equipped to interact with online services and bulletin boards, providing information in the medium necessary for the specific needs of the user. As with local area networks, some technical considerations should be observed when interfacing adaptive technology to an online workstation.

Special attention should be paid when interfacing a modem with any form of adaptive hardware and software. As with any system, the user should avoid interrupt conflicts. Also, special care should be taken to avoid direct conflicts with the modem itself. For example, a speech synthesizer set to operate as communications port 1 will not speak if the modem also is set to this port. All modems use serial ports; therefore, adaptive devices that rely on interfacing to the serial port should avoid the modem port. If the system has only one serial port, adding a second port may be necessary. As with other adapted devices, there must be enough memory to run both mainstream and adaptive applications.

The online world can be fully explored by persons with disabilities. Using available adaptive technology, persons with a variety of disabilities can take advantage of the information and social opportunities waiting online. By creating an adapted workstation, telecommunications can empower individuals to interact with others across town or across the country. The adaptation process can often be accomplished for under several hundred dollars, making the investment well worth executing.

Compact Disks

Throughout recorded history, information storage has been of prime importance. When the printing press became widely available, ideas and information could easily be recorded and reproduced, permitting a machine to do the work that traditionally was done painstakingly by hand. Later, microfilm became an efficient storage technology in which miniature photographs took the place of the bulky printed page. Although microfilm proved highly workable, the computer has proven to be a more efficient storage medium for printed information.

In the early years of computing, magnetic tape was used to store data, a medium that was not efficient for fast retrieval of information because the reels of magnetic tape had to be searched in a linear fashion for the right bit of information. If the desired information was in the middle of the tape, the user had to rewind the tape to that exact point, a process that could take several minutes at best. As storage technology improved, computers began to use cassette tape for storage. Although cassette tape is much less bulky than open-reel tape, cassettes still suffer from the same linear problems as open-reel medium, forcing the user to wind through hundreds of feet of tape to locate an exact file. A method to retrieve information had to be found, one that did not store information in a linear mode.

The floppy disk is such a system—a combination of the tape recorder and the phonograph. Floppy disks soon became the standard for computer storage systems because information could be found much faster. Floppy disks do not store information in a linear format, and intelligent disk drive systems can locate any file on the disk by searching a file allocation table. The file allocation table contains a complete list of every file on the disk and the exact location of every file, permitting the disk head to locate any file in fractions of a second. Although floppy disks proved to be useful for storing and retrieving information, they lack the storage capacity to hold truly large amounts of information. The current state-of-the-art magnetic-based floppy disks can hold about 2.5 megabytes per disk—the size of a novel or small textbook—but not enough for an encyclopedia, dictionary, or other large reference work.

Compact disk read-only memory (CD-ROM) has the fast access time similar to a hard disk coupled with very high storage densities in the hundreds of megabytes range. Information on a CD-ROM is stored using a laser beam rather than a magnetic pulse. The bits of information on a CD-ROM are more closely stored, or tightly packed, than on a floppy disk. The laser burns depressions into the disk that alter the reflective nature of the plastic disk. A CD-ROM disk drive reads the disks using a laser, which interprets the burn holes as part of a binary code.

The CD-ROM can store an entire set of encyclopedias and can transform almost any personal computer into a library databank capable of retrieving vast quantities of information. With the appropriate adaptive hardware and software, the user can create talking dictionaries or encyclopedias for persons who are blind, library computer networks for persons who are deaf or hard of hearing, and accessible libraries for persons with motor impairments. The implications of CD-ROM for persons with disabilities are tremendous because adaptive technology can be interfaced to computers running CD-ROM drives.

CD-ROM Hardware and Software

CD-ROM systems consist of both hardware and software that readily can be interfaced to most personal computers. The hardware consists of the disk drive, circuit card, and interface cable. Once the interface card is installed, the drive can be mounted either internally or externally. An interface cable connects the interface card to the CD-ROM drive, and a second cable connects the drive to the internal power supply of the computer.

CD-ROM software allows the user to control the CD-ROM hardware and to search CD-ROM disks for information. The software can be either a stand-alone application or a memory-resident application. Stand-alone software allows the user to access the CD-ROM software as the computer's primary focus. A memory-resident package allows the CD-ROM software to be loaded into memory with another application. For example, a CD-ROM encyclopedia could be loaded into memory first, then a word processor could be loaded immediately after. Then, the CD-ROM could be accessed while in the word processor by simply striking a function key. A resident package can sit in memory until it is required.

Numerous CD-ROM products are currently on the market on a variety of subjects. Following are two examples of the types of titles available. A more general list appears at the end of this chapter.

Grolier Electronic Encyclopedia

The Grolier Electronic Encyclopedia, from Grolier Electronic Publishing, comes on a single CD-ROM disk. This CD-ROM encyclopedia contains the full text of the *Academic Encyclopedia* and includes a printed reference manual and installation disk. The Grolier CD-ROM is compatible with MS-DOS and Macintosh computers. Although it is not produced specifically for persons with disabilities, it is highly compatible with many forms of adaptive technology including speech synthesis, magnification processing, braille embossing, adapted switches, etc.

The encyclopedia comes with a menu-driven installation program, making it relatively simple to install on most hard disk drives. The installation program asks the user what type of CD-ROM drive he or she is using and automatically copies the proper files to the boot directory on the hard disk. Once the installation process is complete, the system can be started by typing its name on the command line or by clicking with a mouse. When loaded, Grolier displays its title screen and allows the user to select title- or word-search options. The user merely has to key in a word or title and the retrieval software searches the CD-ROM for all occurrences of the target text. Once the search is completed, the software displays a list of titles that match the search pattern. After the user makes a selection, the text can be displayed or printed. Entries also can be printed to disk files, allowing the text to be copied to other systems or printed in braille.

Microsoft Bookshelf

The Microsoft Bookshelf, by Microsoft Corporation, offers a dictionary, thesaurus, almanac, and other reference works. Bookshelf can be loaded into memory in the background, allowing it to be used with most word processors and other applications programs. While the word processor is active, the user moves the cursor to the word to look up and strikes a hot-key sequence to activate the dictionary. Then Bookshelf displays the dictionary page for that word and the user "cuts and pastes" the definition into the text. Similar actions activate the Bookshelf thesaurus and other reference works stored on the CD-ROM.

Interfacing Adaptive Technology with a CD-ROM

CD-ROM systems are compatible with a wide variety of assistive hardware and software including speech synthesis, magnification systems, braille devices, voice recognition, adapted keyboards, and alternative input devices. The CD-ROM system's ability to store vast amounts of information in a small space and to quickly and easily retrieve that information is an empowering technology for persons with vision impairments, who have traditionally had difficulty accessing the printed word. CD-ROM systems are also powerful for persons with hearing impairments, as the systems present text and graphics in an interactive format. For persons with motor impairments, CD-ROM replaces heavy stacks of books and allows the user to flip electronic "pages" with the click of an adapted switch or with voice command.

As with networks and modems, when installing a CD-ROM system special care should be taken to avoid interrupt and memory conflicts. A typical CD-ROM installation involves plugging in a circuit card and attaching the CD-ROM drive to the card. Since these cards often use interrupts, special care should be taken to avoid conflicts. Also, the user should determine that there is enough memory to run both mainstream and adaptive software.

The CD-ROM is a highly useful tool for persons with disabilities. It requires some basic skill with adaptive hardware and software, but the work is well worth the result. Software companies are beginning to supply software on CD-ROM, which is most useful for packages that fill many disks. Games are also migrating to CD-ROM, providing text, graphics, and sound on a single compact disk. At present, more CD-ROM titles are appearing on the shelves, and this trend shows little sign of abatement.

Telecommunications Services and CD-ROM Products

Online Service Providers

The following is a listing of the major online services. Most services offer electronic mail, conferencing, and live chatting. Many of these services have disability-related files and areas of interest.

America Online
  8619 Westwood Center Dr.
  Vienna, VA 22182
  800-227-5938
  703-448-8700

AT&T Mail
  AT&T
  P.O. Box 3505
  New Brunswick, NJ 08903
  800-624-5672
  201-331-4132

BIX
General Videotex Corp.
1030 Massachusetts Ave.
Cambridge, MA 02138
800-544-4005
617-491-3393

BRS/After Dark
BRS INFORMATION
  TECHNOLOGIES
A Division of Maxwell
  Online, Inc.
8000 Westpark Dr.
McLean, VA 22102
800-289-4277
703-442-0900

CompuServe, Inc.
P.O. Box 20212
Columbus, OH 43220
800-848-8199
614-457-0802

DASnet
DA Systems, Inc.
Marketing Dept.
1503 E. Campbell Ave.
Campbell, CA 95008
408-559-7434

DataTimes
14000 Quail Springs Pkwy.,
  Ste. 450
Oklahoma City, OK 73134
800-642-2525
405-751-6400

Delphi
General Videotex Corp.
1030 Massachusetts Ave.
Cambridge, MA 02138
800-544-4005
617-491-3393

DIALCOM
2560 N. First St.
San Jose, CA 95161-9019
800-872-7654
408-922-6051

Dialog Information Services
3460 Hillview Ave.
Palo Alto, CA 94304
800-334-2564
415-858-3810

Dow Jones News/Retrieval
Service
P.O. Box 300
Princeton, NJ 08543
800-552-3567
609-452-5211

EasyNet
Telebase Systems, Inc.
435 Devon Park Dr.,
  Ste. 600
Wayne, PA 19087
800-220-9553
215-293-4700

General Electric Information
Services (GEnie)
401 N. Washington St.
Rockville, MD 20850
800-638-9636
314-340-4000

IQuest
Telebase Systems, Inc.
435 Devon Park Dr.,
  Ste. 600
Wayne, PA 19087
800-220-9553
215-293-4700

Knowledge Index
3460 Hillview Ave.
Palo Alto, CA 94304
800-334-2564
415-858-3810

Lexis and Nexis
Mead Data Central, Inc.
P.O. Box 933
Dayton, OH 45401
800-543-6862
800-227-4908

NewsNet
945 Havorford Rd.
Bryn Mawr, PA 19010
800-345-1301
215-527-8020

PC-Link
8619 Westwood Center Dr.
Vienna, VA 22182
800-458-8532
703-448-8700

Prodigy
445 Hamilton Ave.
White Plains, NY 10601
800-962-0310
800-PRODIGY

Promenade
8619 Westwood Center Dr.
Vienna, VA 22182
800-525-5938
703-448-8700

SprintMail
12490 Sunrise Valley Dr.
Reston, VA 22096
800-736-1130
913-541-6876 (international
calls)

USA TODAY Sports Center
Four Seasons Executive
Center
Terrace Way, Bldg. 9
Greensboro, NC 27403
800-826-9688

The WELL
27 Gate Five Rd.
Sausalito, CA 94965
415-332-4335

Disability-Related Bulletin Board Providers

The following listings include electronic bulletin boards that serve the disabled community around the country and around the world. These systems often go in and out of existence and change phone numbers without warning.

Able Inform BBS
Silver Spring, MD
301-589-3563

ABLED-LINK
Calgary, AB
403-282-4459

ADAnet
Birmingham, AL
205-854-5863

American SITE CBBS
Norman, OK
405-366-1449

ARC BBS
Salem, OR
503-363-7168

Artic Technologies Support
BBS
Troy, MI
313-588-1424

Bay Talk BBS
San Francisco, CA
415-864-6430

Black Bag Medical BBS
Newark, DE
302-994-3772

The Blind Ambition BBS
Rochester, MI
313-651-4009

Blindsights Point-Of-View
Independence, MO
816-254-9116

Blink Connection
San Francisco, CA
415-276-4121

Blink Connection
San Leandro, CA
510-276-4121

BlinkLink
Pittsburgh, PA
412-766-0732

Braille_Inn_Speakout
Jarrettsville, MD
410-893-8944

DDLG Special Needs
Hull, Great Britain
44-482-586711

DeafTek, Inc.
Framingham, MA
508-620-1777

Digex
San Diego, CA
619-454-8078

Dimenet
Taunton, MA
508-880-7340

Disabilities Electronic
Network/DEN
Hackensack, NJ
201-342-3273

Disabled Data Link Group
Lowestoft, Great Britain
44-502-518274

Disabled_Hellas
Thessaloniki, Greece
30-31-245595

DRAGnet BBS
Andover, MN
612-753-1943

4 Sights Network
Detroit, MI
312-272-7111

The Handicap News
Shelton, CT
203-337-1607

Handiline
Arlington, VA
703-536-2052

HandiNet BBS
Virginia Beach, VA
804-496-3320

HcUG BBS
Hong Kong Island, Hong
Kong
852-855-0569

HEX Handicapped Exchange
Rockville, MD
301-593-7357

The Idea Link
Wheaton, MD
301-949-5764

Information 90 BBS
Allentown, PA
215-434-2237

LDS Hospital PC Users Group
Salt Lake City, UT
801-321-5030

Lighthouse
Brewster, MA
508-892-8857

LINC Resources
Columbus, OH
614-885-5551

Mass. Commission for the
Blind
Boston, MA
617-451-5327

Microsystems Software BBS
Framingham, MA
508-875-8009

MicroTalk BBS
Louisville, KY
502-893-2269

MSI SW BBS
Framingham, MA
508-626-2481

National Federation of the
Blind BBS
Baltimore, MD
410-752-5011

Nerve Center
Pikesville, MD
410-655-4708

Project Enable
Dunbar, WV
304-766-7807

SoundingBoard
Pittsburgh, PA
412-621-4604

Special Needs BBS
Phoenix, AZ
602-253-5325

The Special Needs BBS
Whiting, IN
219-659-0112

Square_Hole_BBS
Nanaimo, BC
604-754-0838

Technology Assessment
Program BBS
Washington, DC
202-544-3613

Unique Connections BBS
Brooklyn, NY
718-527-5556

US Department of Justice
(ADA BBS)
Washington, DC
202-514-6193

Virginia School for the Blind
Hampton, VA
804-247-2075

Vision BBS
Ottawa, ON
613-523-8199

Visually Impaired/Blind Users
Group BBS (VI/BUG)
Holbrook, MA
617-767-2909

Yellow Dream Machine
Austin, TX
512-451-3222

Public Access Internet Sites

The selection of public access Internet sites may differ in what they offer. Some include electronic mail and file transfers. Check with the individual provider for additional information.

Anomaly—Rhode Island's
Gateway to the Internet
401-331-3706 (Modem)
401-455-0347 (Modem)
401-273-4669 (Voice)

Colorado SuperNet
303-273-3471 (Voice)

Community News Service
800-876-2373 (Voice)
719-520-1700 (Modem)
719-579-9120 (Voice)
619-634-1376 (Modem)

Cooperative Library Agency
for Systems and Services
800-488-4559 (Voice)

Express Access—Online
Communications Service
301-220-0462 (Modem)
410-766-1855 (Modem)
301-220-2020 (Voice)

Halcyon
206-382-6245 (Modem)
206-426-9298 (Voice)

HoloNet
510-704-1058(Modem)
510-704-0160 (Voice)

The IDS World Network
401-884-9002 (Modem)
401-785-1067 (Modem)
401-884-7856 (Voice)

Netcom Online Communica-
tion Services
310-842-8835
408-241-9760
408-459-9851
415-424-0131
510-426-6860
510-865-9004
408-554-UNIX (Voice)

The Portal System
408-725-0561 (Modem)
408-973-9111 (Voice)

The Whole Earth 'Lectronic
Link
415-332-6106 (Modem)
415-332-4335 (Voice)

The World
617-739-9753 (Modem)
617-739-0202 (Voice)

CD-ROM Providers

The following is a listing of general interest CD-ROM titles. This list is by no means complete and is intended to provide the reader with a general sample of what is available on CD-ROM. Inclusion or omission from this list does not imply endorsement or disapproval.

Bowker Electronic Publishing
121 Chanlon Rd.
New Providence, NJ 07974
800-334-3838
212-734-3855
Books in Print Plus
Childrens Reference Plus
Corporate Affiliations Plus
Directory of Medical Specialists
Library Reference Plus
Marquis Who's Who
Science Technology Reference
Plus
Variety's Video Directory Plus

Facts On File Publications
460 Park Ave. S.
New York, NY 10016
800-322-8755
212-683-2244
Facts On File News Digest

GEOVISION
270 Scientific Dr., Ste. 1
Norcross, GA 30092
404-448-8224
GEOdisc: Windows on the
World

Grolier Electronic Publishing, Inc.
Sherman Turnpike
Danbury, CT 06816
800-356-5590
203-797-3500
The Electronic Encyclopedia
(IBM/Mac)

ICP Software Information
823 E. Westfield Blvd.
Indianapolis, IN 46220
317-251-7727
Software Information
Database

Information Access Co.
362 Lakeside Dr.
Foster City, CA 94404-9888
800-227-8431
415-378-5200
General Periodicals List
National Newspaper Index

Islotech
6520 Edenville Blvd.
Eden Prairie, MN 55346
612-835-5240
PC-Blue: MS-DOS Public
Domain Library
Pravda on CD-ROM
Shareware Grab Bag

McGraw-Hill Book Co.
11 W. 19th St.
New York, NY 10011
800-262-4729
212-337-5907
CD-ROM Science & Technical
Reference Set

Microsoft Corp.
1 Microsoft Way
Redmond, WA 98052-6391
800-426-9400
206-882-8080
Microsoft Bookshelf
Microsoft Word W/ Bookshelf
Stat Pack

Moody's Investors Service
99 Church St.
New York, NY 10007
800-342-5647
Moody's 5000 Plus

Online Computer Library Center
6565 Frantz Rd.
Dublin, OH 43017-0702
800-848-5878
614-764-6000
Environment Library

Optical Media International
180 Knowles Dr.
Los Gatos, CA 95020
408-395-4332
Constitution Papers

Oxford University Press
200 Madison Ave.
New York, NY 10016
212-679-7300
The Oxford English Dictionary
on CD-ROM

Silver Platter Information
100 River Ridge Dr.
Norwood, MA 02062-5026
800-343-0064
617-769-2599
Petersons College Database

Tax Analysts
6830 N. Fairfax Dr.
Arlington, VA 22213
703-532-1850
IRS Letter Rulings
Tax Library

Trace Center
University of Wisconsin
1500 Highland Ave.
Madison, WI 53705
608-262-6966
Cooperative CDROM
Database Distribution
Network for Assistive
Technology

University Microfilms International
300 N. Zeeb Rd.
Ann Arbor, MI 48106
800-521-0600
313-761-4700
Dissertation Abstracts on
Disc
Periodical Abstracts on Disk

Weather Disc Associates
4584 N.E. 89th St.
Seattle, WA 98115
206-524-4314
World WeatherDisc

H.W. Wilson Co.
950 University Ave.
Bronx, NY 10452
212-588-8400
Applied Science &
Technology Index
Biography Index
Book Review Digest
Film Literature Index
Readers' Guide to Periodical
Literature

7

Rehabilitation Engineering, Training, and Technical Support

Analyzing an individual's adaptive technology needs and providing appropriate training are complex, detailed, and time-intensive tasks. Fortunately, the specialists in the fields of rehabilitation engineering and training are available to assist in these tasks. Rehabilitation engineers create technological bridges spanning the turbulent waters of isolation and dependence for persons with disabilities. With the help of the Americans with Disabilities Act, many persons with disabilities are obtaining full- and part-time employment, leading to an increased need for engineering professionals, trainers, and adaptive equipment.

Rehabilitation engineers adapt personal computers and other equipment to make them accessible to persons with disabilities at school, home, and on the job. However, the newly installed adaptive hardware and software will accomplish little if the user does not know how to operate it properly. Training can be performed in the classroom or on the job, providing the knowledge to use mainstream and adaptive technology effectively. Technical support provides ongoing assistance after a training regimen has been completed.

Rehabilitation Engineering

Rehabilitation engineers create pathways through technology that heretofore did not exist and to bring those technologies to life for the betterment of humanity. Rehabilitation engineers provide services for individuals and for organizations large and small. For example, hospitals hire rehabilitation engineers to help speed patients' return to routine functioning after severe illnesses or medical procedures. School districts hire rehabilitation engineers to make classrooms more accessible; companies hire them to adapt job sites for incoming disabled workers or for current workers who have become disabled on the job.

Some rehabilitation engineers specialize in one disability, such as blindness, deafness, or motor impairment. Others specialize in one area of adaptive technology, such as speech synthesis, magnification systems, or communications devices. Depending on the engineer's specific training, he or she may have broad knowledge of other disabilities and other forms of adaptive technology.

Rehabilitation engineers may charge from $50 to $100 per hour. Although this may sound like an extraordinary figure, the demand for these skilled professionals is great, and few can claim to possess the knowledge of this highly specialized field. Rehabilitation engineers often work for a state or federal vocational rehabilitation agency, such as a commission for the blind, hospital, or independent living center, or for a general rehabilitation commission or school system. Free-lance rehabilitation engineers often can be located by calling state rehabilitation commissions or independent living centers to obtain a list of working engineers in a given area of the country. (See Appendix D for a listing of technology assistance states.) Many engineers operate as consultants and are available to large and small companies on an as-needed basis. One source might be to call a rehabilitation engineering professional organization such as the Rehabilitation Engineering Society of North America (RESNA), located in Washington, D.C. The National Rehabilitation Hospital of Washington, D.C., is another reliable source of information, as is the Trace Research and Development Center at the University of Wisconsin–Madison.

The rehabilitation engineering profession requires basic scientific skills and a solid technical education. Many rehabilitation engineers begin with college degrees in electronic engineering, computer science, mechanical engineering, physics, or one of the other hard sciences. A concrete grounding in the physical sciences can be highly valuable to the rehabilitation engineer, as the analytical skills necessary to master the hard sciences will serve the engineer well. The engineer must have a curious mind, one constantly striving for the answer that awaits just over the horizon. The importance of the scientific method cannot be stressed enough in fulfilling the rehabilitation engineer's tasks because he or she must create new devices or modify existing devices.

The rehabilitation engineer's typical job duties are broad based. He or she surveys the needs of the individual, provides the adaptive equipment, installs that equipment, and provides training and technical support.

Job-Site Analysis

Job analysis is the first task for any adaptation. The engineer must first learn all the job duties that are to be undertaken by the person who is disabled. The most efficient way to accomplish this task is to write a work plan of the work week. A complete job analysis is essential so that the consumer is not at risk of being unable to perform the job effectively or of losing the job. (Throughout this section, the term *consumer* describes the rehabilitation engineer's client.)

Security is an important issue for any job adaptation. The engineer must be conscious of security and ethics issues and must never betray proprietary or classified information. These ethics are similar to the ethics followed by members of the medical profession, in which confidentiality is supreme. The engineer may have access to sensitive files and system hardware and may even have access to a company's financial information. For some government or federal jobs, internal security and procedures for some organizations prevent the engineer from performing the adaptation alone. In such cases, the engineer must work closely with the local system administrator or plant manager, often showing the system manager how to install the equipment under supervision.

To analyze a job, the rehabilitation engineer meets with the consumer and the job supervisor and asks many detailed questions. The engineer must have a complete description of the consumer's abilities and basic aptitudes. In addition, the engineer must determine the exact job duties, their priorities, and their time limits, if any. For example, the job of word processing a letter is not a difficult task in itself, but it becomes vastly more difficult if the consumer must generate twenty-five such letters per day while also answering a busy switchboard. Tasks such as data entry, editing, spell checking, and proofreading are made all the more complex by time and quota limits. Jobs that involve only data retrieval require different skills from those that require only data entry. Therefore, the engineer must determine what information is needed to perform the job and what information can be weeded out to increase performance. To illustrate this point, following is a somewhat simplified example of job analysis for a job that is confined to data retrieval. In this example, the worker whose job is being described is blind and is using a speech synthesizer and screen reading software program to read the video screen.

The worker uses an adapted personal computer connected to a mainframe system and reads information from several screens. He relays this information to customers who phone in for specific information. The worker's first step is to answer the telephone and to get the customer's identification number. He then keys the ID number into the computer database to retrieve the customer-data screen that contains all the information on the customer, such as address, phone number, social security number, work history, and other credit information. The worker needs to retrieve only the amount of the last bill and read it to the customer. Therefore, the adaptive equipment should allow the worker to read the exact piece of information he needs without having to scan through the other data. At times the worker also must read the amount of the previous month's bill. Therefore, the adaptive device should present the information in that exact order to maximize efficiency.

To fully accommodate the worker, the engineer must adapt all aspects of the job site, including all office equipment and procedures, making certain that nothing is off-limits to the worker. With the current state of the art of adaptive technology, it is often possible to approach 100 percent accessibility for some positions. For example, the engineer also should adapt the telephone system, as it will be of vital importance on almost every job. The engineer may use low-technology adaptations, such as simply labeling a telephone touch-pad with braille symbols, to make the entire office accessible for the worker. A speaker telephone or headset device is appropriate to make the telephone system accessible for persons unable to hold a standard telephone. For persons with hearing impairments, the engineer should modify smoke alarms and other emergency signals, allowing the person access to this vital information. The engineer should work and think like a private investigator, tracking down all points that prevent access and adapting them to the needs of the consumer.

Figure 2 is a list of data that the rehabilitation engineer should record. Some of the items require short answers, while others may require many paragraphs of description. For example, information about job duties will have lengthy answers and may need to be expanded upon to include multiple job duties. Although this list

Figure 2. Rehabilitation engineering checklist

Personal Data

Consumer name _____

Home address _____

_____

Home phone _____

Primary disability description _____

_____

_____

_____

Secondary disability description _____

_____

_____

_____

Transportation to/from work site _____

_____

Employment Data

Job title _____

Company name _____

Company address _____

Company phone _____

Fax number _____ Modem number _____

Supervisor name _____

Supervisor phone _____

Supervisor job title _____

Job Analysis

Work hours _____ Work days _____

Prior computer experience _____

_____

Main job duty _____

_____

_____

_____

Time limits on main job duty _____

_____

_____

_____

Percentage of main job duty _____

Secondary job duty _____

_____

Time limits on secondary job duty _____

_____

Percentage of secondary job duty _____

Hardware

Computer type _____ CPU type _____

Operating system _____ System memory _____

Monitor type _____ # serial ports _____

parallel ports _____ # expansion slots _____

Modem type _____ Fax type _____

Printer type _____ CD-ROM type _____

Keyboard type _____ # disk drives _____

Hard drive type _____ Hard drive size _____

Network type _____ Mainframe type _____

Other network type _____

Software

Word processor _____

Database _____

Spreadsheet _____

Telecommunications package _____

Utilities _____

Adaptive Equipment

Currently in use _____

_____

_____

Previously used _____

_____

_____

Training required _____

_____

_____

is not exhaustive, it should be used as a guidepost for general considerations.

Coordinating the Adaptation of the Workplace

Once the job-site analysis is complete and the rehabilitation engineer has determined what type of adaptive equipment is necessary, the on-site installation can begin. (The following discussion focuses on personal computer adaptations and assumes that the technology in question is computer compatible.) First, the rehabilitation engineer must contact the person responsible for the existing computer hardware. The engineer must gain the confidence of office management, the consumer's supervisor, and, of course, the consumer. Since communication is crucial, the engineer must keep all parties informed, especially the supervisor and the consumer, particularly if any significant changes are to be made. The engineer will arrange an initial planning meeting to discuss the expectations for all concerned. On the day of the system installation, the engineer must consult the consumer and supervisor during the installation to assure that all job functions are under adaptation. The engineer should also role play with the consumer, assuring that the equipment will work appropriately.

Training

Unfortunately, training is often the weakest link in most computer purchases, either adaptive or mainstream in nature. Although thousands of dollars may have been expended on computers, software, printers, modems, and other equipment, the computer purchaser habitually leaves training as the last item on a shopping list—if it is even present on the list at all. Training is one of the most important parts of the adaptation process because the user has a more complex system than generally is found in the mainstream, a system with many more commands and peripherals. Users of adaptive equipment must receive proper training for both the mainstream and adaptive equipment if both are to operate smoothly in tandem.

There are three basic types of training that will be discussed in the following sections: classroom, on-the-job, and follow-up. These training methods differ, and it is up to the rehabilitation engineer and user to decide which type of training is needed and when to start it.

Classroom Training

The benefits of classroom training are many. In the classroom-training group environment, students learn as much from each other as they do from the instructor. Students can work in a hands-on environment with the actual mainstream and adaptive equipment, guided all the way by instructors who are familiar with the subject. One of the most valuable benefits of classroom training is that it takes workers away from their job sites and into an environment in which they can learn without phones ringing or distractions from fellow workers.

If the person has little or no computer knowledge, then a full regimen of classroom training is in order. This training should include an overview of the computer hardware, the disk operating system, all applications programs, and all adaptive hardware and software.

Sometimes it is not possible for the worker to be trained away from the job for many weeks at a time. In that case, the rehabilitation engineer must make recommendations to satisfy the needs of the employer and the worker. If a long classroom training period is not possible, then a combination of classroom and on-the-job training might be a viable alternative.

On-the-Job Training

As its name implies, on-the-job training takes place at the actual work site, usually in a one-on-one situation between trainer and worker. On-the-job training has advantages and disadvantages, and the individual to be trained should consider them carefully.

A primary advantage of on-the-job training is that the training involves the actual equipment and procedures the worker needs to know. If the worker needs to run a software package stored on a centralized mainframe computer system, then the actual mainframe computer is available to practice on. In contrast, a classroom setting would not include access to the mainframe unless the trainer could arrange for a modem hookup.

On the other hand, on-the-job training may be inappropriate for a worker with little or no computer experience. It may take anywhere from one to several weeks to build basic skills— a task accomplished more successfully in a classroom environment in which the person could concentrate on the lesson plan uninterrupted.

Continuing Training

Continuing training is used after the adaptive equipment has been installed for a few weeks or a month. The trainer builds upon or refreshes skills or helps the user find more efficient methods to accomplish a job task. Continuing training can be most valuable when performed at the job site, allowing the trainer to fine-tune the adaptive and mainstream hardware and software for maximum efficiency. For example, the trainer can work with the rehabilitation engineer to write macros to shorten complicated procedures that require repeated keystrokes.

Training Materials

Users need not rely solely on instructors to increase their skills. The learning process can continue efficiently with the help of training materials and tutorials provided by trainers, manufacturers of software and hardware products, and computer trade books available from bookstores. Of course, the training materials must be in an accessible form for the user. Formats that may be available for training and tutorial materials include audiocassettes or videocassettes, printed books, and floppy disks. Each format has advantages, disadvantages, and adherents.

Audiocassettes are one of the most efficient training formats in use today because they can hold hours of information and can be transported easily. They can be copied (if this does not infringe on copyright) or shared with others, and inexpensive playback machines are readily available. For persons who are visually impaired, the audiocassette has been used effectively for many years. Audiocassettes require little training to use. Videocassettes are a popular training format because they provide both sound and images. Playback devices are widely available and are becoming less expensive than in the past. For persons who are blind or visually impaired, descriptive video systems bring the power of pictures to life with verbal descriptions. For individuals who are deaf or hard of hearing, the videocassette represents a medium where visual concepts can be stressed to maximum advantage. Closed or open captioning may be available for some videocassettes.

The oldest training medium of all is the printed book. The basic advantage of printed books is that they do not require mechanical or electronic equipment to access; thus, they can be used almost anywhere. However, as discussed in Chapter 1, the printed word can be a barrier for persons who have disabilities. Those who are blind or visually impaired must use a reader or adaptive technology to access books. For persons who are deaf or hard of hearing, the printed word presents few physical barriers unless the individual has not been trained with the written form of the language, as may be the case for some individuals schooled in sign language or lip reading. For persons who are motor impaired, printed books also may require adaptive technologies to hold and turn the pages of a textbook.

Disk-based tutorials allow users to run interactive learning programs on their personal computers. The user can answer the on-screen questions by typing answers on the computer keyboard. The computer then processes the input and displays the results of the interactive session, perhaps informing the user of weak points to brush up on or altering the training style to meet individual needs. Disk-based tutorials may present text, sound, and graphics–each of which may be a barrier to some persons with disabilities. For persons who are blind, or visually impaired, some disk-based tutorial programs are not accessible due to their reliance on graphics, especially if the individuals use speech synthesis as their primary method of computer access. Therefore, these users should preview disk-based training materials to see if they are appropriate. For persons who are deaf or hard of hearing, disk-based tutorials offer much opportunity for learning, provided the individual is comfortable with reading print. (For some individuals who are deaf, English is a second language, with sign language or lip reading being the primary mode of communication.) For the person who is motor impaired, the disk-based tutorial can offer a medium free from the weight of heavy textbooks, where the person can scan electronic pages with the simple press of a key or mouse button.

Technical Support

Technical support has become a common buzzword in the computer trade. It refers to assistance provided to the user after equipment has been purchased. Technical support is a necessary form of hand-holding that can make or break users' ability to operate their computers successfully. No matter how much training is provided, the user will always need to ask technical questions relating to the system, although these questions will become less frequent as the user gains confidence. Perhaps the first person the user will turn to is the one who holds key knowledge of the equipment and its exact configuration—the rehabilitation engineer who installed it and performed the initial training. In addition, technical support may come from manufacturers, outside contractors, users' groups, and built-in help screens.

Vendor Technical Support

Although they may not be aware of the fact, users are entitled to technical support from the companies that manufactured their adaptive and mainstream equipment. When purchasing a piece of hardware or software, the user is buying much more than what is in the box—the invisible addition is technical support. Different vendors will be involved with the overall technical support issue, one for each software program and one for each hardware or adaptive device. The user can expect to call a vendor during select times and ask technical questions, usually free of charge, of one of the company's trained technical support staff.

To ensure that they will receive technical support from a given company, users should fill out all required forms and warranty cards for the adaptive and mainstream hardware and software installed on the job site. This will entitle them to the vendors' technical support hot lines. Users should keep these hot line phone numbers handy for ready reference.

Third-Party Technical Support

Technical assistance also can be purchased through companies that make their living selling technical support. The user pays a fee to access a toll-free telephone number to call for help. Through third-party services, the user can get technical support for a wide variety of products in one telephone call. However, these companies generally are unable to assist with adaptive hardware or software questions. The technical support industry focuses chiefly on mainstream hardware and software packages to appeal to the widest market share possible.

Users' Groups and Special Interest Groups

User groups are a widely available, cost-effective method for obtaining technical support on a variety of subjects. People who have limited budgets but still need much technical support can look to a users' group or to a special interest group for assistance. These groups often are sponsored by schools and other institutions. Often, special interest group members are those who have a fondness for computers and who are more than willing to share their knowledge with others.

Users' groups can be located by contacting a local university or by calling local computer stores. The problem may not be in locating a user group but in deciding which group is most beneficial, simply because a flood of such organizations exist in most cities. For example, the Boston Computer Society of Cambridge, Massachusetts, is the largest computer support group in the United States with its approximately 30,000 members in the Massachusetts area. The Society has users' groups on almost every computer platform, including two groups aimed at the special needs community: the Visually Impaired and Blind Users Group (VIBUG) and the Disabled Special Needs Users Group (DSNUG). Both of these groups can assist novices and professionals with technical questions regarding adaptive computer technology and its many uses at home, school, and work.

Help Screens

One type of continuous technical support is as close as the computer monitor. The Help screen is a source of vital assistance for most software packages, allowing the user to receive help while running a particular application. Nearly every software package has some form of built-in help, and this assistance varies from package to package. The user is urged to explore the help system provided by his or her word processor, database, spreadsheet, or other application software, as these systems can provide invaluable information.

As an example, the WordPerfect word-processing program contains a series of Help screens. At the press of a function key, the user can display many screens of valuable technical information, all presented in plain, easy-to-understand text. The user can even use the help system to obtain help on any function key on the system simply by pressing that key while in the help system. The user can also press alphabetic keys to look up commands via their name, such as Print, Copy, or Delete. The WordPerfect help facility is also context sensitive; that is, it tracks the user's progress through the software and provides different assistance depending on where the user is within the program. For example, if the user is about to print a document, pressing the Help key will display different help information than if the user were about to save a document. Context sensitive help is being built into most applications software as standard equipment.

One example of a database program that contains an extensive help system accessible to the user employing adaptive equipment is that of dBASE. In contrast to the WordPerfect help facility, dBASE help is command driven, similar to the MS-DOS disk operating system. The user can access help by typing "help" at the command prompt followed by a word or phrase. This brings up a screen or screens of useful information on that topic or command.

With the appropriate adaptive equipment and training, the user can achieve far-reaching educational and career goals. See Appendix D for a listing of technology assistance states, as many of these programs provide technical assistance and training to users on various forms of adaptive hardware and software.

8

Funding Adaptive Technology

Since many adaptive devices can be beyond the financial reach of consumers, the acquisition of adaptive technology can sometimes lead to anxiety and frustration. Fortunately, numerous funding options are available to the consumer from both private and government sources. A complete treatment on funding would fill a book by itself; therefore, the following overview of funding is restricted in scope.

As explained in Chapter 1, the Americans with Disabilities Act (ADA) injects important considerations about the provision of assistive technology. Although the ADA is not a funding source, it is an impetus to others to supply adaptive technologies under certain circumstances. The act does this by requiring that private employers (Title I) and government employers (Title II) provide "reasonable accommodations" to achieve equal access and compliance with the law. In many cases, the definition of such reasonable accommodations will involve the provision of assistive devices. In simple terms, the ADA states that the employer must provide reasonable accommodation to a new or existing disabled worker. This does not always translate into technology, but the provision of technology is often the result. However, technology does not have to be provided if its provision would impose an "undue burden" or "undue hardship" upon the provider. When a burden or hardship is not the case—which is typical—technology may be indicated.

This chapter presents common sense cost-savings suggestions and describes how to use personal, private-sector, and government-sector funding options. Examples of funding providers are given for their model status. Readers are encouraged to contact the various funding sources directly or to locate the twin of that funding source in their home states.

Cost-Saving Ideas

Prior to purchasing adaptive technology, the consumer should do as much initial research as possible into both the companies and the equipment. A solid knowledge of the technology available will empower the consumer to choose the least expensive device for the job. For example, since software is often less expensive than hardware, the consumer should purchase adaptive software rather than hardware whenever possible. An example of this would be to choose a less expensive software-based screen magnification program instead of a more expensive hardware-based magnification processor. The consumer also is encouraged to use shareware and freeware software packages whenever possible to further cut costs.

As emphasized earlier, consumers should get as much hands-on experience with as many products as possible to judge the basic capabilities of each device. They should be familiar with more than just one device that seems to fit their individual needs to determine if a less expensive device will suffice.

Another way to cut costs is to purchase less equipment at the outset. For example, the consumer who wants to purchase a computer system equipped with a speech synthesizer, braille printer, magnification system, optical scanner, modem, and laser printer could spend as much as $10,000, depending on the exact system configuration. But if the purchase is scaled back to a more-affordable level, the person may be able to obtain a starter system—say, the computer with a speech synthesizer or braille printer—and then build up to the dream system.

Consumers should look for special deals, such as vendor sales and special promotions. The time of year also can affect the price. For example, prices are usually lower before or just after the holiday season. Purchasing discontinued products, such as last year's models, saves even more money.

Demonstration equipment is frequently less expensive than new devices, and it even may come with a full manufacturer's warranty. Although many consumers reject this out of hand, previously owned equipment can result in dramatic savings—as long as the equipment is purchased from a reputable private source or company. For the consumer who may not be fully familiar with computer systems, it is wise to have a reliable, knowledgeable third party inspect the equipment first. The consumer can often find previously owned equipment through the local newspaper, and there are numerous buying guides offering used equipment. In addition, many brokers also offer previously owned equipment to consumers at substantial cost savings.

Personal Funding Sources

All consumers have their own personal financial resources, and these assets will obviously vary greatly from person to person. If the consumer has significant financial resources, it is a simple matter merely to write a check for any required assistive technology. But since most people do not fit in this enviable category, other methods must be explored in earnest. Many purchasers of adaptive equipment have access to various personal credit sources, including friends and family members who may be in a position to grant a loan or cash advance. Although this may not be feasible for most consumers, it deserves mentioning as part of any funding plan.

Family and Friends

Family members or even friends may be sought out to provide low-interest loans. The loan might be worked out so that the consumer pays a small amount of interest with a long-term payment plan. If the consumer is working, this arrangement often can be very successful. For the consumer who is not working full time or who is on social security, an outright grant of funds from a family member might be explored, although this is not realistic for every individual.

Lending Institutions and Credit Unions

Lending institutions such as banks, savings and loan institutions, credit unions, and finance companies are logical places to seek capital to finance adaptive technology. These lending institutions offer credit cards, cash loans, and other revolving loan programs. Consumers may have to prove employment or to provide collateral to the lending institution. Consumers should consider that if they purchase adaptive equipment through a loan, they will have to pay back the loan along with any interest charges. Interest rates vary, and the final amount paid will depend on the amount borrowed, the interest rate, and the time taken to pay back the loan.

Would-be technology purchasers sometimes encounter problems getting loans or opening charge accounts because of their credit histories, which may be spotty due to unemployment and the like. The consumer should strive to get any credit reports and records amended to mitigate any adverse information. If that cannot be done, the individual should meet with loan officers to explain any negative information. It is also vital to develop a good credit history by making regular payments on any existing loans or credit card charges to assure loan officers that a loan for adaptive equipment will be repaid.

Credit Cards

Credit cards can also be used to purchase both mainstream and adaptive technology. For credit card purchases, the consumer charges the amount of the purchase, and interest is applied to the balance each month. As with bank loans, credit card companies will require that the applicant be employed.

The faster the consumer pays back the purchase, the smaller the amount paid for interest charges. Some credit cards carry rather hefty interest rates, so it is wise to shop around for a card with the most-affordable interest rate. Some credit cards also have users' fees that the consumer must pay on a regular basis.

Mainstream vendors accept most of the major credit cards, including MasterCard, Visa, and Discover Card, but not all cards are accepted at all vendors. Consult with the individual vendor before planning to make a purchase by credit card.

If the adaptive or mainstream vendor does not accept credit card purchases, the consumer may be able to make the purchase by using a cash advance from the credit card for that particular purchase. The amount the credit card advances depends on the line of credit or open balance of the credit card. However, the consumer should be aware that large cash advances usually invoke higher interest rates than normal charges on the card.

Of course, consumers also may use a combination of personal resources and credit resources to purchase the desired equipment. This indicates that the consumer should assemble as much ready cash as possible and combine that with a cash advance from a credit card or other funding source.

Government-Sponsored Funding Sources

Federal and state governments have long been sources of funding for adaptive technology. They are always good places for consumers to seek funding, especially if personal resources are minimal or if the consumer does not have a great deal of credit or a good credit rating. The federal government sponsors numerous grant programs that offer different funding options to consumers. Some programs offer cash at low interest rates, while others offer actual equipment. Some grants are available only to low-income individuals, while others are not means-tested at all. Following are several government-sector funding sources.

Federal Vocational Rehabilitation Program

A specific piece of adaptive equipment needed for obtaining a job or attending school is often covered by the federally funded Vocational Rehabilitation Program. Local rehabilitation agencies or state rehabilitation commissions can provide further information. For example, the local commission for the blind, commission for the deaf, or rehabilitation service agency is always a good place to find these programs. Individuals can become consumers of these services by obtaining a letter of referral from a physician to prove the existence of the disability. Many such agencies can provide adaptive equipment and other services to the consumer, but exact services offered vary greatly from state to state. Examples of other services are funding for school or college, mobility and orientation, independent travel, and assistance around the home for daily living. Addresses for programs are listed at the end of this chapter.

Maine Adaptive Equipment Loan Program

Designed to provide loans for the purchase of adaptive equipment, the Adaptive Equipment Loan Program is administered by the government-funded Alpha One Independent Living Center. The program is open to all residents of Maine who have disabilities and who are of legal age. The fund can provide capital to both businesses and private citizens. For businesses, the maximum amount that can be borrowed is $50,000; the amount varies for individuals, depending on the exact equipment needs. Interest rates are based on the prime interest rate. All types of adaptive equipment—home modifications, computers, driving, hearing aids, etc.—can be funded by the loan as long as they advance the independence of an individual.

Massachusetts Commission for the Blind

As with other rehabilitation agencies, the Massachusetts Commission for the Blind operates an adaptive technology program for consumers. The Commission program, which is both federally and state funded, provides adaptive equipment to state residents who are visually impaired and who register with the Commission. The adaptive technology program provides job-site analysis, adaptive equipment installation, and follow-up training in the field through a team of rehabilitation engineers. Its annual operating budget pays for both engineering and equipment. Intended for vocational rehabilitation, consumers entering the workforce, and college students, the program helps consumers obtain equipment on loan. Examples of equipment available are speech synthesizers, magnification software, braille displays and printers, talking calculators, tape recorders, and other low- and high-technology equipment.

Readers should check with their local state rehabilitation commissions for similar programs, as many states have such adaptive technology assistance programs funded with either federal or state dollars. Many of these programs will loan or grant adaptive equipment to consumers free of charge if they meet the specific criteria of employment or education. In other words, if the consumer is working, about to obtain work, or in school, he or she may qualify for equipment through one of the state programs.

Medicaid

The federally funded Medicaid program offers opportunities for obtaining technology on behalf of persons with disabilities who are eligible for Medicaid services. If adaptive equipment is deemed by a physician to be medically necessary, Medicaid may be required to provide adaptive technology to the consumer. Under the Medicaid program, adaptive technology often can be classified as durable medical equipment. This term can encompass a wide variety of adaptive technology, including speech synthesis systems for the blind and communications devices for persons with speech impairments. A great deal of persistence may be necessary, but many devices have been obtained through this resource. If the person can meet the definition of medical necessity, then adaptive equipment can be provided by Medicaid.

Nevada Assistive Technology Loan Program

Similar to the equipment loan fund based in Maine, the Nevada Assistive Technology Loan Program provides low-interest loans for adaptive equipment to persons of all ages with disabilities. The interest rate is based on the prime rate. The typical range of the loans is from $1,000 to $5,000. The consumer must first provide a written estimate of all equipment. The loan is then based on this written estimate. The loan can be paid back in 12 to 36 months. The fund is limited to residents of Nevada. The program is administered through United Cerebral Palsy of Nevada.

New York Equipment Loan Fund

The New York Equipment Loan Fund is administered by the Department of Social Services and is funded out of state dollars. The total amount of the fund monies available per year is $50,000. The fund is designed to provide low-interest loans to consumers for the purchase of adaptive equipment. It is open to all disabilities and all ages. Interest rates are based on the prime interest rate. Loans can range from $500 to $4,000 to be repaid within two to eight years as selected by the consumer. The loan fund is a payer of last resort, meaning that consumers must show proof of refusal from other sources.

Special Education

Implemented in each state under the provisions of the federal Individuals with Disabilities Education Act (IDEA), the special education system is an important source for technology. Every student who qualifies for special education services by reason of a disability will have the nature and extent of those services determined by an Individualized Education Plan (IEP). If technology represents the best means for achieving or for setting viable educational goals, its inclusion among IEP services is appropriate—and perhaps even mandatory. That is, if a student needs adaptive technology to achieve his or her goals, then the school must provide the technology. School districts may resist supplying adaptive technology by denying there is a substantive need or by questioning the educational appropriateness of the equipment when, in reality, their resistance may be due to budgetary concerns. School districts that claim that technology is never appropriate for inclusion in special educational services are clearly misinformed about the requirements of the federal law.

Social Security Administration PASS Program

The Social Security Administration is a source of funding for adaptive technology for persons with disabilities. The Plan to Achieve Self Support (PASS) is available for those on supplemental security income; thus, it is aimed at low-income individuals. With its emphasis on self-support, the PASS program also can be used to purchase adaptive equipment or to start a small business. This plan is not widely known to the general public and may not be known to every Social Security representative. Consumers may have to aggressively seek out Social Security claims representatives who can guide them through the PASS process.

PASS allows consumers of adaptive equipment to save for their purchases by obtaining funds from Social Security. Individuals can save this money in a bank or other kind of interest-bearing account and not have it count against their current Social Security income. In other words, the money saved through PASS is invisible money and will not result in cuts to supplemental security income or Social Security disability insurance benefits. The plan can last for several years, allowing the consumer to save thousands of dollars to be put toward the purchase of expensive adaptive systems.

To apply to the program, consumers must write a detailed proposal outlining how much money must be saved, exactly what equipment will be purchased, and how this equipment will allow the consumer to become self-supporting or gainfully employed. If the consumer can persuade the Social Security Administration that a particular piece of adaptive equipment will lead to self-sufficiency, there is a good chance the plan will be approved.

When the plan comes to completion, the consumer is free to expend the saved funds toward the purchase of appropriate adaptive equipment. If the plan is violated, the Social Security Administration can levy an overpayment against the consumer for all monies received.

The Technology-Related Assistance Act

The Technology-Related Assistance for Individuals with Disabilities Act of 1988 (Tech Act, for short) provides grant money to selected states to further the cause of adaptive technology and to provide information about it. The Tech Act was the first federal law to cover all disabilities and all ages. It also was the first piece of legislation that used the term *consumer responsive*; that is, it mandated that consumers be on the advisory boards guiding the policies. The Tech Act is funded under the National Institute on Disability and Rehabilitation Research (NIDRR). Under the Act consumers can receive information and referral on adaptive technology services.

Tech Act assistance includes training opportunities, development of surveys, on-site consultation in the area of project needs assessments and evaluations, and project planning. Tech Act states mainly provide information to consumers and professionals within their respective states. The Tech Act programs also promote interagency coordination and conduct policy analysis with the goal of spreading the word about assistive technology services. The Tech Act programs are developing strategies to accomplish the goal of statewide consumer-responsive systems of assistive technology delivery.

From some Tech Act states, consumers may be able to obtain actual adaptive equipment. (See Appendix D for a list of Tech Act states.) If it is not possible to obtain equipment, Tech Act states typically have information and networking capabilities. Consumers who live in a Tech Act state should contact the agency operating the program for guidance about possible funding sources. If the consumer's state is not listed, contact the Rehabilitation Engineering Society of North America (RESNA) office in Washington, D.C.

Veterans Benefits

For veterans of the United States armed services, military insurance policies and the Department of Veterans Affairs often can provide adaptive equipment and other services. The Department will supply training and other equipment as long as the disability is service connected. If the disability is not service connected, the Department will treat consumers at its facilities on a space-available basis and on a sliding scale for fees. The term service connected is defined as "any disease or condition that can be directly traced to military service." For further information, readers can contact the local office of the Department of Veterans Affairs or the central office in Washington.

Private-Sector Funding Sources

The private sector offers many programs for consumers interested in financing adaptive technology. These programs may provide helpful guidance, actual equipment, or low-interest loans to individuals. Some of the programs are means tested; that is, consumers must qualify by submitting to a personal income review to determine if they qualify for the funding. Other programs are not means tested, and almost anyone can qualify for the funding. Following are several examples of private-sector funding sources. (See also Appendix A: Organizational Resources for Persons with Disabilities and Appendix B: Assistive Technology Conferences for additional resources that may provide funding information.)

American Foundation for the Blind

The American Foundation for the Blind (AFB) sponsors a low-interest loan program for U.S. citizens who are legally blind and who wish to purchase a Xerox/Kurzweil reading machine. The program is means tested, and the user must provide a 10 percent down payment with the balance to be financed over 4 years at an interest rate based on general interest rates in the banking industry. The average monthly payment is about $125. The loan is financed through the Bank of Boston.

Easter Seals Society

The Easter Seals Society is a national organization that sponsors various regional technology assistance centers. Each center is independent, and services vary from state to state. Some states offer actual adaptive technology, while others offer engineering and training services only. Readers are advised to contact their local Easter Seals Society for specific information.

Lions Clubs

Lions Clubs can be found in almost every community, and these civic groups frequently provide adaptive equipment to persons with disabilities. Although most of their donations have been focused on persons with vision impairments, the Lions Clubs also assist persons with other disabilities. Since policies differ from club to club, check with the local organization.

Prentke Romich

Prentke Romich, a manufacturer of adaptive devices, will assist persons with disabilities in locating funding from various sources including Medicaid and private insurance. It also offers a free 23-page booklet on funding that explains how to write successful letters of request to obtain funding for adaptive equipment.

TeleSensory Optacon Loan Program

TeleSensory, a manufacturer of adaptive technology for the visually impaired, offers a funding program for its Optacon reading machine. (See Chapter 3.) The Optacon Finance Plan is a funding program with a maximum limit of $3,200. Since the total cost of the Optacon is $3,695, the consumer must place a down payment of $500, bringing the total amount financed to $3,200. The loan program is a joint venture among TeleSensory, Canon, and General Electric Credit Corporation. The payment schedule is about $100 per month for a total of 34 payments. The interest rate is 3.96 percent. The loaning company prefers a limited credit history on the part of the borrower, such as credit cards or other small loans. In some cases, a co-signer may be necessary. The loan is applicable only for the Optacon unit and any Optacon accessories.

In summary, a variety of funding sources are available for adaptive technology within the public and private sectors. Consumers should research their funding options and should commit to writing a solid plan of attack. Those who complete this necessary homework will increase their chances of reaching a positive outcome.

Financial Aid Resources

Addresses of Funding Sources

The American Foundation for the Blind
15 W. 16th St.
New York, NY 10011
212-620-2000

Department of Veterans Affairs
Office of Public Affairs
810 Vermont Ave. N.W.
Washington, DC 20420
800-827-1000

Lions Club Intl.
300 22nd St.
Oakbrook, IL 60521
708-571-5466

Maine Adaptive Equipment Loan Program
Alpha One
85 E St.
South Portland, ME 04106
207-767-2189

Massachusetts Commission for the Blind
88 Kingston St.
Boston, MA 02111
617-727-5550

National Institute on Disability and Rehabilitation Research (NIDRR)
U.S. Dept. Education
400 Maryland Ave. S.W.
Washington, D.C. 20202-2572
202-205-5449

Nevada Assistive Technology Loan Program
United Cerebral Palsy of Nevada
1500 E. Tropicana, Ste. 230
Las Vegas, NV 89119
702-798-4433

New York Equipment Loan
Fund
  Office of Financial Management
  Dept. of Social Services
  40 N. Pearl St.
  Albany, NY 12243

Prentke Romich Co.
  1022 Heyl Rd.
  Wooster, OH 44691
  216-262-1984

RESNA Technology-Related
Assistance Project
  1101 Connecticut Ave. N.W.,
  Ste. 700
  Washington, DC 20036
  202-857-1140 (Voice or
    TDD)

TeleSensory
  455 N. Bernardo Ave.
  P.O. Box 7455
  Mountain View, CA 94039
  415-960-0920

Books on Funding Sources

American Foundation for the Blind. *Designing a Program for Financing Assistive Technology: The AFB Loan Program Model.* New York: The Foundation, 1993.

Mendelsohn, S. *Financing Adaptive Technology: A Guide to Sources and Strategies for Blind and Visually Impaired Users.* New York: Smiling Interface, 1987. (Available in print, braille, four-track cassette and IBM-compatible floppy disk)

_____ . *Tax Options and Strategies for People with Disabilities.* New York: Demos Publications, Inc., 1993. (Available in print, on audiocassette, and on IBM or Macintosh floppy disk)

Prentke Romich. *How to Obtain Funding for Augmentative Communication Devices.* Wooster, Ohio: Prentke Romich, 1989. (Free through the company)

Superintendent of Documents. *Federal Benefits for Veterans and Dependents.* Washington, D.C.: U.S. Government Printing Office, 1993. (Available at government bookstores)

Organizational Resources for Persons with Disabilities

The following listing may be used as a resource for locating specific national organizations, information networks, and referral centers that focus on specific disability-related issues. This listing is by no means complete, as there are many local and community organizations that may provide the same information. Inclusion of any resource on this listing does not indicate an endorsement.

A comprehensive resource entitled *Directory of National Information Sources on Disabilities* is available through the National Rehabilitation Information Center (NARIC) by calling 800-346-2742.

The National Institute on Disability and Rehabilitation Research (NIDRR) has funded numerous rehabilitation engineering centers, research and training centers, state technology-related assistance projects, and special demonstration and innovation projects. NIDRR's *Program Directory* lists current NIDRR-funded centers and projects. For a complete listing of rehabilitation engineering centers and research and training centers contact NIDRR at 202-732-1134. For a complete listing and information regarding state technology-related assistance projects contact RESNA's Technology-Related Assistance Project at 202-857-1140.

Accent on Living Publishers
  P.O. Box 700
  Bloomington, IL 61702
  309-378-2961

Adaptive Environments
  Center
  374 Congress St.,
  Ste. 301
  Boston, MA 02110
  617-695-1225 (Voice or
  TDD)

Affiliated Leadership League
for the Blind of America
1030 15th St. N.W.
Washington, DC 20005
202-775-8261

Alexander Graham Bell Assn.
for the Deaf
3417 Volta Pl. N.W.
Washington, DC 20007
202-337-5220 (Voice or
TDD)

Alzheimer's Disease Assn.
70 E. Lake St.
Chicago, IL 60601
312-853-3060

American Academy of
Orthotists and Prosthetists
717 Pendleton St.
Alexandria, VA 22314
703-836-7118

American Academy of Pain
Medicine
5700 Old Orchard Rd.,
1st Fl.
Skokie, IL 60077
708-966-9510

American Academy of
Physical Medicine and
Rehabilitation
122 S. Michigan Ave.,
Ste. 1300
Chicago, IL 60603
312-922-9366

American Amputee
Foundation, Inc.
P.O. Box 250218
Little Rock, AR 72272
501-666-2523
800-553-4483

American Assn. for
Respiratory Care
11030 Ables Lane
Dallas, TX 75229
214-243-2272

American Assn. for the
Advancement of Science
(AAAS)
Project on Science,
Technology, and Disability
1333 H St. N.W.
Washington, DC 20005
202-326-6672 (Voice or
TDD)

American Assn. of Retired
Persons (AARP)
601 E St. N.W.
Washington, DC 20049
202-434-2277

American Burn Assn.
Baltimore Regional Burn
Center
4940 Eastern Ave.
Baltimore, MD 21224
800-548-2876

American Cancer Society
Ntl. Office
1599 Clifton Rd. N.E.
Atlanta, GA 30329
404-320-3333
800-ACS-2345

American Chronic Pain Assn.
P.O. Box 850
Rocklin, CA 95677
916-632-0922

American Congress of
Rehabilitation Medicine
Assn. Management Center
5700 Old Orchard Rd.
Skokie, IL 60077
708-965-2776

American Council of the
Blind
   1155 15th St. N.W., Ste. 720
   Washington, DC 20005
   202-467-5081
   800-424-8666

American Deafness and
Rehabilitation Assn.
   P.O. Box 251554
   Little Rock, AR 72225
   501-663-7074

American Diabetes Assn., Inc.
   Ntl. Center
   1660 Duke St.
   Alexandria, VA 22134
   800-232-3472

American Epilepsy Society
   638 Prospect Ave.
   Hartford, CT 06105
   203-232-4825

American Foundation for the
Blind
   15 W. 16th St.
   New York, NY 10011
   212-620-2000
   800-232-5463

American Geriatrics Society
   770 Lexington Ave.,
     Ste. 300
   New York, NY 10021
   212-308-1414

American Lung Assn.
   1740 Broadway
   New York, NY 10019
   212-315-8700

American Occupational
Therapy Assn.
   1383 Piccard Dr.
   P.O. Box 1725
   Rockville, MD 20850
   301-948-9626

American Paralysis Assn.
   500 Morris Ave.
   Springfield, NJ 07081
   800-225-0292
   201-379-2690

American Parkinson Disease
Assn.
   60 Bay St.
   New York, NY 10301
   718-981-8001

American Physical Therapy
Assn.
   1111 N. Fairfax St.
   Alexandria, VA 22314
   703-684-2782

American Printing House for
the Blind
   1835 Frankfort Ave.
   P.O. Box 6085
   Frankfort, KY 40206
   502-895-2405

American Speech-
Language-Hearing Assn.
   10801 Rockville Pike
   Rockville, MD 20852
   301-897-5700 (Voice or
     TDD)

American Spinal Injury Assn.
   250 E. Superior St., Rm. 619
   Chicago, IL 60611
   312-908-3425

Amyotrophic Lateral
Sclerosis (ALS) Assn.
   21021 Ventura Blvd.,
     Ste. 321
   Woodland Hills, CA 91364
   818-340-7500

Arthritis Foundation
1314 Spring St. NW
Atlanta, GA 30309
404-872-7100
800-283-7800

Associated Services for the
Blind
919 Walnut St.
Philadelphia, PA 19107
215-627-0600

The Assn. for Persons with
Severe Handicaps (TASH)
7010 Roosevelt Way N.E.
Seattle, WA 98115
206-523-8446 (Voice)
206-524-6198 (TDD)

Assn. for the Retarded
Citizens of the United States
2501 Ave. J
P.O. Box 6109
Arlington, TX 76005-6109
817-640-0204

Assn. of Higher Education
and Disability (AHEAD)
P.O. Box 21192
Columbus, OH 43221
614-488-4972 (Voice or
TDD)

AT&T Ntl. Special Needs
Center
2001 Route 46, Ste. 310
Parsippany, NJ 07054
800-233-1222 (Voice)
800-833-3232 (TDD)

Better Hearing Institute
5012 B Backlick Rd.
Annandale, VA 22003
703-642-0580
800-424-8576

Computer Retrieval of
Information Scientific
Projects (CRISP)
Information Systems
Branch
Div. of Research Grants
Ntl. Institutes of Health
U.S. Dept. of Health &
Human Svcs.
Bethesda, MD 20892
301-496-7543

Council of State
Administrators of Vocational
Rehabilitation
P.O. Box 3776
Washington, DC 20007
202-638-4634

Courage Center
3910 Golden Valley Rd.
Golden Valley, MN 55422
612-588-0811

Deafpride, Inc.
1350 Potomac Ave. S.E.
Washington, DC 20003
202-675-6700 (Voice or
TDD)

Direct Link for the Disabled,
Inc.
P.O. Box 1036
Solvang, CA 93464
805-688-1603 (Voice or
TDD)

Disability Rights Education
and Defense Fund (DREDF)
2212 Sixth St.
Berkeley, CA 94170
415-644-2555 (Voice or
TDD)

Disability Statistics Program
1995 University Ave.,
Ste. 215
Berkeley, CA 94704
415-644-9904

Dole Foundation for
Employment of Persons with
Disabilities
1819 H St. N.W., Ste. 850
Washington, DC 20006
202-457-0318

Epilepsy Foundation of
America
4351 Garden City Dr.,
Ste. 406
Landover, MD 20785
301-459-3700
800-332-1000 (Info. &
Referral)
800-332-4050 (Library
Services)

4 Sights Network
Ntl. Information Systems
for the Visually Impaired
16625 Grand River
Detroit, MI 48227
313-272-3900

Goodwill Industries of
America, Inc.
9200 Wisconsin Ave.
Bethesda, MD 20814
301-530-6500

HEATH Resource Center
Ntl. Clearinghouse on
Post-Secondary Education
for Handicapped
Individuals
One Dupont Cir. N.W.,
Ste. 800
Washington, DC
20036-1193
202-939-9320
800-54-HEATH (Outside of
DC)

Helen Keller Ntl. Center
for Deaf/Blind Youths and
Adults
111 Middleneck Rd.
Sands Point, NY 11050
516-944-8900 (Voice or
TDD)

Housing for Elderly and
Handicapped People
Division (HUD)
451 7th St. S.W., Rm. 6116
Washington, DC 20410
202-718-2866

IBM Independence Series
Information Center
Bldg. 5
P.O. Box 1328
Boca Raton, FL 33429
800-426-4832

Independent Living Research
Utilization (ILRU)
Institute for Rehabilitation
and Research
2323 S. Shepherd, Ste. 1000
Houston, TX 77019
713-520-0232 (Voice)
713-520-5136 (TDD)

Job Accommodation Network
(JAN)
  809 Allen Hall
  West Virginia U.
  Morgantown, WV 26506
  800-526-7234
  800-526-4698 (in WV)

Muscular Dystrophy Assn.
  3561 E. Sunrise Dr.
  Tucson, AZ 85718
  602-529-2000

Ntl. AIDS Information
Clearinghouse
  P.O. Box 6003
  Rockville, MD 20850
  800-458-5231 (Voice)
  800-243-7012 (TDD)

Ntl. Amputation Foundation
  12-45 150th St.
  Whitestone, NY 11357
  718-767-0596

Ntl. Arthritis and
Musculoskeletal and Skin
Diseases Information
Clearinghouse
  9000 Rockville Pike
  Box AMS
  Bethesda, MD 20892
  301-495-4484

Ntl. Assn. for the Visually
Impaired
  22 W. 21st St.
  New York, NY 10010
  212-889-3141

Ntl. Assn. of Rehabilitation
Facilities
  P.O. Box 17675
  Washington, DC 20041
  703-648-9300

Ntl. Assn. of the Deaf
  814 Thayer Ave.
  Silver Spring, MD 20910
  301-587-1788 (Voice)
  301-587-1789 (TDD)

Ntl. Clearinghouse on
Technology and Aging
  University Center on Aging
  U. of Massachusetts
    Medical Center
  55 Lake Ave. N.
  Worcester, MA 01655
  508-856-3662

Ntl. Council on Aging, Inc.
  409 3rd St. S.W., 2nd Fl.
  Washington, DC 20024
  202-479-1200

Ntl. Council on Disability
  800 Independence Ave. S.W.,
    Ste. 814
  Washington, DC 20591
  202-267-3846 (Voice)
  202-267-3233 (TDD)

Ntl. Council on Independent
Living
  2539 Telegraph Ave.
  Berkeley, CA 94704
  415-849-1243 (Voice)
  415-848-3101 (TDD)

Ntl. Diabetes Information
Clearinghouse
  1801 Rockville Pike,
    Ste. 500
  Rockville, MD 20852
  301-468-2162

Ntl. Easter Seal Society
  70 E. Lake St.
  Chicago, IL 60601
  312-726-6200 (Voice)
  312-726-4258 (TDD)
  800-221-6827

Ntl. Federation of the Blind
1800 Johnson St.
Baltimore, MD 21230
301-659-9314

Ntl. Foundation of Dentistry
for the Handicapped
1600 Stout, Ste. 1420
Denver, CO 80202
303-573-0264

Ntl. Head Injury Foundation
(NHIF)
1140 Connecticut Ave. N.W.,
Ste. 812
Washington, DC 20036
202-296-6443
800-444-NHIF

Ntl. Industries for the
Severely Handicapped
2235 Cedar Lane
Vienna, VA 22182-5200
703-560-6800

Ntl. Information Center for
Children and Youth with
Disabilities
P.O. Box 1492
Washington, DC 20013
703-893-6061 (DC only)
800-999-5599 (Outside DC)
703-893-8614 (TDD)

Ntl. Information Center on
Deafness
Gallaudet University
800 Florida Ave. N.E.
Washington, DC 20002
202-651-5052 (TDD)
202-651-5000 (Voice)

Ntl. Information System
Center for Developmental
Disabilities
Benson Building, 1st Fl.
U. of South Carolina
Columbia, SC 29208
803-777-4435
803-777-6058 (fax)
800-922-9234 (ext. 301)
800-922-1107 (in SC)

Ntl. Institute on Disability
and Rehabilitation Research
(NIDRR)
U.S. Dept. of Education
400 Maryland Ave. S.W.
Washington, DC. 20202
202-732-1134

Ntl. Multiple Sclerosis
Society
205 E. 42nd St., 3rd. Fl.
New York, NY 10017
212-986-3240
800-624-8236 (Information
Resource Center)

Ntl. Organization on
Disability (NOD)
910 16th St., Ste. 600
Washington, DC 20006
202-293-5960
202-293-5968 (TDD)

Ntl. Parkinson's Foundation
1501 N.W. 9th Ave.
Miami, FL 33136
800-327-4545
800-433-7022 (in FL)
305-547-6666

Ntl. Rehabilitation Assn.
633 S. Washington St.
Alexandria, VA 22314
703-836-0850
703-836-0852 (TDD)

Ntl. Rehabilitation
Information Center (NARIC)
  8455 Colesville Rd.,
    Ste. 935
  Silver Spring, MD
    20910-3319
  301-588-9284
  800-346-2742 (Voice or
    TDD)

Ntl. Spinal Cord Injury Assn.
  600 W. Cummings Park,
    Ste. 2000
  Woburn, MA 01801
  800-962-9629

Ntl. Spinal Cord Injury
Hotline
  American Paralysis Assn.
  2201 Argonne Dr.
  Baltimore, MD 21218
  800-526-3456 (Outside MD)
  800-638-1733 (MD only)

Ntl. Stroke Assn.
  300 E. Hampden Ave.,
    Ste. 240
  Englewood, CO 80110
  303-762-9922

Ntl. Technical Information
Service
  U.S. Dept. of Commerce
  5285 Port Royal Rd.
  Springfield, VA 22161
  703-487-4600 (General
    Info.)
  703-487-4642 (Searches)
  703-487-4650 (Documents)

Orthotic and Prosthetic Assn.
  717 Pendleton St.
  Alexandria, VA 22314
  703-836-7116

Paralyzed Veterans of
America
  801 18th St. N.W.
  Washington, DC 20006
  202-872-1300

Polio Information Center
  510 Main St., Ste. A446
  Roosevelt Island, NY 10044
  212-223-0353

President's Committee on
Employment of People with
Disabilities
  1331 F St. N.W.
  Washington, DC 20004
  202-376-6200

Registry of Interpreters for the
Deaf, Inc.
  8719 Colesville Rd.,
    Ste. 310
  Silver Spring, MD 20910
  301-608-0050

Rehabilitation Engineering
Society of North America
(RESNA)
  1101 Connecticut Ave. N.W.,
    Ste. 700
  Washington, DC 20036
  202-857-1140
  202-775-2625 (fax)

Resources for Rehabilitation
  33 Bedford St., Ste. 19A
  Lexington, MA 02173
  617-862-6455

Self-Help for Hard of Hearing
People, Inc. (SHHH)
  7800 Wisconsin Ave.
  Bethesda, MD 20814
  301-657-2248 (Voice)
  301-657-2249 (TDD)

Sensory Aids Foundation
385 Sherman Ave., Ste. 2
Palo Alto, CA 94306
415-329-0430

Spina Bifida Assn. of America
(SBAA)
1700 Rockville Pike,
Ste. 250
Rockville, MD 20852
301-770-7222
800-621-3141

Spinal Network
P.O. Box 4162
Boulder, CO 80306
303-449-5412

Technical Aids and
Assistance for the Disabled
1950 W. Roosevelt Rd.
Chicago, IL 60608
312-421-3373
800-346-2959

Tele-Consumer Hotline
1910 K St. N.W., Ste. 610
Washington, DC 20006
800-332-1124 (Voice or
TDD)
202-223-4371 (Voice or
TDD)

Trace R&D Center
S-151 Waisman Center
1500 Highland Ave.
Madison, WI 53705
608-262-6966 (Voice)
608-263-5408 (TDD)

United Cerebral Palsy Assn.
1522 K St. NW, Ste. 1112
Washington, DC 20005
202-842-1266
800-872-5827

World Institute on Disability
510 16th St., Ste. 100
Oakland, CA 94612
510-763-4100

Appendix B

Assistive Technology Conferences

The following alphabetical list includes conferences that encourage the use of assistive technology aids and devices to enhance the daily lives of persons with disabilities. This is a general listing of the major conferences on assistive technology and is by no means complete. Omission or inclusion of any conference does not indicate endorsement or rejection of that conference.

Abilities Expo
RCW Productions, Inc.
1106 2nd St., Ste. 118
Encinitas, CA 92024
Abilities Expo is held in St. Louis and in Los Angeles on an annual basis. Vendors, dealers, and manufacturers of durable medical equipment display new products and their standard merchandise. Some seminars take place, but this is primarily a product demonstration conference.

American Occupational Therapy Assn. (AOTA) Annual Conference
1383 Piccard Dr.
P.O. Box 1725
Rockville, MD 20850
AOTA's annual professional meeting includes seminars and product demonstrations.

American Physical Therapy Assn. (APTA) Annual Conference
Official Meeting Services
1111 N. Fairfax St.
Alexandria, VA 22314
APTA's annual professional meeting is primarily seminar based with product demonstrations.

American Society of Mechanical Engineers (ASME) Annual Meeting
22 Law Dr.
P.O. Box 2300
Fairfield, NJ 07007-2300
The annual professional meeting of ASME features seminars.

American Speech-Language-Hearing Assn. (ASHA) Annual Meeting
Convention and Meetings Div.
10801 Rockville Pike
Rockville, MD 20852
ASHA's annual meeting features seminars with minimal product demonstrations.

The Assn. for Persons with Severe Handicaps (TASH) Annual Conference
7010 Roosevelt Way N.E.
Seattle, WA 98115
The TASH conference features product demonstrations and a variety of seminars.

California State University at Northridge (CSUN) Technology and Persons with Disabilities Annual Conference on Contemporary Applications of Technology
Office of Disabled Student Services
California State U. at Northridge
1811 Nordhoff St.-DVSS
Northridge, CA 91330
The large CSUN conference includes seminars, poster sessions, and product demonstrations of various assistive devices.

Closing the Gap Conference

P.O. Box 68

Henderson, MN 56044

This annual conference focuses on the use of microcomputer technology for persons with disabilities. It places a strong emphasis on products (magnification devices and augmentative communication) for the visually impaired and blind as well as on educational products.

Council for Exceptional Children (CEC) Annual Conference

Dept. for Professional Development

1920 Association Dr.

Reston, VA 22091

The annual meeting of the CEC features seminars and poster sessions.

The Institute of Electrical and Electronics Engineers, Inc. (IEEE)

The IEEE Engineering in Medicine and Biology Society Annual Conference

345 E. 47th St.

New York, NY 10017

This technical information conference focuses on seminars, studies in the field, and poster sessions.

Intl. Society for Augmentative and Alternative Communication (ISAAC) Conference

The Institute for Integration

Norrmalmstorg 1

114 46 Stockholm, Sweden

This large international conference is held in different worldwide locations. It features poster sessions, seminars, and demonstrations of assistive devices.

Ntl. Home Health Care Exposition

1130 Hightower Trail

Atlanta, GA 30350-1220

The annual home health care conference is very large. It features a medical equipment show of durable products. Numerous new products are first presented at this exposition.

Ntl. Rehabilitation Assn. (NRA) Training Conference

1910 Association Dr., Ste. 205
Reston, VA 22091
The annual professional meeting of the NRA features seminars
and poster sessions in rehabilitation counseling, etc.

Ntl. Symposium on Information Technology (NSIT)

Conference Information
The U. of South Carolina
Center for Developmental Disabilities
Benson Bldg., 1st Fl.
Columbia, SC 29208
NSIT's annual meeting includes persons interested in access to information on assistive technology resources, literature, databases, etc.

President's Committee on Employment of People with Disabilities (PCEPD) Annual Meeting

1331 F St. N.W., 3rd Fl.
Washington, DC 20004
This large annual meeting includes top government speakers in the area of vocational rehabilitation, law, and legislation. Seminars and product demonstrations are the main attractions.

Rehabilitation Engineering Society of North America (RESNA) Conference

1101 Connecticut Ave. N.W., Ste. 700
Washington, DC 20036
The RESNA annual conference focuses on the use of rehabilitation engineering services and their application to assistive and rehabilitation technology. Product demonstrations, seminars, and poster sessions are all part of this conference. RESNA also offers regional conferences that take place during various times throughout the year and include poster sessions and seminars with limited product demonstrations. Contact RESNA at the address indicated above for a listing of regional conferences.

Journals and Newsletters on Assistive Technology

Accent on Living Magazine
P.O. Box 700
Bloomington, IL 61702

American Rehabilitation
Rehabilitation Services
Admin.
330 C St. S.W.
Washington, DC
20202-2531

*Assistive Device Center
Newsletter*
California State U. at
Sacramento
School of Engineering &
Computer Science
650 University Ave.,
Ste. 101B
Sacramento, CA 95825

Assistive Devices News
Pennsylvania Assistive
Device Center
Elizabethtown Hospital and
Rehabilitation Center
Elizabethtown, PA 17022

*Assistive Technology
Information Network
Newsletter*
U. of Iowa
Rehabilitation Engineering
U. Hospital School
Iowa City, IA 52242

*Assistive Technology Journal
(RESNA)*
Demos Publications
156 Fifth Ave., Ste. 1018
New York, NY 10010

*Augmentative
Communication News*
c/o Sunset Enterprises
One Surfway, Ste. 215
Monterey, CA 93940

Closing the Gap News
P.O. Box 68
Henderson, MN 56044

*Communication Outlook
Newsletter*
Artificial Language
Laboratory
405 Computer Center
Michigan State U.
East Lansing, MI
40824-1042

Computer Disability News
  The Ntl. Easter Seal Society
  2023 W. Ogden Ave.
  Chicago, IL 60612

*The Exceptional Parent
  Magazine*
  Psy Ed Corp.
  605 Commonwealth Ave.
  Boston, MA 02215

First Dibs Newsletter
  P.O. Box 1285
  Tucson, AZ 85702-1285

*Handicapped Requirements
  Handbook*
  Thompson Publ. Group
  1725 K St. N.W., Ste. 200
  Washington, DC 20006

Homecare Magazine
  Miramar Publ. Co.
  6133 Bristol Parkway
  Culver City, CA 90230

*International Journal of
  Technology & Aging*
  Human Sciences Press
  72 Fifth Ave.
  New York, NY 10011

*Mainstream Magazine of the
  Able Disabled*
  Exploding Myths, Inc.
  P.O. Box 2781
  Escondido, CA 92025

Paraplegia News
  PVA Publ.
  5201 N. 19th Ave., Ste. 111
  Phoenix, AZ 85015

Rehabilitation Brief
  Ntl. Inst. on Disability and
  Rehabilitation Research
  Dept. of Education
  Washington, DC 20202

Rehabilitation Digest
  Canadian Rehabilitation
  Council for the Disabled
  One Yonge St., Ste. 2110
  Toronto, ON M5E 1E5
  CANADA

*Rehabilitation Gazette
  International*
  4502 Maryland Ave.
  St. Louis, MO 63108

The Sloane Report
  P.O. Box 561689
  Miami, FL 33256

*Social Issues and Health
  Review*
  Equal Opportunity Publ.,
  Inc.
  Circulation Dept.
  44 Broadway
  Greenlawn, NY 11740

Sports N' Spokes Magazine
  PVA Publ.
  5201 N. 19th Ave., Ste. 111
  Phoenix, AZ 85015

*Technology Update
  Newsletter*
  Sensory Aids Foundation
  399 Sherman Ave., Ste. 12
  Palo Alto, CA 94306

Window on Technology
  Program Technology
  Branch
  Ministry of Community
  and Social Services
  16 Breadalbane St.
  Toronto, ON M4Y 1C3
  CANADA

Technology Assistance States

Following is a listing of states that are funded under the National Institute on Disability and Rehabilitation Research (NIDRR) to provide assistive technology service delivery to persons with disabilities. These are known as the Tech Act states, with the goal of ultimately having one in every state. For further information contact the local state program. If a state is not listed, contact the RESNA Technical Assistance Project, which oversees all of the Technology-Related Assistance States.

RESNA Technical Assistance Proj.
  1101 Connecticut Ave. N.W., Ste. 700
  Washington, DC 20036
  202-857-1140 (Voice or TDD)
  202-223-4579 (Fax)

Alaska
Assistive Technologies of Alaska
  400 D St., Ste. 230
  Anchorage, AK 99501
  907-274-0138 (Voice or TDD)
  907-274-1399 (BBS)
  907-274-0516 (Fax)

Arkansas
Arkansas Increasing Capabilities Access Network (ICAN)
  Dept. of Human Svcs.
  Div. of Rehabilitation Svcs.
  2201 Brookwood Dr., Ste. 117
  Little Rock, AR 72202
  501-666-8868 (Voice or TDD)
  501-666-5319 (Fax)

Colorado
Colorado Assistive Technology Project
  Rocky Mountain Resource and Training Inst.
  6355 Ward Rd., Ste. 310
  Arvada, CO 80004
  303-420-2942 (Voice)
  303-420-8675 (Fax)

Connecticut
Connecticut Assistive
 Technology Proj.
  Bureau of Rehabilitation
  Svcs.
  10 Griffin Rd. N.
  Windsor, CT 06095
  203-298-2042 (Voice)
  203-298-9590 (Fax)

Delaware
Delaware Assistive
 Technology Initiative
  Applied Science and
  Engineering Labs.
  U. of Delaware/A. I. duPont
  Inst.
  1600 Rockland Rd.,
  Rm. 154
  P.O. Box 269
  Wilmington, DE 19899
  302-651-6790 (Voice)
  302-651-6794 (TDD)
  302-651-6793 (Fax)

Florida
Florida Assistive Technology
 Proj.
  Florida Dept. of Labor &
  Employment
  Div. of Vocational
  Rehabilitation
  Bureau of Client Svcs.
  Rehabilitation Engineering
  Technology
  1709-A Mahan Dr.
  Tallahassee, FL 32399-0696
  904-488-6210 (Voice)

Georgia
Georgia Tools for Life
  Div. of Rehabilitation Svcs.
  878 Peachtree St. N.E.,
  Rm. 711
  Atlanta, GA 30309
  404-894-6655 (Voice)
  404-894-9669 (Fax)

Hawaii
Hawaii Assistive Technology
 Svcs. (HATS)
  677 Ala Moana Blvd.,
  Rm. 403
  Honolulu, HI 96813
  808-532-7110 (Voice or
  TDD)
  808-532-7120 (Fax)

Idaho
Idaho Assistive Technology
 Proj.
  129 W. Third St.
  Moscow, ID 83843
  208-885-6849 (Voice)
  208-885-6624 (Fax)

Illinois
Illinois Assistive Technology
 Proj.
  411 E. Adams
  Springfield, IL 62701
  217-522-7985 (Voice or
  TDD)
  217-522-8067 (Fax)

Indiana
Indiana ATTAIN Proj.
(Indiana Accessing
Technology through
Awareness in Indiana)
  Family & Social Svcs.
  Admin.
  Div. of Aging &
  Rehabilitative Svcs.
  402 W. Washington St.,
  Rm. W453
  P.O. Box 7083
  Indianapolis, IN
  46207-7083
  800-545-7763 (Voice)

Iowa
Iowa Program for Assistive
Technology (IPAT)
  Iowa Univ. Affiliated
  Program
  Univ. Hospital School
  Iowa City, IA 52242-1011
  800-331-3027 (Voice or
  TDD)
  319-356-8284 (Fax)

Kentucky
Kentucky Assistive
Technology Svcs.
(KATS-Network)
  427 Versailles Rd.
  Frankfort, KY 40601
  502-564-4665 (Voice or
  TDD)
  502-564-3976 (Fax)

Louisiana
Louisiana Technology
Assistance Network (LA
TAN)
  P.O. Box 3455, Bin #14
  Baton Rouge, LA
  70821-3455
  504-342-2471 (Voice)
  504-342-4419 (Fax)

Maine
Maine Consumer Information
and Technology Training
Exchange (CITE)
  Maine CITE Coordinating
  Ctr.
  Univ. of Maine at Augusta
  University Heights
  Augusta, ME 04330
  207-621-3195 (Voice or
  TDD)
  207-621-3193 (Fax)

Maryland
Maryland Technology
Assistance Program (TAP)
  300 W. Lexington St.
  P.O. Box 10
  Baltimore, MD 21201
  410-333-4975 (Voice)
  410-333-6674 (Fax)

Massachusetts
Massachusetts Assistive
Technology Partnership
(MATP-Center)
  Children's Hospital,
  Gardner 529
  300 Longwood Ave.
  Boston, MA 02115
  617-735-7820 (Voice)
  617-735-7301 (TDD)
  617-735-6345 (Fax)

Michigan
Michigan Assistive
  Technology Project
  Michigan Dept. of
  Education
  Rehabilitation Svcs.
  P.O. Box 30010
  Lansing, MI 48909
  517-373-4058 (Voice)

Minnesota
Minnesota STAR Program
  300 Centennial Bldg.
  658 Cedar St.
  St. Paul, MN 55155
  612-296-2771 (Voice)
  612-296-9962 (TDD)
  612-297-7200 (Fax)

Mississippi
Mississippi Proj. START
  P.O. Box 1698
  300 Capers Ave., Bldg. 3
  Jackson, MS 39215-1698
  601-354-6891 (Voice or
  TDD)
  601-354-6080 (Fax)

Missouri
Missouri Assistive
  Technology Proj.
  Univ. of Missouri-Kansas
  City
  5100 Rockhill Rd., Rm. 117
  EDUC
  Kansas City, MO
  64110-2499
  816-235-5337 (Voice)
  800-647-8558 (TDD)
  816-235-5270 (Fax)

Montana
MonTech
  The Univ. of Montana,
  MUARID, MonTECH
  634 Eddy Ave.
  Missoula, MT 59812
  406-243-5676 (Voice)
  406-243-2349 (Fax)

Nebraska
Nebraska Assistive
  Technology Proj.
  301 Centennial Mall S.
  P.O. Box 94987
  Lincoln, NE 68509-4987
  402-471-0734 (Voice or
  TDD)
  402-471-0117 (Fax)

Nevada
Nevada Assistive Technology
  Proj.
  Rehabilitation Div.
  Community Based Svc.
  Development
  711 S. Stewart St.
  Carson City, NV 89710
  702-687-4452 (Voice)
  702-687-3388 (TDD)
  702-687-3292 (Fax)

New Hampshire
New Hampshire Technology
  Partnership Proj.
  Inst. on Disability
  10 Ferry St., #14
  The Concord Ctr.
  Concord, NH 03301
  603-224-0630 (Voice)
  603-228-3270 (Fax)

New Jersey
New Jersey Technology
 Assistive Resource Program
 (TARP)
  Labor Bldg., Rm. 806
  CN 938
  Trenton, NJ 08625
  609-292-3604 (Voice)
  609-292-4616 (Fax)

New Mexico
New Mexico Technology
 Assistance Program
  435 St. Michael's Dr.,
  Bldg. D
  Santa Fe, NM 87503
  505-827-3533 (Voice or
  TDD)
  505-827-3746 (Fax)

New York
New York State TRAID Proj.
  NYS Office of Advocate for
  the Disabled
  One Empire State Plaza,
  10th Fl.
  Albany, NY 12223-0001
  518-474-2825 (Voice)
  518-473-4231 (TDD)
  518-473-6005 (Fax)

North Carolina
North Carolina Assistive
 Technology Proj.
  Div. of Vocational
  Rehabilitation Svcs.
  1110 Navaho Dr., Ste. 101
  Raleigh, NC 27609
  919-850-2787 (Voice or
  TDD)
  919-850-2792 (Fax)

Ohio
Ohio Assistive Technology
 Proj.
  400 E. Campus View Blvd.,
  SW5F
  Columbus, OH 43235-4604
  614-438-1474 (Voice)
  614-438-1257 (Fax)

Oklahoma
Oklahoma Assistive
 Technology Proj.
  Div. of Rehabilitation Svcs.,
  RS #24
  P.O. Box 25352
  Oklahoma City, OK 73125
  405-424-4311 (Voice)
  405-427-2753 (Fax)

Oregon
Oregon Technology Access
 through Life Needs
 (TALN-Project)
  Dept. of Human Resources
  Human Resources Bldg.
  Vocational Rehabilitation
  Div.
  500 Summer St. N.E.
  Salem, OR 97310-1018
  503-945-6265 (Voice)
  503-378-2756 (Fax)

Pennsylvania
Pennsylvania's Initiative on
 Assistive Technology (PIAT)
 Institute on
  Disabilities/UAP
  Ritter Annex 433 004-00
  Temple Univ.
  Philadelphia, PA 19122
  215-204-1356 (Voice)
  215-204-6336 (Fax)

South Carolina

South Carolina Assistive
 Technology Proj.
  Dept. of Vocational
  Rehabilitation
  1410-C Boston Ave.
  P.O. Box 15
  West Columbia, SC
  29171-0015
  803-822-5404 (Voice)
  803-822-4301 (Fax)

South Dakota

DakotaLink
  1925 Plaza Blvd.
  Rapid City, SD 57702
  605-394-1876 (Voice)
  605-394-5315 (Fax)

Tennessee

Tennessee Technology Access
 Proj.
  Office of Assistive
  Technology—Central
  Office
  706 Church St., Doctors'
  Bldg.
  Nashville, TN 37243-0675
  615-741-7441 (Voice)
  615-741-0770 (Fax)

Texas

Texas Assistive Technology
 Proj.
  The Univ. of Texas at
  Austin
  UAP of Texas
  Dept. of Special Education
  EDB 306
  Austin, TX 78712
  512-471-7621 (Voice)

Utah

Utah Assistive Technology
 Program
  Utah State Univ.
  Center for Persons with
  Disabilities
  UMC 6855
  Logan, UT 84322
  801-750-3824 (Voice)
  801-750-2355 (Fax)

Vermont

Vermont Assistive
 Technology Proj.
  103 South Main St.,
  Weeks Bldg., 1st Fl.
  Waterbury, VT 05671-2305
  802-241-2620 (Voice or
  TDD)
  802-241-3052 (Fax)

Virginia

Virginia Assistive Technology
 System (VATS)
  4900 Fitzhugh Ave.
  Richmond, VA 23230
  804-367-2445 (Voice or
  TDD)
  804-367-2440 (Fax)

West Virginia

West Virginia Assistive
 Technology System (WVATS)
  Univ. Affiliated Ctr.
  for Developmental
  Disabilities
  Airport Research and Office
  Park
  955 Hartman Run Rd.
  Morgantown, WV 26505
  304-293-4692 (Voice)
  304-293-7294 (Fax)

Wisconsin
Wisconsin Assistive
  Technology Program
  (WisTech)
  Div. of Vocational
    Rehabilitation
  P.O. Box 7852
  1 West Wilson, Rm. 950
  Madison, WI 53707-7852
  608-267-6720 (Voice)
  608-266-9599 (TDD)
  608-267-3657 (Fax)

Note: Photographs are designated by bold type.

abacus, 15

abbreviation-expansion software, 134–135

Accent PC (speech synthesis hardware), 50, 56

Accent SA (speech synthesis hardware), 50, **51**

AccessDOS (key modifier software), 128–129

AccessDOS ShowSounds (visual beep indicator software), 102

accessibility
  defined, 1
  determining in job-site analysis, 187

ADA. *See* Americans with Disabilities Act

adapted keyboards, 6, 121, 122–125
  described, 122
  King Keyboard, 123, **123**
  PC Mini Keyboard, 123
  product providers, 145–147
  Unicorn Membrane Keyboards, 123–124
  Unicorn Smart Keyboard, 124

adapted switches
  described, 130–132, 141
  Freewheel, 131
  HeadMaster, 131, **132**
  See also scanning keyboards

adaptive devices, connecting to computer, 25
  See also circuit cards

Adaptive Firmware Card (Morse code system), 133

adaptive technology, xiii–xiv, 2–4
  Americans with Disabilities Act provisions for, 7–9
  applications for, 157–183
  computer memory requirements for, 27
  computer power requirements for, 20–21
  cost-saving ideas for, 198–199
  funding for, 197–207
  interfacing with CD-ROM, 175–176
  interfacing with online services, 172–173
  in networks, 162, 164
  rehabilitation engineering for, 184–186
  role of keyboard in, 22
  selecting, 41
  technical support for, 193–194
  for vision impairment, 3, 23–24, 45–88

addresses
  for circuit cards, 31
  for electronic mail, 166

alarm clocks
  adapted, 108
  signaler for, 108
Alt key, 22, 56, 127–128
  See also sticky key software
Altair computer, **19**
alternative communications
    devices, 6, 121–122
  Dynavox, 141–142
  IntroTalker, 142, **142**
  Liberator, 142–143
  Polycom, 143
  product providers, 153–154
  RealVoice, 143
American Foundation for the
    Blind, 205
American Sign Language (ASL),
    104, 105
  computer training for, 89
  Computerized Animated
    Vocabulary of American
    Sign Language (training
    software), 105
  Elementary Signer (training
    software), 105
  See also hearing impaired; sign
    language
American Standard Code for
    Information Interchange. *See*
    ASCII language
Americans with Disabilities Act
  affecting employment, 9–11
  discussion of, 7–9, 197
  and text telephones, 93
  workplace requirements of,
    xiii, 13
  See also rehabilitation engi-
    neering; training
amplification systems, elec-
    tronic, 4, 5, 89, 111–115
  assistive listening devices,
    113–114
  hearing aids, 112–113
  history of, 111

product providers, 118–119
  telephone amplifiers, 114–115
An Open Book (optical character
    recognition system), 82
Apple Computer, 14
Apple IIGS, 37–38
  expansion slots in, 30
  graphics-based system for, 34
  magnification software for, 67
applications programs, 34–37
  See also software
architectural barriers, affecting
    motor impaired, 6
Arkenstone Reader (optical char-
    acter recognition system), 82
arrow keys
  functions for, 22
  as mouse replacement, 55,
    125, 129
  in screen magnification sys-
    tem, 66
Artic Business Vision (speech
    synthesis hardware), 48
Artic Transport (speech synthe-
    sis hardware), 51
Artic 215 (speech synthesizer),
    56
ASCII language, 26
  modem use of, 89, 97–98
  text telephone use of, 91
ASCII-TDD Software (text tele-
    phone software), 100–101
assistive listening devices, 111–
    114
  Easy Listener, 113–114
  Personal FM System, 114
  Pocketalker, 114
  Sound Enhancement System,
    114
  Telex TW 3, 114
assistive technology. *See* adap-
    tive technology
attitude, affecting disability
    barriers, 13

Audapter (speech synthesizer), 56
audiocassettes, for computer training, 192
Audiotone A-526 (hearing aid), 112

Babbage, Charles, 15
babies, signaling system for, 107–109
Bank Street Writer, 133
banks, as funding sources, 199–200
barriers, xiv, 1–3
    attitudinal, 13
    architectural, 6, 10
    for blind/visually impaired, 2–3
    for deaf/hearing impaired, 4
    for motor/speech impaired, 6–7
    of standard keyboard, 22, 102, 122, 125, 127–128
    See also keyboards; monitors; mice
BASIC computer language, 36
baud rate, for modem, 26
Baudot/ASCII modems, 89, 97–98
    ASCII-TDD Software, 100–101
    CM-4, 98
    Futura-TDD, 101
    Intele-Modem, 98, **99**
    MIC 3001, 98–99
    Phone Communicator, 99–100
    Phone TTY Multi Bulletin Board, 101
    Pop-up-TDD, 101
    Smart Modem 85, 100
    software, 100–102
    talking on, 102
Baudot language, 91

BBS. See bulletin boards
beep (computer)
    software for indicating visually, 102–103
    software for initiating, 129
Bell, Alexander Graham, 111
binary code, 46
    in CD-ROM, 174
    See also Morse code
binary language, Baudot, 89, 91
binary notation, 15
bit, defined, 27
BIX (online service), 165, 168
blindness, 2–3
    See also vision impaired
body movement, for controlling computer operation, 6
    See also adapted switches
BookMaker (braille printer), 77
books
    braille transcription for, 2
    closed circuit TV magnification for, 63
    for computer training, 192–193
    magnification systems enhancing, 3
    scanning procedure for, 84
    See also compact disks
Boston Computer Society, 42, 195
braille, history of, 71–72
Braille Blazer (braille printer), 75
braille cell, 71, 78
braille computers
    Braille 'n Speak, 80
    BrailleMate, 80, **81**
    portable, 80, **81**
    Type 'n Speak, 80
braille displays
    for computer output, 3
    KeyBraille, 79
    Navigator, **79**, 80
    product providers, 87–88

refreshable, 78–80
  for text telephones, 93–96, **95**
Braille Edit Express (magnified
  editor), 67
Braille Express (braille printer),
  77
Braille 'n Speak (pocket braille
  computer), 80
braille printers, 3, 75–78
  BookMaker, 77
  Braille Blazer, 75
  Braille Express, 77
  Everest, 78
  features of, 45
  heavy-duty, 76–77
  Juliet, 75
  Marathon, 78
  medium-weight, 75–76, **77**
  on networks, 163
  PED-30, 77
  Perkins Brailler, 72
  personal-class, 75
  product providers, 87–88
  Romeo, 76
  TED-600, 77
  VersaPoint, 76, **77**
braille slate, 72
braille systems, 71–72
braille text telephones, 93–96
  See also text telephones
braille transcription, 2
  See also transcription
braille translation, 23
braille translators
  computer memory require-
    ments, 27
  Duxbury Braille Translator, 74
  Hot Dots, 74
  Mega Dots, 74
  PC-Braille, 74
  Ransley Braille Interface, 74
  software for, 72–74
BrailleMate (pocket braille com-
  puter), 80, **81**

bulletin boards (BBS)
  accessing, 167–170
  disability-related providers,
    178–180
  freeware distribution of, 33
  Internet access, 181
  as online service, 165–166
  text-telephone accessible, 101
Butler in a Box (environmental
  control system), 144
byte, defined, 27

C computer language, 36
Caption Maker, 110–111
Caption Maker Plus, 110–111
captioning systems, 5, 89, 109–
    111, **110**
  Caption Maker, 110–111
  Caption Maker Plus, 110–111
  captioning videotapes, 110
  product providers, 118
  TELECAPTION 4000, 109
  VR 100, 109
cathode ray tube, 23
CCD. *See* charged-couple device
CCT Environmental Control,
    144
CCTV. *See* closed circuit televi-
    sion
CD-ROM. *See* compact disks
central processing unit (CPU),
    20–21
character recognition. *See* opti-
    cal character recognition
charged-couple device (CCD), 64
checklist
  for computer purchase, 42–44
  for rehabilitation engineering,
    188–189
circuit cards, 29–32, **30**, 130
  for CD-ROM, 174
  for hardware-based magnifica-
    tion systems, 69

installing, 30–32
for networks, 158
for optical character recognition, 82, 83
for screen magnification, 66, 67
for speech synthesis, 46–47, **47**
for voice recognition, 136–137
closed circuit television (CCTV), 62–65
Magni-Cam, 63
Meva ME2A, 63–64
20/20, 64
Vantage CCD, 64, **65**
Voyager, 64–65
CloseView (magnification software), 67
CM-4 (Baudot/ASCII modem), 98
color
speech synthesis recognition of, 52
tracking with braille display, 78–79
communications devices. *See* alternative communications devices; speech synthesis; text telephones; voice recognition systems
Compact (text telephone), 91–92
compact disks (CD-ROM), 29, 173–176
adaptive technology interfacing for, 175–176
Grolier Electronic Encyclopedia, 175
hardware, 174–176
Microsoft Bookshelf, 175
product providers, 182–183
software, 174–176
compatibility issues, 31, 37, 39, 41
Baudot/ASCII, 91, 97–98, 102

CD-ROM, 176
local area networks, 159–161
macro programs, 126–127
online services, 167, 172
speech synthesizers, 47
sticky key and keyboard modification programs, 128
voice recognition systems, 136
Compu-Lenz (optical aid), 62
CompuServe, 165
computer-aided transcription, 89, 103–104, **104**
RAPIDTEXT, 104
Computerized Animated Vocabulary of American Sign Language (training software), 105
computers, 5–6, 14–44
adaptive technology compatibility for, xiii, 14, 26
applications programs, 34–36
central processing unit (CPU), 20–21
checklist for, 42–44
circuit cards, 29–32
disk operating system, 33–34
expansion slots, 29–32
hardware, 20–32
history of, 15–19
input devices, 21–23
input/output ports, 25–26
job training for use of, 190–193
kits, 19
laptops/notebooks, 39–41
local area networks, 157–164
mainframe, 16–17
manufacturers, 36–41
memory requirements, 27, 47–49, 161, 164
minicomputer, 17, 19
modems, 26
output devices, 23–25
personal computers, 19

selecting, 41–44
selecting for networks, 159–160
software, 32–36
storage devices, 27–29, 173
technical support for, 193–194
See also local area networks
conferences
  assistive technology, 218–221
  electronic, 165, 171
Control key, 22, 69, 125, 127–128
  modification for, 128
  See also sticky key software
correspondence, 2–3
CPU. *See* central processing unit
credit cards
  as funding source, 200
  Special Touch Talking Credit Card Reader, 60
cursor, 22
  in braille display, 79
  movement with mouse, 23
  in screen magnification, 66
  screen reader tracking for, 54
  in screen review, 53

daisy wheel printer, 25
data, computer ports directing, 25
  See also files; information
database, functions of, 35
  See also online databanks
dBASE (database software), 35, 196
deaf-blind, 93–96, 97, 119–120
deafness
  barriers in, 1
  defined, 3–4
  speech impairment affecting, 5
  See also hearing impaired

DECtalk (speech synthesis hardware), 56, 142
DECtalk PC (speech synthesis hardware), 48
Delphi (online service), 165, 168, 169
descriptive video service, 60–61
  See also video
desktop publishing, 35
  See also word processing
dictionary
  The Franklin Language Master Special Edition (talking dictionary), 60
  Microsoft Bookshelf (CD-ROM), 175
  in word-prediction software, 134
Difference Engine, 15, **16**
disabilities, xiii–xiv, 2, 3–4, 5, 121
  Americans with Disabilities Act components, 7–9
  evaluation of, 93
  rehabilitation engineering for, 184–186
Disabled Special Needs Users Group (DSNUG), 195
disk drive, 27–28
disk operating system, 33–34
Display Processor 11 (magnification hardware), 70
documents
  printing procedures, 22
  word processing options for, 35
  See also files
doorbell signaling systems, 107–109
DOS. *See* disk operating system
dot matrix printer, 24
DragonDictate (voice recognition system), 139
DSNUG. *See* Disabled Special Needs Users Group

Duxbury Braille Translator, 74
DVS. *See* descriptive video service
Dynavox (alternative communications device), 141–142

ear trumpet, 111
Easter Seals Society, for equipment funding, 205
Easy Listener (assistive listening device), 113–114
Echo PC (speech synthesis hardware), 51
Echo II (speech synthesis hardware), 49
EGA monitor, magnification software compatibility with, 66
electronic conferences, with online service, 165, 171
See also electronic mail; Internet; online services
electronic mail
in networks, 163
as online service, 165, 166
See also live chatting; online services
Elementary Signer (training software), 105
employment
Americans with Disabilities Act provisions, 7–10
job-site analysis concerns, 186–190
rehabilitation engineering for, 184–186
encyclopedia (CD-ROM), 175
End key
functions of, 22
in screen magnification, 66
ENIAC, 15
Environmental Control System, 144

environmental control systems, 6–7, 122, 143–145
Butler in a Box, 144
CCT Environmental Control, 144
Environmental Control System, 144
Ez-Control, 144
HandiPHONE, 145
product providers, 154–156
essential functions, defined, 8
Everest (braille printer), 78
Excel (spreadsheet software), 35
expansion slots, 29–32
in Apple IIGS, 37
installing circuit cards in, 30–32
for network workstation, 160–161
See also circuit cards
Ez-Control (environmental control system), 144

facsimile communication. *See* fax
family, as source for funds, 199
fax
and hearing impaired, 5, 96–97
and modems, 26
in online service, 167
Federal Vocational Rehabilitation Program, 201
Filch (key modifier software), 129–130
file sharing, in networks, 162
files
defined, 33
shared, in network, 162
shared, online, 162, 165
synthesized speech for, 143
finances, 3
See also funding sources

finger spelling, 104–105
  Fingernumbers, 105
  Fingerspeller, 105
  FingerZoids, 105–106
  Micro-Interpreter I Finger-
    speller, 106
  PC-Fingers, 106
  Talking Hands, 106
  training for, on computer,
    104–106
  training software providers,
    117
  See also sign language
Fingernumbers (training software), 105
Fingerspeller (training software),
  105
FingerZoids (training software),
  105–106
flat-filing systems, 35
floppy disks, 28–29, 173
Fox Base (database software),
  35
Franklin Language Master Special Edition (talking dictionary), 60
freeware, 33, 198
Freewheel (adapted switch), 131
friends, as source for funds, 199
function keys, 22, 123, 125
funding sources
  addresses of, 206–207
  American Foundation for the
    Blind, 205
  and Americans with Disabili-
    ties Act, 197
  books on, 207
  cost-saving ideas, 198–199
  Easter Seals Society, 205
  Federal Vocational Rehabilita-
    tion Program, 201
  financial aid, 206–207
  government, 200–204
  Lions Clubs, 205
  Maine Adaptive Equipment
    Loan Program, 201
  Massachusetts Commission
    for the Blind, 201–202
  Medicaid, 202
  Nevada Assistive Technology
    Loan Program, 202
  New York Equipment Loan
    Fund, 202
  personal, 199–200
  Prentke Romich, 205
  private-sector, 204–206
  Social Security Administra-
    tion PASS Program, 203–
    204
  special education, 203
  Technology-Related Assis-
    tance Act, 204
  TeleSensory Optacon Loan
    Program, 205–206
  veterans benefits, 204
Futura-TDD (text telephone
  software), 101

GEnie (online service), 165, 168,
  170
Gopher (online service), 172
graphical user interface (GUI),
  33–34
  in Macintosh computer, 38
  screen readers for, 54–57
graphics
  from braille printer, 77
  dot matrix printers for, 24
  magnification systems en-
    hancing, 3
  screen readers for, 54–57
  speech synthesis for, 51–52,
    54–57
Grolier Electronic Encyclopedia
  (CD-ROM), 175
GS/OS, 34
GUI. *See* graphical user interface

HandiCODE (Morse code system), 133
HandiPHONE (environmental control system), 145
HandiSHIFT (sticky key software), 130
HandiWORD (word-prediction software), 135
hard disks, 28–29
hardware, **21**, **24**, **30**, **31**
  for adapted keyboards, 122–124, **123**
  for Baudot/ASCII modems, 97–100, **99**
  braille computers, pocket, 80, **81**
  for braille printers, 75–78, **77**
  for CD-ROMs, 174–175
  central processing unit, 20–21
  checklist, 43–44
  circuit card, 29–32
  computer memory, 27
  expansion slot, 29, 32
  input device, 21–23
  input/output port, 25–26
  for magnification systems, 69–71, **70**
  modem, 26
  for networks, 158–161, **159**, **160**
  output device, 23–25
  for refreshable braille displays, 78–80, **79**
  for speech synthesis, 46–51, **47**, **51**
  storage device, 27–29
  for voice recognition, 136–137, 139–141, **140**
HeadMaster (adapted switch), 131, **132**
hearing aids, 5, 111–113
  Audiotone A-526, 112
  HSI Model P, PLP, EP, EC, EZ, 112
  Panasonic WHO1, 112
  Siemens 408 W-H, 113
  See also electronic amplification systems
hearing impaired, xiv, 3–5, 85–90
  captioning systems for, 109–111
  computer-assisted access for, 97–106
  computer barriers, 22, 122
  electronic amplification systems for, 111–115
  facsimile communication for , 96–97
  product providers for, 115–120
  signaling systems for, 106–109
  text telephones for, 90–96, 100–101
Help key, 56
Help screen
  menus, 52, 53
  providing technical support, 195–196
  screen reader, monitoring of, 52
Home key, 22, 66
Hot Dots (braille translator), 74
hot key, for screen reader, 58, 59
HSI Model P, PLP, EP, EC, EZ (hearing aid), 112

IBM PC, 14, 20, **24**
  clock speeds, 20
  disk operating system, 34
  expansion slots, 30
  features, 38–39
  graphics screen reader for, 56
  macro program for, 127
  magnification software for, 67
  See also individual products
icons
  in graphical user interface, 33
  screen readers for, 54, 55

Individualized Education Plan
(IEP), 203
Individuals with Disabilities
Education Act (IDEA), 203
information, 2, 6, 89
in computer storage devices,
27–29
input devices for computer
input, 21–23
modem for movement of, 26
See also compact disks; data;
files; online services
InfoTouch (braille text telephone), 94–95
ink-jet printer, 25
inLARGE (magnification software), 67
input devices
adapted switches, 130–132
alternative, 121–122, 130–135
alternative, product providers,
149–150
keyboards, 21–22
mice, 23
input ports
for network workstation, 161
parallel, 25–26
selecting for adaptive devices,
172
SCSI, 26
serial, 25–26
input/output ports, 25–26, 161
Insert key, functions for, 22
installation
adapted keyboards, 122
adaptive technologies, on local
area networks, 164
CD-ROM hardware and soft-
ware, 174, 176
circuit cards, 30–32, 48
macro programs, 126
magnification software, 68–69
network software, 161–162
refreshable braille displays, 79

screen readers, 57–59
signaling systems, 107
voice recognition systems,
136–138
integrated circuit, development
of, 17, **18**
Intele-Modem (Baudot/ASCII
modem), 98, **99**
International Business Machines. *See* IBM PC
Internet, 158
electronic mail facility, 166
features of, 171–172
live chatting on, 172
public access sites, 181
Relay Chat, 172
interrupt, 31–32, 48
IntroTalker (alternative communications device), 142

job discrimination, ADA provisions against, 7–10
job-application practices, 9
job-site analysis, by rehabilitation engineer, 186–190
journals, on assistive technology, 222–223
Juliet (braille printer), 75

key modifier software, 127–128
AccessDOS, 128–129
Filch, 129–130
HandiSHIFT, 130
product providers, 147–148
keyboard keyguards, 124–125,
124
Keyguard, 125
keyboards
adapted for motor/speech
impaired, 121, 122–125
adapted keyboard providers,
145–147

adaptive modifications for, 38
alternative input providers,
    149–152
alternatives to, 130–141
functions of, 21–22
modification software for,
    125–130
modification software
    providers, 147–149
redefining, 126
templates for, 121
See also specific keys
keyboards, adapted. *See* adapted
    keyboards
keyboards, scanning. *See* scan-
    ning keyboards
KeyBraille (refreshable braille
    display), 79–80
Keyguard, 125
keypad, numeric, 22
keys, 22
  hot key, 58
  identifying for voice recogni-
    tion, 138
  locked down, 27, 125, 127–130
  for Morse code, 133
  sticky, 121, 125, 128–130
  See also specific keys
keystrokes
  computer feedback for, 22
  computer verbalization of, 3,
    46–59
  redefining, 125–127
  and word-prediction software,
    134–135
kilobyte, defined, 27
King Keyboard (adapted keyboard), 123, **123**
Kurzweil Reading Machine, 81–
  82

LAN. *See* local area network
laptop computers

features of, 39–41
  speech synthesizer for, 51
laser printer, 25
legislation, for disabled, 7–12,
    93, 96, 109, 197, 201–204
lending institutions, 199–200
Liberator (alternative communi-
    cations device), 142–143
lighting fixtures, operation by
    motor impaired, 7
Lions Clubs, for equipment
    funding, 205
lip reading
  assisting hearing impaired, 4
  as primary language, 193
live chatting online, 165, 167
local area networks (LANs)
  electronic mail feature, 163
  file server, 158–159, **160**
  file sharing in, 162
  hardware for, 158–161
  operation of, 157–159
  peer-to-peer, 158–159, **159**
  printer sharing in, 163
  software for, 161–162
  troubleshooting, for adaptive
    technologies on, 164
Lotus 1-2-3 (spreadsheet soft-
    ware), 35, 126
low-vision aids. *See* optical aids

Macintosh, 14, 19, 38
  adapted keyboards for, 123–
    124
  compatibility with voice
    recognition, 136
  disk operating system, 34
  expansion slots in, 30
  macro program for, 127
  magnification software for, 67
  screen readers for, 54–55
Macintosh Speaker (visual beep
    indicator software), 102–103

macro programs, 121
  advantages of, 125
  compatibility with adaptive
    technology, 126–127
  ProKey Plus, 127
  QuicKeys 2, 127
  for redefining keyboard, 126
  software for, 125–127
magazines, braille transcription
  for, 2
MAGic (magnification software),
  68
magnetic media, for storage
  devices, 16, 28, 173
Magni-Cam (closed circuit television), 63
magnification systems, 3, 45,
  61–71
  Braille Edit Express, 67
  closed circuit television, 62–
    65
  CloseView, 67
  computer memory require-
    ments, 27
  Display Processor 11, 70
  hardware-based, 69–71
  inLARGE, 67
  large monitors, 62
  in Macintosh, 38
  MAGic, 68
  for monitor enhancement,
    23
  optical aids, 61–62
  product providers, 86–87
  software-based, 65–69
  Vista, 70, **70**
  ZoomText, 68
mail, vision impaired barriers
  with, 2–3
  See also electronic mail
Maine Adaptive Equipment
  Loan Program, 201
mainframe computer, 16–17
Marathon (braille printer), 78

Massachusetts Commission for
  the Blind, 201–202
Medicaid, as funding source, 202
medical examination issues, 9–
  10
meetings, barriers of for hearing
  impaired, 4, 103–104
Mega Dots (braille translator), 74
megabyte, defined, 27
megahertz (MHz), 20
memory, computer
  for local area networks, 161,
    164
  for speech synthesizer, 47, 48,
    49
  types and requirements for, 27
  See also computers
Memory Printer (text telephone),
  92
menu, speech synthesis recognition of, 52, 53
  See also Help screen
Meva ME2A (closed circuit
  television), 63–64
mice, 23
  arrow keys replacing, 125, 129
  for graphical user interface, 33
  screen reader tracking for, 54,
    57
  use in magnification program,
    66, 69
  use with Macintosh, 38
MIC-3001, 98–99
Micro-Interpreter I Fingerspeller
  (training software), 106
microprocessor, **21**
  See also central processing
    unit; computer
Microsoft Bookshelf (CD-ROM),
  175
Microsoft Windows, 34
  using magnification software
    with, 69
  See also windows

Microsoft Word (word processing software), 35
MindReader (word-prediction software), 135
Minicom (text telephone), 92
minicomputer, development of, 17, 19
modems, 26
  Baudot/ASCII, 89, 97–100, **99**
  interfacing with adaptive hardware, 172
  operating, 102, 167–170
  See also bulletin boards; online services; text telephones
money
  Note Teller (speech synthesis device), 60
  vision impaired barriers with, 3
  See also credit cards; funding sources
monitors, 3, 23–24
  for closed circuit television, 63
  large, for vision impaired, 62
  for network workstation, 161
  software magnification factors, 66
  See also screen reading software
Morse code systems
  Adaptive Firmware Card, 133
  for alternative input device, 132–134
  for computer operation, 6, 121–122
  HandiCODE, 133
  Morse Code WSKE, 133
  Morsek, 134
Morse Code WSKE (Morse code system), 133

Morsek (Morse code software), 134
motherboard, 20
motor impaired, xiv, 1, 5, 121–122
  adapted keyboards for, 122–125
  adaptive technology assisting, 6
  alternative communications devices for, 141–143
  alternative input systems for, 130–135
  computer requirements for, 29
  environmental control systems for, 143–145
  keyboard barriers for, 22
  keyboard modification software for, 125–130
  product providers for, 145–156
  voice recognition systems for, 136–141
MS-DOS, 34

National Institute on Disability and Rehabilitation Research, regional centers, 10–12
National Rehabilitation Hospital, 185
Navigator (refreshable braille display), **79**, 80
networks. *See* local area networks
Nevada Assistive Technology Loan Program, 202
newsletters, on assistive technology, 222–223
NIDRR. *See* National Institute on Disability and Rehabilitation Research
Norton Utilities, 36
Note Teller (paper money identifier), 60
notebook computers, 39–41

OCR. *See* optical character
recognition
office equipment, use by motor
impaired, 6
online databanks, xiv, 165
accessing, for vision impaired,
3
assisting hearing impaired, 5
for shareware availability, 32
software for accessing, 36
See also bulletin boards
online services
accessing, 167–170
adaptive technology interfacing for, 172–173
bulletin boards, 33, 101,
165–166
electronic conferencing,
171
electronic mail, 166
fax, 167
Internet, 171–172
live chatting, 165, 167
providers, 176–178
Optacon (scanner), 83
optical aids
Compu-Lenz, 62
in magnification systems, 61–
62
optical character recognition
(OCR), 3, 45
An Open Book, 82
Arkenstone Reader, 82
history of, 81–82
Optacon, 83
OsCaR, 83
product providers, 88
Reading Edge, 83
scanning text, 83–84
organizations, for persons with
disabilities, 209–217
OS/2, 34, 56
See also disk operating system; IBM PC

OsCaR (optical character recognition system), 83
output devices
monitors, 23–24
printers, 24–25
output ports, 25–26
for network workstation, 161
parallel, 25–26
SCSI, 26
selecting for adaptive devices,
172
serial, 26
outSPOKEN (speech synthesis
software for graphics), 54–55,
55

Pagedown key, 22
Pageup key, 22
PAL. *See* Profile Access Lan-
guage
Panasonic WHO1 (hearing aid),
112
parallel ports, 25–26
PASS. *See* Plan to Achieve Self
Support
Pay Phone Text Telephone, 93,
94
PC compatibles, 39
See also computers; IBM PC
PC Mini Keyboard (adapted
keyboard), 123
PC-Braille (braille translator), 74
PC-DOS, 34
PC-Fingers (training software),
106
PC-Tools (utility program), 36
PED-30 (braille printer), 77
Perkins Brailler (braille writer),
72
personal-care attendants, for
motor impaired, 6
Personal FM System (assistive
listening device), 114

Phone TTY Multi Bulletin Board (text telephone software), 101

PhoneCommunicator (modem), 99–100

phonemes, in speech synthesis, 46

Plan to Achieve Self Support (PASS), 203–204

Pocketalker (assistive listening device), 114

Polycom (alternative communications device), 143

Pop-up-TDD (software), 101

portability
of adaptive speech devices, 59–60
of low-vision aids, 62–64
of optical character recognition systems, 83
of software magnification systems, 66
of voice recognition systems, 138

Portaview (text telephone), 92

ports. *See* input ports; output ports

Prentke Romich, for funding assistance, 205

printers, 24–25
daisy wheel, 25
dot matrix, 24
ink-jet, 25
laser, 25
selecting, 41–44
sharing, in networks, 158, **159**, **160**, 163
See also braille printers

privacy, 3

Procomm (telecommunications software), 36

Prodigy, 165

Profile Access Language (PAL), 56

programming
for adapted keyboards, 122, 123–124
languages for, 36, 56
for speech synthesizers, 52

ProKey Plus (macro software), 127

public accommodations, Americans with Disabilities Act affecting, 10

public gatherings, barriers for hearing impaired, 4

punched cards, 15

Qmodem (telecommunications software), 36

Quattro Pro (spreadsheet software), 35

QuicKeys 2 (macro software), 127

random-access memory (RAM), 27
See also memory

Ransley Braille Interface (braille translator), 74

RAPIDTEXT (transcription software), 104

Reading Edge (optical character recognition system), 83

read-only memory (ROM), 27
See also memory

RealVoice (alternative communications device), 143

reasonable accommodation, defined, 8–9

refreshable braille displays, 78–80
KeyBraille, 79
Navigator, **79**, 80
product providers, 87–88

rehabilitation engineering, 184–186
checklist for, 188–189

job-site analysis concerns, 186–190
workplace adaptation, 190
See also training
Rehabilitation Engineering Society of North America (RESNA), 185
relational databases, 35
relay services, for hearing impaired, 89, 96
See also text telephones
RESNA. *See* Rehabilitation Engineering Society of North America
review mode. *See* screen review
ROM. *See* read-only memory
Romeo (braille printer), 76

SAP button. *See* secondary audio program channel
scanning devices, for vision impaired, 3
See also optical character recognition
scanning keyboards, 130–132, 141
TetraScan Keyboard, 132
scanning text, with optical character reader, 83–84
screen magnifier. *See* magnification systems; optical aids
Screen Reader/2 (speech synthesis software for graphics), 56
screen reading software, 3, 51–54
adapting for mainstream software, 57–59
for graphics, 54–57
outSPOKEN, 54–55, **55**
Screen Reader/2, 56
Tiny Talk, 54
use with scanned documents, 84

Vocal-Eyes, 54, 139
Window Bridge, 56–57
See also speech synthesis
screen review
by magnification program, 66
by speech synthesizer, 53, 57
SCSI ports, 26
See also input ports; output ports
security
and job-site analysis, 186
on local area networks, 162
secondary audio program channel (SAP button), 61
SeeBEEP software, 103
serial ports, 25–26
setups, 123–124
shareware, 32–33, 198
See also freeware; software
Shift key, 22, 125, 127–128
See also sticky keys
Siemens 408 W-H (hearing aid), 113
sign language, 4, 89, 193
American, 89, 104
Computerized Animated Vocabulary (training software), 105
Elementary Signer (training software), 105
training for, on computer, 104–106
training software providers, 117
See also finger spelling
signaling systems, 5, 106–109
product providers, 117–118
Super Signal, 108
Super Signal Clock, 108
Watchman, 108–109
small computer systems interface. *See* SCSI ports

Smart Modem 85, 100
Social Security Administration
 PASS Program, 203–204
software
 adapting screen readers to, 57–
  59
 applications program, 34–36
 braille translation, 72–74
 captioning, 110–111
 for CD-ROM, 174–175
 checklist, 42–44
 for computer-aided transcription, 103–104
 disk operating system, 33–34
 key modifier, 127–128
 for keyboard modification,
  125–130
 macros, 125–127
 for magnification systems, 65–
  69
 memory requirements for, 27
 for Morse code, 133–134
 for networks, 161–162
 programming languages, 36
 selecting, 41–44
 speech synthesis, 51–54
 for teaching sign language,
  105–106
 text telephone, 100–101
 types of, 32–33
 visual beep indicator, 102–103
 voice recognition, 137–141
 word-prediction, 134–135
software drivers, for speech
 synthesizer, 48
Sound Enhancement System
 (assistive listening device),
 114
sound (environmental)
 barriers for hearing impaired,
  4
 signaling systems for, 5
Speaqualizer (speech synthesis
 hardware), 49

Special Education, sources for
 funding, 203
Special Touch Talking Credit
 Card Reader, 60
speech impaired, xiv, 5–6
 alternative communication
  product providers, 153–154
 alternative communications
  devices, 141
 Baudot/ASCII modems, 97–
  100
 DECtalk PC, 48
 Dynavox, 141–142
 IntroTalker, 142, **142**
 Liberator, 142–143
 Polycom, 143
 RealVoice, 143
 relay services, 96
 text telephones, 90–96, 100–
  102
 See also motor impaired
Speech Plus synthesizer circuit
 card, **47**
speech synthesis, 23, 45, 46
 Accent PC (hardware), 50, 56
 Accent SA (hardware), 50, **51**
 adapting, with mainstream
  software, 57–59
 adaptive applications for, 59–
  61
 Artic Business Vision (hardware), 48
 Artic Transport (hardware), 51
 braille pocket computer for, 80
 computer memory require-
  ments, 27
 DECtalk PC (hardware), 48
 Echo PC (hardware), 51
 Echo II (hardware), 49
 in environmental control
  systems, 144
 external hardware, 49–51, **51**
 internal hardware, 46–48, **47**
 of Macintosh, 38, 54–55

modem use with, 99, 172
outSPOKEN (graphics soft-
    ware), 54–55, **55**
product providers, 84–86
Screen Reader/2 (graphics
    hardware and software),
    56
silencing, 53
software, 51–54
Speaqualizer (hardware), 49
Tiny Talk (software), 54
use with scanned documents,
    84
VertPro (hardware), 49
Vocal-Eyes (software) 54, 139
Window Bridge (graphics soft-
    ware), 56–57
speech synthesizer card, **30**
    installing, 30–32
spell checker, screen reader
    adaptation for, 59
    See also dictionary; word
        processing
split-screen image, with
    magnification systems, 69
spreadsheets, functions of, 35
sticky keys, 121, 125, 129–
    130
storage devices, 27–29
    compact disks, 29, 173–176
    criteria for selecting, 28
    floppy disks, 28–29, 173
    hard disks, 28–29
    tape drives, 28, 29, 173
students
    communications barrier af-
        fecting, 2
    computer use by, 14
substantial impairment, defined,
    8
Super Signal (signaling system),
    108
Super Signal Clock (signaling
    system), 108

Supercom (text telephone), 92–
    93
Superprint (text telephone), 92
switches, adapted. *See* adapted
    switches
Syntha-Voice (speech synthe-
    sizer), 56
System 7, 34

Talking Hands (training soft-
    ware), 106
tape drives, 28, 29, 173
task switching, 33
TDD. *See* text telephones
technical support, 193–194
    Help screens, 195–196
    special interest groups, 194–
        195
    technology assistance states,
        224–230
    third-party, 194
    users' groups, 194–195
    vendor, 194
technology assistance states,
    224–230
Technology-Related Assistance
    Act, 204
TED-600 (braille printer), 77
TeleBraille (text telephone), 95–
    96, **95**
TELECAPTION 4000, 109
telecommunications software,
    functions of, 36
telecommunications technology.
    See online services
telephone
    amplification systems, 89,
        112, 114–115
    barriers for hearing impaired,
        4, 187
    HandiPHONE (environmental
        control system), 145
    signaler for, 108

use of by motor impaired, 6
Volume Control Handset, 115
Walker Clarity (amplifier), 115
See also Baudot/ASCII
    modems; modems; text
    telephones
telephone, text. *See* text tele-
    phones
television, 3–4
    captioning systems for, 5, 89,
        109–111
    closed circuit, 62–65
    descriptive video service for,
        60–61
Television Decoder Circuitry
    Act, 109
Telex TW 3 (assistive listening
    device), 114
Telix (telecommunications
    software), 36
TetraScan Keyboard, 132
text
    assistive technology for, 45
    barriers to blind, 2
    entering with Morse code, 133
    magnification systems en-
        hancing, 3
    scanning for word processing,
        83–84
    word processing for, 34–35
    See also magnification sys-
        tems; speech synthesis
text telephones (TDD), 5, 89,
    90–93, **90**, 100–102
    and Americans with Disabili-
        ties Act, 93
    ASCII-TDD Software, 100–101
    braille, 93–96, **95**
    Compact, 91–92
    and computers, 97–102
    Futura-TDD (software), 101
    InfoTouch (braille), 94–95
    Memory Printer, 92
    Minicom, 92

Pay Phone Text Telephone, 93,
    94
Phone TTY Multi Bulletin
    Board (software), 101
Polycom, 143
Pop-up-TDD (software), 101
Portaview, 92
product providers, 115–117
relay services for, 96
software for, 100–101
Supercom, 92–93
Superprint, 92
talking on, 91, 102
TeleBraille, 95–96, **95**
See also Baudot/ASCII
    modems; modems
text-based operating system, 33–
    34
text-enlargement software, 69
See also magnification sys-
    tems
thesaurus, talking, 60
Tiny Talk (speech synthesis
    software), 54
Trace Research and Develop-
    ment Center, 185
training, for adapted technology
    and computer use, 190
    audiocassettes, 192
    in classroom, 191
    continuing, 192
    disks, 193
    materials, 192–193
    on-the-job, 191
    technology assistance states,
        224–230
transcription, computer-aided
    for hearing impaired, 89,
        103–104, **104**
    RAPIDTEXT, 104
    See also braille transcription
transistor
    development of, 17, **18**
    in Intel microprocessor, **21**

transportation
  Americans with Disabilities
    Act affecting, 10
  vision impaired barriers with,
    3
TSR utilities. *See* utilities, memory resident
TTY. *See* text telephones
tutorials, for computer training,
  193
20/20 (closed circuit television),
  64
Type 'n Speak (pocket braille
  computer), 80
typewriter, vision impaired
  barriers with, 3

Unicorn Membrane Keyboard
  (adapted keyboard), 123–124
Unicorn Smart Keyboard
  (adapted keyboard), 124
UNIX, 34
USENET, 171
utilities
  adaptive software, 65–66
  functions for, 35–36
  memory resident, 128

vacuum tubes, 15
Vantage CCD (closed circuit
  television), 64, **65**
vaporware, 33
VersaPoint (braille printer), 76,
  77
VertPro (speech synthesis hardware), 49
Veterans Benefits, as funding
  source, 204
VGA monitor, magnification
  software compatibility, 66
  See also monitors
VIBUG. *See* Visually Impaired
  and Blind Users Group

video
  captioning systems for, 5, 89,
    109–111
  closed circuit television, 62–
    65
  for computer training, 192
  descriptive video service for,
    60–61
  providing captions for, 110–
    111
video cards
  for hardware-based magnification systems, 69
  for screen magnification, 66,
    67
  See also circuit cards
video system, for network workstation, 161
vision impaired, xiv, 1–3
  adaptive speech applications
    for, 59–61
  adaptive technology for, 23–
    24, 45
  braille systems for, 71–80
  computer keyboard barriers
    for, 22
  computer requirements for,
    28–29
  magnification systems for, 61–
    71
  optical character recognition
    systems for, 81–84
  product providers for, 84–88
  speech synthesis systems for,
    46–61
Vista (magnification hardware),
  70, **71**
visual beep indicator software,
  102–103
  AccessDOS ShowSounds, 102
  Macintosh Speaker, 102–103
  SeeBEEP, 103
Visually Impaired and Blind
  Users Group (VIBUG), 195

Vocal-Eyes (speech synthesis software), 54, 139
Voice Navigator SW (voice recognition system), 139–140
Voice Navigator II (voice recognition system), 139, **140**
voice recognition systems, 26, 122, 136, 140–141
   continuous-utterance, 137–138
   discrete utterance, 138
   DragonDictate, 139
   hardware for, 136–137
   installing, 136–137
   product providers, 151–152
   speaker dependent/independent, 137, 138
   training, 138
   Voice Navigator SW, 139–140
   Voice Navigator II, 139, **140**
   VoiceType, 140
voice synthesis. *See* speech synthesis
VoiceType (voice recognition system), 140
Volume Control Handset (telephone amplification system), 115
Voyager (closed circuit television), 64–65
VR 100 (captioning system), 109

Walker Clarity (telephone amplification system), 115
Watchman (signaling system), 108–109
Weitbrecht, Robert, 90
wheelchair, for motor impaired, 6

Window Bridge (speech synthesis software for graphics), 56–57
windows
   screen reader adaptation for, 58, 59
   screen readers for, 54–57
   speech synthesis recognition of, 52
   See also Microsoft Windows
word processing, 34–35
   adapting screen readers for, 57–59
   Bank Street Writer, 133
   braille displays for, 78–80
   Microsoft Word, 35
   scanning text to, 83–84
   use with braille translators, 74
   WordPerfect, 35, 57–59, 126, 195
WordPerfect (word processing software), 35, 126
   adapting screen readers for, 57–59
   Help screens in, 195
   macros, 126
word-prediction software, 134
   HandiWORD, 135
   MindReader, 135
workers, 2, 7
   See also Americans with Disabilities Act; rehabilitation engineering; training
workplace. *See* employment
workstations. *See* local area networks

ZoomText (magnification software), 68

Joseph J. Lazzaro is director of the Adaptive Technology Program housed at the Massachusetts Commission for the Blind in Boston. He recommends, installs, and trains on assistive systems interfaced to personal computers, networks, and mainframe computer platforms for visually impaired workers and students. He is also a freelance author, writing frequently for numerous computer trade magazines in the United States and Europe. His articles and product reviews have appeared in *Byte*, *Time Life Access Newsletter*, *InCider*, *Home Office Computing*, *CD Data Report*, *LAN Technology*, *Windows User*, and *Computer Shopper* in the United States and *PC World* and *PC Dealer* in the United Kingdom. Mr. Lazzaro is also moderator of the Adaptive Technology conference on BIX, a forum dedicated to assistive technology and its benefit to persons with disabilities. He has a BS in Physical Science Information Systems from the University of Massachusetts. A frequent visitor to the online world, Mr. Lazzaro can be found on BIX, GEnie, Delphi, and The World. His electronic mail addresses are:
LAZZARO@BIX.COM and
LAZZARO@WORLD.STD.COM.